Irked by Kirk

by

Kirk Dunkirk
Scott Linyard
Owen Wade

or

"The Funniest Book in the World"

or

"My Gift to Humanity"

Irked by Kirk
Nutty Prank Letters From Japan

- or -

My Gift to Humanity

- or -

The Funniest Book in the World

In memory of Roman "Jerky" Meshon
(1971 ~ 2007)

First Print Edition © 2012

Acknowledgments

Thanks to: Elmer, Erik Nielsen, Evan Coombes, Mr. Fantastico, Mark Zuckerberg, Prince Charles and the Nomuras (not a band.)

No thanks to Chook.

To Tom for his perseverance and Mineko for her patience

Intro by Scott Linyard

When Kirk First asked me to take a look at his letters, I had no idea the wild ride on which we were about to embark.

Since then, I have lost my home, my job, my way, several games of scrabble, Patience but never Hope (two pet goldfish), part of my sanity – but not my mojo.

We got shipwrecked off Indonesia, lost a fortune when the EMP blast went off over Frankfurt then won it back at poker …one stinking nursing home at a time. I survived a blizzard inside the carcass of an alpaca, and helped prevent an alien invasion using nothing but a borrowed UFO and a dial-up modem. I drove trucks in the desert, tended bar in New Orleans, jumped from planes into forest fires, danced for the GOP and wrote speeches for mobsters. I once got caught stealing cough drops dressed as Santa, but I never stooped so low to have to teach kids English in Japan. In short, I've been to paradise but I've never been to me.

I learned the true meaning of ASICS, how Mitsuya Cider is older than Coke and the role golf pants played in the development of canned coffee. By the time my team of Exterminators entered the Vortex I was no longer the same man.

Through it all, the thing that kept me going was the belief that this book, this book that we started with faces in it, faces so that our friends at Harvard could check each other out, this "face book" with letters as well could make the world a better place.

Scott Linyard
March 2012

Foreword by Owen Wade

This book is good. I like this book. It is like other books in some ways but also a little different in other ways. There are many new ways to make books. Some books aren't even books cause they aren't made of paper they are made out of electricity. Same as money. Money is electric now. Pictures too. The Romans made books out of rocks.

Peepul said that cause books are easy to make now, any one can make a book easy so there will be lots of bad books. Well I am telling you they are dead wrong. What you hold hear in your hands is nothing short of revalushinary. If you keep it it might be worth something someday. Like three bucks at a garage sale or to prop up a wobbly table. Ha ha. No, I'm serious, This book prooves that the new technolagy will herald a golden age of creative innovashun unseen since the Rennisans. So here it is, my gift to humanity. I hope you like it. My friends say it is funny.

Owen Wade
President, KENSA
March 2012

Kirk Dunkirk
✈ ✈ ✈ ✈ ✈
Kochi City, Japan
780-✗ ✗ ✗

All Nippon Airways Co., Ltd.
Fukuoka Asahi Building
2-1-1 Hakataekimae
Hakata-ku, Fukuoka City

October 10, 2000

Dear Customer Service Representative:

I will be flying home to my native Oklahoma for Thanksgiving soon and therefore have a request.

I have a glass eye and due to the dry air inside an airplane, my eye socket shrinks a little and forces it out. If I'm not paying attention, like when I'm falling asleep, my eye may pop out and roll down the aisle.

Normally I take my eye out and wear a patch but at the moment I have an infection and the doctor recommended I keep it in. Again, that dry air is the culprit. It might cause my infection to bleed, and I think a fat American with blood coming out of his empty eye socket is the last thing your customers want to see.

I am asking about this beforehand so the airplane staff will be prepared. If my glass eye pops out, I would like the flight attendants to retrieve it and return it to me quietly. People who don't wear glass eyes have no idea how embarrassing it is to have it pop out in a public place.

I flew Singapore Airlines about two weeks ago and my eye popped out and the flight staff humiliated me. One of them screamed and most of the others wouldn't help look for my eye, and the woman who found it wouldn't even pick it up. It is supposed to be such a good airline but let me tell you I will never fly Singapore Airlines again. And I'm telling my friends and putting it on my homepage too.

I haven't reserved my flight yet but when I do I will tell you the details.

Thank you very much.
Sincerely,

Kirk Dunkirk

All Nippon Airways Co., Ltd.
2-1-1Hakataekimae Hakata-Ku
Fukuoka, Japan 812-0011

Mr. Kirk Dunkirk

Kochi, Japan 780-

Dear Mr. Dunkirk:

We appreciate for your concerned letter.   It is our privilege for our customers to provide the special service for the special demands.   We are here to meet your satisfactions.   Your concerns may easily be taken care by our special staffs.   At this time, we informed your request to our related customer service and the flight attendant department in Narita.

Please feel free to contact the following number for more details. This toll free number will give you an idea how much we care about you. All requests including your reservation will be taken care of.

It is our pleasure to help you experience a safe and a comfortable journey. If you have any further questions, please do not hesitate to contact us.

ANA SKY ASSIST DESK
Open: Daily 09:00-17:00
Telephone number (Toll-free service) 0120-029-377

Sincerely, Yours

M. Sugi

Masazumi Sugi
Manager,
TEL 092-471-5134

```
                                                    O/REF:JAS BTR 12-390
                                                    October.18.2000
```

Dear Kirk Dunkirk,

    Let us begin by thanking you for your inquiry.

    Unfortunatery, we have no flights bound for Oklahoma, so we can not help you at this time.
Plese consult with other Airlines.
We are looking forward to our next opportunity to be helpful.

    Thank you again for your interest in Japan Air Seystem.

                                             Sincerely yours,

Keiichi Kawaguchi
Keiichi Kawaguchi
General Manager
"Rainbow" Customers Service Office
JAPAN AIR SYSTEM Co., Ltd.

Kirk Dunkirk
x x x x x x
Kochi City 780

Asahi Breweries, Co.
1-23-1 Azumabashi
Sumida-ku, Tokyo
130-8606

Sept 11, 2000

To the Director of Marketing,

First of all I must say that I am a big fan of all of your products, especially Asahi Super Dry. However, now that I am no longer young it is beginning to show on my waistline.

I write this letter for two reasons, the first of which is a sincere but rather arcane question. I have noticed that on your television commercials, Asahi, like other beverage makers, has a loud and obvious gulping noise while the people on screen are consuming the product. This is true whether the product is tea, sports drink, or beer, but seems to be particularly important, and I might add, loud, in the case of beer during the summer months.

Please tell me more about the history of this phenomenon. Has it always been like this with Japanese beer commercials? Was it the brainchild of the beverage companies or the advertisers? Did one company start the "gulping" practice and have others followed suit? How about in the days before television: was there a gulping noise on the radio? Also, the gulp sounds the same in every commercial spot, except for its volume. Is there one agreed- upon "gulp" by all the beverage companies and if so, does someone receive royalties for the original recording?

You may be surprised by my interest in this matter but I assure you it is wholly academic. I am not a corporate spy. After volleyball, my favorite hobby is studying the history of television commercials, especially in other countries. I consider myself a bit of an amateur expert on the matter of alcohol commercials in particular. For example, did you know that in Russia it is common to show the consumer so zealous in his imbibing that the product, usually vodka, spills down his neck so he must wipe it away with the back of his hand in the "finale?"

As a final note, I must add that though I appreciate the gulping noises in your commercials, I think they would work better if toned down a bit. Most of my young Japanese friends, male and female alike, agree. If the current gulp were rated a "10", I'd say bump it down to a "7" or "8." Just an idea.

anyway, sorry for such a long letter but I truly hope you can shed some light on this matter for me.

sincerely,

Kirk Dunkirk

Kirk Dunkirk 様

　拝復　時下ますますご清祥のこととお慶び申し上げます。
　日頃は弊社製品をご愛顧いただきまして、厚く御礼申し上げます。
　さて、この度はCMに使用している「ゴクッ」という効果音についてのご質問のお便りをお寄せいただきまして、誠にありがとうございました。
　弊社では、お客様の豊かな消費生活に少しでもお役立ち出来るようにとお客様のニーズに添った商品開発と広告制作に努めております。それだけにお客様からのこのようなお便りをお寄せいただきますことは、大変有り難いと感謝致しております。
　さて、ご質問についてですが、弊社のわかる範囲でご返事させて頂きます。
○日本のビールCMでは昔から使用されていたのか？
　→弊社のTVCMでは１９７４年のものから使用されていました。
○これは飲料会社のアイデアかそれとも広告代理店のアイデアか？
　→どちらかには違いないと思いますが、弊社ではわかりかねます。
○誰かがはじめて他社が追随したのか？
　→弊社ではわかりかねます。
○ラジオ全盛期にもあったのか？
　→古いラジオの記録が残っておらず、弊社ではわかりかねます。
○全社共通の「ゴクッ」があるのか？
　→それぞれのブランドの表現ルールや、CM企画意図に基づいて個々に制作しています。
　　似ておりますが微妙に違い、同じ音ではありません。
○原盤を録音した誰かがロイヤリティを受け取っているのか？
　→効果音等を専門に制作している会社があり、そこに広告代理店を通じてロイヤリティを支払っております。
　Kirk Dunkirk 様のご質問に１００％お応えできるものではないと思いますが、ご了承下さい。
　弊社はこれからも品質の向上と皆様にお喜びいただけるよい商品と広告の提供に努力致して参りますので、今後ともご厚情賜りますよう、宜しくお願い申しあげます。
　末筆ながら、Kirk Dunkirk 様の今後ますますのご健勝をお祈り申し上げます。

敬具

平成１２年９月２９日
アサヒビール株式会社
マーケティング部宣伝課長
友野宏章

Mr. Kirk Dunkirk,

Greetings and well wishes.

We highly appreciate your regular consumption of Asahi Breweries' products.
Thank you very much for your letter inquiring about the 'gulp' sound effect we use in our commercials.

At Asahi Breweries, we strive to produce products and advertisements that meet the needs of our customers in an attempt to enhance their plentiful lives as consumers, if only a little. To that extent, we are extremely grateful to receive such a letter from you.

Let me answer your questions to the best of my knowledge.

○Has it always been like this with Japanese beer commercials?
→Asahi Breweries has used the sound in TV commercials since 1974.
○Was it the brainchild of the beverage companies or the advertisers?
→I can't answer that question, but I'm sure it was one of them.
○Did one company start 'gulping' and others followed?
→I don't know.
○Was it used in the days of radio?
→I don't know as there is no record of old radio programs.
○Do all companies use the same 'gulp' sound?
→Each company produces it own sound effect based on the intentions of the commercial and the expressive theme of the brand. They are slightly different, even though they may sound similar.
○Does someone receive royalties for the original sound?
→Royalties are paid through our advertising agencies to the companies that specialize in producing such sound effects.

We ask for your understanding in not being able to reply fully to your questions.
Asahi Breweries is committed to improving quality and offering great products and advertisements to the delight of our customers, and we sincerely hope for your continuing patronage.

In conclusion, Mr. Kirk Dunkirk, we would like to wish you the best of health in the future.

Regards,
September 29, 2000
Asahi Breweries, Ltd.
Chief of Marketing

Hiroaki Tomono

(Asahi Breweries reply, translation: Evan Coombes)

Kirk Dunkirk
Forestry & Agriculture Dept.
♣♣♣♣♣♣ University
♣♣♣♣♣♣♣♣♣♣♣♣♣
Kochi City 780

June 17, 2001

FedEx
WBG Marive West
2-6 Nakase, Mihama-ku
Chiba City, Chiba Prefecture

To Whom it may Concern,

I am a graduate exchange student in the Food Preservation Programme at ♣♣♣♣♣♣ University. It has become necessary for us to send specimens to London for testing, but they require special shipping consideration.

The articles in question are the mummified remains from a hill tribe in Indonesia. These include: 2 forearms with hands and the near complete remains of one woman, small and elderly at the time of death, approximately 145 cm tall. (We call her "Betty")

The articles have little smell, no disease or parasites and pose no health risk to workers. We can provide appropriate containers, but we need to verify the shipping condition in your warehouses and planes. The mummified remains need to be kept in a dry environment with no rapid changes in temperature. Can your company provide these conditions?

Another consideration is the threat posed by a national extremist. Due to our close ties with the hill tribe region, our university has a cultural exchange programme. There is one exchange student opposed to any research on these mummies, and he has resorted to petty acts of sabotage to disrupt our work. He is rather small and nervous, and therefore poses little physical threat to workers, but he may attempt something foolish at the airport.

If you can assure special shipping consideration for our work, please contact me and I can provide more details about Betty et al. and about our cultural extremist's modus operandi.

thank you for your time.
Sincerely

Kirk Dunkirk

FedEx Express

Federal Express
World Business Garden Marive West
2-6 Nakase, Mihama-ku, Chiba-shi
Chiba 261-7110 Japan

June 28, 2001

Mr. Kirk Dunkirk
Forestry and Agriculture Department.
　　　　University

Kochi City 780

Dear Mr. Dunkirk

I am writing to inform you that shipping mummified remains from Japan to Great Britain is unacceptable by our door to door service. Commodity such as human corpses, human organs or body parts; cremated or disinterred human remains are prohibited under FedEx International Express Service.

As far as I have checked regarding your commodity, you need to further check on the following points:

1. You need to check with Indonesian Government if mummified remains are allowed to ship out to Great Britain (Third country) even for the purpose of research.

2. On your letter, you have stated that there are no diseases, no health risks etc..., but you need to check with customs in Great Britain if they allow your shipment into their country. Recently Quarantine and Customs in Great Britain are very strict due to "Foot and mouth Disease" affair.

3. You also need to check with Japanese Ministry of Economy, Trade & Industry, if your shipment can be shipped out from Japan.

As for my conclusion, unfortunately it is difficult to send out your shipment by FedEx. I would like to suggest you to contact Japan External Trade Organization (JETRO) and also an airline cargo company (such as Japan Airlines Co Ltd). There companies might provide you with a better information/suggestion regarding your shipment.

Sincerely

Toru Ichige
Specialist, Customer Service
Federal Express Corporation

Mar. 21, 2000

Krik Dunkirk
Forestry & Agriculture Dept.
▓▓▓▓University
▓▓▓▓▓▓▓▓▓▓▓▓▓▓▓▓

Dear Dunkirk,

Your letter dated June 18 has been received.
We must say thank you for your interest in our service and we're very glad to have a inquiry from you but at the same time, we regret to say that iit is impossible for us to respond to your request.
DHL Japan Inc. are not able to have special shipping arrangements for such contents you mentioned on your letter.

We look forward to provide our service for you in the near future and wising you great success in your study.

Sincerely Yours

DHL Japan Inc.
Osaka Customer Service
Phone:0120-39-2580

Mika Ohtsuki

13 July 2001

UPS YAMATO EXPRESS CO., LTD.
2-3-34 Tosabori Nishi-ku
Osaka 550-0001
Tel 06(4803)5757
Fax 06(6459)4085
Email upsosa@mx1.alpha-web.ne.jp

Mr. Kirk Dunkirk
Forestry & Agriculture Dept.
███ University
████████████████████

Dear Sir,

We received your letter with reference to your special shipping needs as of 18 June 2001. Thank you for your attention to our company. We apologize for our delay to reply to you.

First of all, we have to tell you that unfortunately, we cannot accept your shipping request because of our terms and conditions. Our service is just door-to-door express delivery service for small packages and documents and some articles are prohibited from handling such as foods, dangerous goods, invaluable things, animals or plants. The articles in question, the mummified remains must be extremely delicate and perishable in a sense so that they need a special care in every process for transportation. We cannot provide any suitable services like a special container nor facility in the aircraft nor at the airports and warehouses.

The enclosed please find our service guide and rate chart for your reference. It includes the information about the articles that we cannot accept. However, should you have any further inquiry about our service, please do not hesitate to contact us at your convenience. We will be pleased to be your help for another shipping needs in the future.

Finally, thank you for your attention again and we hope you can find a forwarder who can satisfy your shipping needs.

Yours Faithfully,

Hitoshi Sakai
Osaka Branch
UPS Yamato Express Co., Ltd.

Miki Dunkirk
Evergreen Dive School
☺ ☺ ☺ ☺ ☺ ☺ ☺
Kochi City 780- ☺ ☺ ☺ ☺

TeleMotion
600 Longfellow Dr.
---------, CA ----

June 24, 2002

Dear Dr. Longfellow,

Do you print original telephone cards?

I am belong to the elite extreme scuba team what creates custom dives for people all over Japan who have passionate feelings for marine animals.

We want create souvenirs for our customers soon trip to USA and members but other companies have turned us down. Because this may be misunderstanding about the nature about our design.

We believe in the unitedness of all being that aliveing. Humans come from and will finally return to a sea like our mothers uterus. We are just a passionate club, not a religion or a cult, but like before religions, we do represent such the union through the act of sexual intercourse.

We have many of variety souvenir designs, made by our members who is professional artist. What they all in common of is graphic depictions of people, sometimes in scuba gear, sometimes naked, while act of copulation with marine animals. Men, women, dolphin, turtle, it depending on a design. I'm explain this in you for a professional manner so you are not be put off, because but when you see the designs for one's self I'm sure you'll very agree are pretty design.

I also must addition that those design are drawn of artists hands and computer enhanced and no depiction real person or animals. There are no famous likenesses to problematic either. In 1998 such image were posting on our web site of Julia Roberts with manta ray caused a legal fuss, but the webmaster responsible was reprimand and is no longer working from us.

Some telephone card companies don't have very wide minds. But if you are wide and would like our business, please send a hasty reply to the above address.

Thank you so much
Sincerely

Miki Dunkirk
Live Love and Dive, Extreme Marine Pleasure Club

                        2002 Challenge the Humpback!

July 2, 2002

Miki Dunkirk
Evergreem Dive School
████████████ 4F
Kochi City, 780-████
Japan

Dear Miki:

Thank you for your letter of June 24, 2002 inquiring our custom prepaid phone card. We are one of few companies who make custom prepaid phone card for souvenirs or product/service promotion.

You can use any one of our stock cards and add your message or use white blank card to add your custom artwork or messages. You can send us your custom artwork via e-mail to ████████@adelphia.net or send us a camera-ready artwork. We will send you a fax proof for your approval before we go into production.

Our phone card is good for one year from your purchase date and good for the origination from USA to destination at anywhere in the world. "Minutes on each card" on the enclosed price matrix indicate the USA domestic call minute. If you decided to order our phone card, please let us know how many card and how many minute you need on each card and send us your check with your order.

If you have any questions, please call us or send us e-mail.

Sincerely,

Henry H. ████████
Manager, Customer Service

600 Longfellow Drive, ████████ • (888)604-████ • ████████0141 • Fax ████████0398 • ████████@aol.com

Kirk Dunkirk Visionary Business Solutions
Evergreen Resources
XXXXXXXXXX
XXXXXXXXXXXX 4F
Kochi City 780

Sept. 1, 2004

Central Krankenversicherung AG
Hansaring 40-50 50670
Köln, Germany

To Whom It May Concern,

I will be moving to Germany soon and am very interested in acquiring automobile collision insurance from your esteemed company. Please send me a brochure -- in English if you have one but German is all right as someone at my agency can translate.

As a proud member of my ancient profession, though, I am bound by the Oath of the Oracle to tell you the following: My ability to glimpse the future affects my driving, though usually in a positive way.

In fact, I was involved in a landmark case in California (Dunkirk v. Orange County, 1973) in which I was released from paying damages to the police department for running over one of their K-9 squad members (a dog) in order to avoid a larger accident that I foresaw coming at that time.

I have long admired the deep passion of the German people for safety and can't help but wonder if my ability might affect my rates? If not, it's probably just my karma, as I was a tax collector in Elizabethan England in a former Life.

Thanks in advance.
Sincerely,

Kirk Dunkirk

ps: Did you know that Clairvoyants are used by some insurance companies in the UK to screen policy applicants? Please let me know if you are interested and I can forward a CV!

"Don't Procrastinate – Prognosticate!"

Evergreen Resources
XXXXXXXXXX
XXXXXXXXXXXX 4F
Kochi City 780

Visionary Business Solutions

Sept. 1, 2004

Central Krankenversicherung AG
Hansaring 40-50 50670
Köln, Germany

To Whom It May Concern,

I will be moving to Germany soon and am very interested in acquiring automobile collision insurance from your esteemed company. Please send me a brochure -- in English if you have one but German is all right as someone at my agency can translate.

As a proud member of my ancient profession, though, I am bound by the Oath of the Oracle to tell you the following: My ability to glimpse the future affects my driving, though usually in a positive way.

In fact, I was involved in a landmark case in California (*Dunkirk v. Orange County, 1973*) in which I was released from paying damages to the police department for running over one of their K-9 squad members (a dog) in order to avoid a larger accident that I foresaw coming at that time.

I have long admired the deep passion of the German people for safety and can't help but wonder if my ability might affect my rates? If not, it's probably just my karma, as I was a tax collector in Elizabethan England in a former Life.

Thanks in advance.
Sincerely,

Kirk Dunkirk

ps: Did you know that Clairvoyants are used by some insurance companies in the UK to screen policy applicants? Please let me know if you are interested and I can forward a CV!

Kirk Dunkirk

"Don't Procrastinate – Prognosticate!"

CENTRAL KRANKENVERSICHERUNG AG · 50593 Köln

AIRMAIL Japan

Evergreen Recources
Mr Kirk Dunkirk

4F
Kochi City 780

Hansaring 40-50
50670 Köln
Telefon (02 21) 16 36 0
Telefax (02 21) 16 36-2 00
Internet www.central.de
E-Mail info@central.de

Postanschrift:
**CENTRAL
KRANKENVERSICHERUNG AG
50593 Köln**
Konto:
COMMERZBANK AG, Köln
(BLZ 370 400 44)
Konto-Nr. 120 1276 00
STADTSPARKASSE KÖLN
(BLZ 370 501 98)
Konto-Nr. 11772027

Ihre Zeichen	Ihre Nachricht vom	GS./Versicherungsschein-Nr.	Unsere Zeichen	☎ Durchwahl 16 36/	Tag
			UK/MA-MU-bid	2319	20.09.2004

Fax: 16 36/223
E-Mail: jana.biedka@central.de

Your letter of September 1, 2004

Dear Mr Dunkirk,

thank you for your letter received on September 7, 2004. We regret to inform you that we are a health insurance company and therefore don't offer automobile insurances.

Yours sincerely,

Jana Biedka
Unternehmenskommunikation/Marketing

Ein Unternehmen der Generali Gruppe.

Vorsitzender des Aufsichtsrates:
Dr. iur. Dr. h. c. Wolfgang Kaske
Vorstand: Willi Alfter (Vorsitzender)
Dr. Wolfgang Havenith, Alexander Mante
Sitz: Köln, Amtsgericht Köln HR B 93

Miki Dunkirk
Beneficial Bottoms Association
☺☺☺☺☺☺☺ Club Room 4F
Kochi City 780
Japan

Aug 29, 2004

Prince Charles
Clarence House
St. James's Palace
London SW1A 1BA

Dear Mr. Prince Charles,

Hello. How are you? I'm fine thank you.

Thank you for find a time reading my letter apart from your busy schedule.

I am president of the ☺☺☺☺☺☺☺ University Beneficial Bottoms Association. We are female group of students dedication for raising money to charity.

Our founding member had great idea three years ago. While exchangeing student in Buffalo she become member of Walk-a-Thon. She very exciting has been and America has many good ideas but so do we Japan of asian race for example the Sony Walkman, instant noodles and now "Bow Lingual" dog translator.

Because we are busy students we haven't times about walking. Because, we made original Japanese charity: Annual Spank-a Thon.

Our college students get financial promise from local citizens then famous celebrity and mayor etc. comes to our city and spanks us in public square with many audiences. Donations are proportion to spanks.

We are hope you will consider are request and spank us for good cause next May. We learn about you in our english converation text. Japanese people also having royal families but they are not cool. You are so cool. And your horse riding is especially wondering. You experting the polo. So cool~! (Sorry don't know many words) If you can't come please may we some auto- and photographs? Perhaps we auction those :)

Thank you in advance for your kind consideration.

Miki Dunkirk

CLARENCE HOUSE
LONDON SW1A 1BA

From: The Office of HRH The Prince of Wales

16th September, 2004

Dear Miss Dunkirk,

    The Prince of Wales has asked me to thank you for your letter of 29th August in connection with the ⬚⬚⬚⬚⬚⬚⬚ University Beneficial Bottoms Association.

    It was kind of you to write as you did and The Prince of Wales has considered your request; however I regret to inform you that on this occasion he is unable to help. As I am sure you will appreciate, The Prince of Wales receives a great many requests for deserving causes such as yours but is unfortunately unable to accede to them all.

    I am sorry to send you what I appreciate will be a disappointing reply. Nevertheless, His Royal Highness has asked me to send his best wishes for your fundraising which he hopes is a great success.

Yours sincerely,

Mrs. Claudia Holloway

Miss Miki Dunkirk

Kirk Dunkirk
☀-☀-☂-☀-☀-☂-☀
Kochi City 780
Japan

April 17, 2003

Petline Uosama Cat Food
Petline Kabushiki Kaisha
2-5-5 Yoyogi
Shibuya-ku, Tokyo-to

To Whom it May Concern,

    I love cats. I often took walks with them across the heath in my native Scotland. Oh yes, it's true -- cats enjoy taking walks with big people, if they respect you! When the winds blew over the highlands I'd shelter them under my tartan kilt.

    As you can see, I'm a cat lover. And tho' the whisky leaves something to be desired I am also a Japan lover. Now I call it my home with my wife Miki. She too is something of a cat lover. That's how we met.

    As a cat lover and a Japan lover, I have cats now in my Japanese home. But my cats haven't adjusted well to the move to Japan. My pretty little ones, Angus, Braveheart, Bilbo, Nebuchadnezzar and Wasabi fight all the time now. They didn't used to fight back in their native Scotland.

    Perhaps it's because I have to keep them locked up in a box when I'm at work. We can't take long walks together over the heath anymore. I gave up wearing a tartan kilt as school boys always poked me up the bum while I waited for the streetcar. So I can't cuddle my pretty little ones under my kilt like I did back in my native Scotland. As a cat lover, this has me distressed.

    My cats here sometimes won't eat. I always buy your cat food but often they refuse to eat it. When we have this problem back in my native Scotland, we cat lovers usually mix a little blood sausage in with the food and eat together with the cats. Then the wee pussies respect you.

    So please write me back and let me know if I can eat your cat food. I don't know if Japanese cat food is edible for humans like cat food is back in my native Scotland. If so, would you kindly tell me a few Japanese cat food recipes? I checked your home page but can't make sense of it. My Japanese neighbor, also a cat lover, doesn't know either. I don't have any blood sausage but some of your local dishes with leftover fish parts should do the job.

Sorry for the long letter. Me and the wee ones look forward to your reply.
Sincerely,

Kirk Dunkirk.

April 26, 2003

Dear Mr. Dunkirk

[ ]

Kochi City 780

Thank you very much for your interesting letter. I could imagine you holding your cute cats with your traditional Scotch clothes. Anyway please let me answer your questions. I am not sure which product your have your interests in, but basically cat wet food can be eaten by human. The following is the ingredients in case of the our Uomasa.

1. Uomasa maguro(red label)

    Yellowfin tuna, Skipjack tuna, Bonito tuna, gel powder(derived from sea weeds) VitaminE

2. Uomasa katsuo(green label)

    Almost same as 1. except this one does not include Yellowfin tuna.

3. Uomasa shiromizakana(blue label)

    Almost same as 1. except this one also includes white fish such as sea bream.

4. Uomasa chicken(orange label)

    Basically same as 1, but this one contains about 15% of chicken-by-product.
    Personally, I would not eat this No.4, but it should be OK because it is cooked.

In my experience cat wet food sold here in Japan are made with fishes in many cases, but in the Western nations they are made with meat in general. If we look at the evolution of cats, they should be eating meat in stead of fishes. But cats tend to prefer to eat food they were eating when they were babies.

So this may be the reasons your cats sometimes do not eat fish-based food.

By the way I have no idea about your blood sausages, it sounds scary though.

Sincerely

Norihiko Tsuji
Planning & Development Dept.
PETLINE
AC building 2-5-5 Yoyogi
Shibuya-ku Tokyo
E-mail   norihiko_tsuji@petline.co.jp

Kirk Dunkirk
☹☹☹☹☹☹☹☹
Kochi City 780
Japan

Sharp Corporation
22-22 Nagaike-cho, Abeno-ku
Osaka 545-8522
Japan

April 21, 2003

Dear Sharp,

We have one of your copy machines in my office. It's a Sharp AR-S507.

The quality of the copies are ok, but this machine has a MAJOR DESIGN FLAW!

Look at the picture(s) I have attached. Whenever I need to make a copy, the book I am copying covers the control panel! I can't choose paper size, zoom, and so on because the book is in the way. You should have put the control panel off to the side. I am a busy office worker and this is a BIG WASTE OF TIME!

I can't believe you let such a serious design flaw out of your factory. Whoever approved this design should send me an apology immediately. I am VERY ANGRY about this. This is not acceptable behavior in the twenty-second century. This would never happen in Scotland! All of your employees should be ASHAMED of themselves. How dare you!

regretfully yours,

Kirk Dunkirk

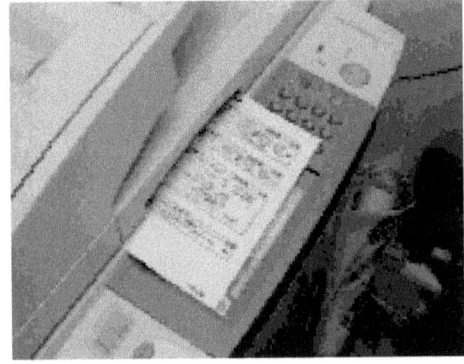

SHARP

Sharp Corporation
Page : 1 / 1
3-1-72, Kita-Kamei-cho, Yao-shi, Osaka581-8585, Japan
Phone : +81 6-6792-1001   Fax :+81 6-6792-0416
Date : May 17, 2003

Mr / Ms. Kirk Dunkirkb   Kochi City 780)

〒780 -
高知県高知市

REF: YOUR LETTER
      Our ref. 305131

Dear Sir / Madam,

Thank you very much for using Sharp products.

We refer to your letter concerning to the sharp AR-S507.

We are sorry that our product could not obtain your satisfaction.

We understand your problem, but it is difficult to change the design of this product.

However, your claim has been passed to our factory in consideration of future design.

We appreciate your constructive complaint.

                                    Yours truly,

                                    Sharp Corporation
                                    Customer Assistance Center
                                    W.Kohzai

3-1-72, Kita-Kamei-cho, Yao-shi, Osaka 581-8585, Japan
Tel: 06-6792-1001   Fax: 06-6792-0416   E-mail : customer@cmn.hirano.sharp.co.jp

JTB Corp., International Travel Division
2-3-11 Higashishinagawa, Shinagawa-ku,
Tokyo 140-8604 Japan

April 23, 2003

To Whom It May Concern,

 Your travel company has a good reputation. My Japanese mother-in-law always says how good JTB is, especially its tour guides. She says they are the best. You are overpriced, but she always uses you anyway because you are the best.

 On her first tour with you, one of the members tried electrocuting her husband in the hotel Jacuzzi but since the tour conductor had already taken her passport, she couldn't escape from Hong Kong. Good thinking, JTB.

 I am an actor. Not just any actor, but a method actor. As a method actor I must wholly prepare myself before a role and never change character. For my role in "The Pirates of Penzance" at the Sydney Playhouse, I wore a patch over my eye for 5 weeks and walked with a wooden leg. In "Cannibal Cruise 3" an independent New Zealand film, I ate moths and my own fingernails for breakfast. We method actors love a challenge.

 For my next film role I play a spy who goes undercover as a Japanese tour guide, whose mission is to stop a communist revolution in Guam. Since I am a method actor, I want to join one of your tours to Guam as a tour conductor. I have no tour guide experience but I was a summer camp counselor for emotionally disturbed children, so I think I'll be ok. I can't speak Japanese but I assure you that as a method actor, between now and August, I will speak nothing but Japanese in my house, to my dog, and at the pool hall until I get it right.

 So what do you think? Can I be a tour guide? I won't need a salary and I can bring my own snacks. There will be another method actor in Guam and he will sometimes jump out of the bushes and throw knives at me. He will also drown me in the pool. Since I am a method actor I will pretend to die until I am taken to the hospital where I come back to life (It's just a ruse to throw off the terrorists.) To keep it realistic, please don't say anything to the guests until I'm already in the ambulance. Once they understand, I'm sure they'll agree it was the best tour ever!

 Please write me back about becoming a temporary tour conductor. Also, please have more tours to American Indian Reservations and Macau as my mother-in-law loves to gamble at new places.

Sincerely,

Kirk Dunkirk (not a stage name)

JTB CORP.
International Travel Division
Planning and Development

4/30/2003

Dear Mr. Dunkirk

Thank you for your interest with our company. While your background and qualifications are impressive, I regret to inform you that JTB International Travel Division has no position for tour conductor now.

Your letter will be kept on file for future consideration once an position with your background and experience becomes available.

Again, your interest with our company is truly appreciated.

Sincerely yours.

Takuya Kako

Kako Takuya
Manager, Purchasing and Development
JTB International Travel Division

Kirk Dunkirk
¥¥¥¥¥¥¥¥¥¥
Kochi City 780
Japan

Office of the Cabinet, Public Relations, Cabinet Secretariat
1-6-1 Nagata-cho, Chiyoda-ku
Tokyo 100-8968

April 30, 2003

Dear Mr. Prime Minister Koizumi,

    You may have received a strange letter recently from my wife Miki asking you to participate in a charity fundraiser at her university. Just for the record, her university is ✻✻✻✻✻ University and the fundraiser is called a "Spank-a-Thon."

    At a Spank-a-Thon, famous people spank university students on stage while other people donate money. Her explanation in Japanese may be a little different, but you get the idea.

    I'm writing to ask you to please not come to the Spank-a-Thon. My wife invited you out of spite. You see, she's a second-year economics major and she thinks she has all the answers. Personally, I'm a fan of yours and think you're doing a great job. It's not your fault the economy is so bad and keeps getting worse, month after month, year after year. It's the damn Chinese! Their biggest export is deflation.

    But my wife, Miki, doesn't see it that way. She wants to embarrass you somehow. I'm not sure how, but it's probably at the Spank-a-Thon. This is also her way of getting back at me, too; We often fight about economic theory (she's definitely not a Keynesian!) and she always concludes by throwing the DVD remote-control at me and sleeping with my friends. That's what I get for marrying someone 15 years younger.

    Well, anyway, if you do get a letter from her or anyone else inviting you to come to ✻✻✻✻✻ University, please don't come. I'd love to meet you, but perhaps under better circumstances. So help me out here, extend more loans to medium-size businesses and get the economy rolling again. This will strengthen my argument and perhaps even save my marriage.

Sincerely,

Kirk Dunkirk
(a supporter)

Spank Koizumi:

No reply

:(

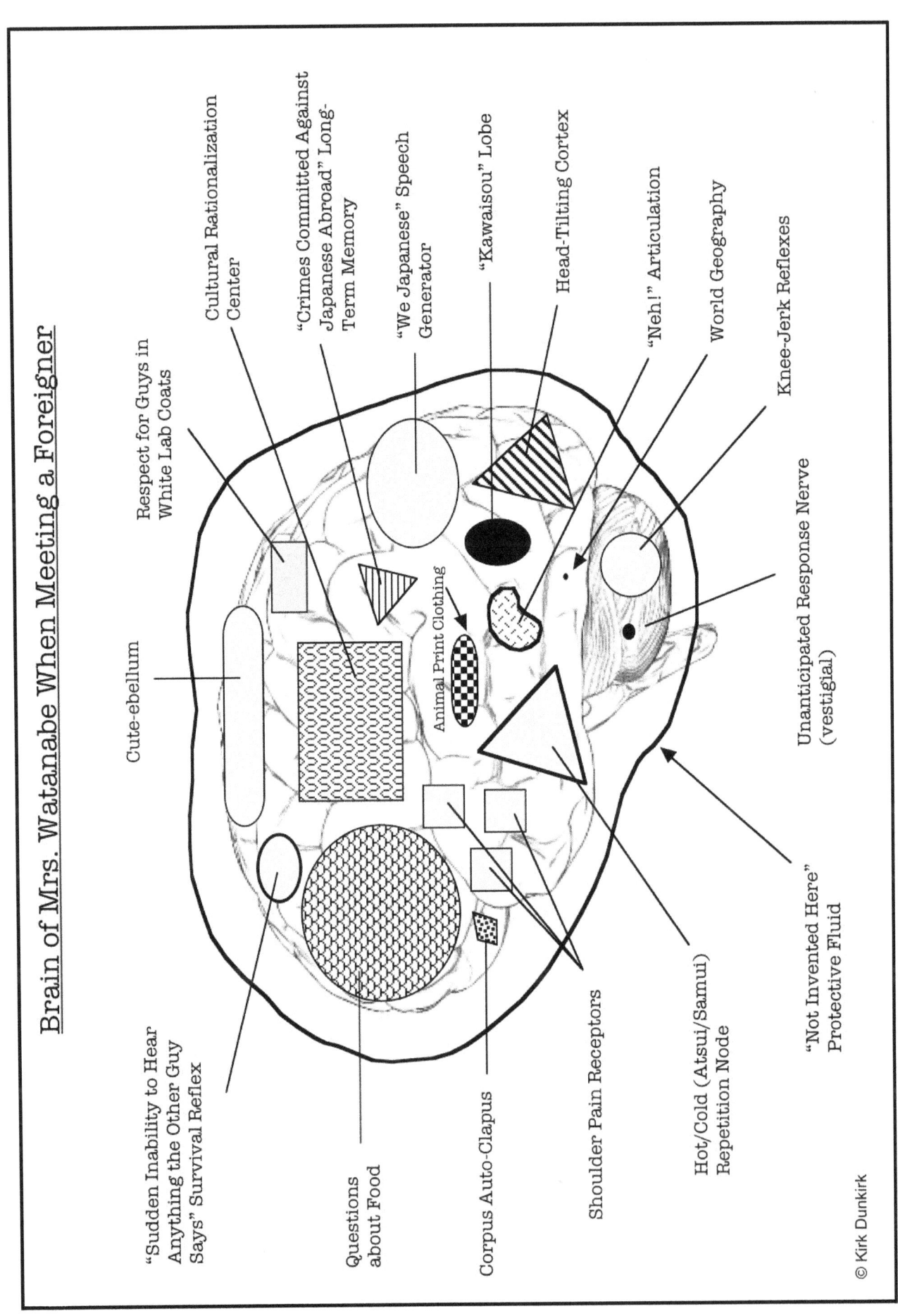

Kirk Dunkirk
☠☠☠☠☠☠☠
Kochi City 780
Japan

Fuji Xerox Co. Ltd.
2-17-22 Akasaka
Minato-ku, Tokyo
107-0052

May 7, 2003

To the Director of Marketing,

I have recently retired from the Royal Canadian Navy and just moved here with my Japanese wife. The transition to my new life was going swimmingly until she broke her ankle and I had to do the shopping yesterday. I was shocked and aghast when I discovered your product in the corner of my local convenience store.

Your design and names are obvious rip-offs of the real Xerox, a Canadian company. Even your big "X" symbol is a cheap imitation. Have you no shame? How fitting that the company you copy is our copying company -- you probably used one of our copiers to copy it. It would be funny if it weren't a crime.

I realize that Asia is still getting used to western concepts such as copyright, but I didn't spend 27 years defending the St. Lawrence Seaway from foreign invaders just so you folks could get rich off hardworking Canadians and our original ideas.

I suggest you stop this illegal profiteering immediately. I have many friends in the Royal Canadian Navy, who in turn have friends in Ottawa who know many influential people who can contact powerful government lobbyists and intellectual property lawyers.

In the meantime I refuse to use your products and have told everyone I know about this injustice. My mechanic needed a new copy machine and I even talked him into buying one from another company (which shall remain nameless for fear of reprisal.)

We in the Royal Canadian Navy pride ourselves on integrity and honor. I have the same impression of the Japanese but obviously your company is the exception.

Dismayed,

Kirk Dunkirk, Lieut.(Ret.) RCN

THE DOCUMENT COMPANY
FUJI XEROX

May 13, 2003

Mr. Kirk Dunkirk, Lieut. (Ret.)
[redacted]
Kochi City 780

Dear Mr. Dunkirk;

This letter is in response to your May 7, 2003 letter to the Director of Marketing at Fuji Xerox (FX). My name is Ryoichi Hirano and I am the Manager of Fuji Xerox's License Group in Japan. Trademark licensing is one of among several of types of intellectual property licensing matters, which I oversee.

With regards to your letter, I think that there are a number of facts that you were perhaps unaware of at the time you sent it, that if you had been apprised of, would have lead you to reconsider some of your allegations. So please allow me this chance to inform you of some of these facts.

First of all, the Xerox trademarks such as the big "X" that you saw used with our products are licensed to us from the Xerox Corporation (XC), a New York company, under arrangement we have with XC and its affiliates. FX, itself is an affiliate of XC established over 40 years by another Xerox affiliate with Fuji Photo Film to conduct the xerography copier business in East Asian. Hence our name, "Fuji Xerox." Further please know that three of the twelve members of our Board of Directors are XC executives, including XC Chairman & CEO Anne M. Mulcahy. All three of them know, approve and in some hypothetical cases would probably insist on our continued use of the big "X" symbol.

Although currently XC only owns 25% of our stock, we still maintain close relations with them and build many of the products that you can see, in Japan, Canada and throughout the world, in close collaboration with them. As such FX believes, and we think XC concurs as well, that our intimate relationship with them has enabled us to share the benefits of technology and business practices developed in both East Asia and North America.

So in conclusion, keeping the above facts in mind, we think that you ought to feel delight, and not dismay the next time you see the big "X" at your local convenience store. Not only has FX compensated XC amply for the right to use the big "X" in East Asia but we have also contributed significantly to the spread and use of superb big "X" products around the world.

Hope your wife recovers soon from her ankle injury.

Best wishes,

[signature]

Ryoichi Hirano
License Group Manager
Center for Intellectual Resources
Fuji Xerox Co., Ltd.

Fuji Xerox Co., Ltd. 2-17-22 Akasaka, Minato-ku, Tokyo, 107-0052 JAPAN TEL 81-3-3585-3211 FAX 81-3-3585-8321

Kirk Dunkirk
☠ ☠ ☠ ☠ ☠
Kochi City 780
Japan

Iams Japan,Inc.
Osaki New City 8F
1-6-1,Osaki
Shinagawa-ku
Tokyo 141-0032 Japan

May 9, 2003

To the Director of Marketing,

I have recently retired from the Royal Canadian Navy and just moved here with my Japanese wife. The transition to my new life was going swimmingly until she broke her ankle and I had to do the shopping yesterday. I was shocked and aghast when I discovered your products on the shelves of my local supermarket.

Your packaging and product names are obvious rip-offs of the real Iams cat food, a Canadian company. Even your cute "paw print" symbol is a cheap imitation. Have you no shame?

I realize that Asia is still getting used to western concepts such as copyright, but I didn't spend 27 years defending the St. Lawrence Seaway from foreign invaders just so you folks could get rich off hardworking Canadians and our original ideas.

I suggest you stop this illegal profiteering immediately. I have many friends in the Royal Canadian Navy, who in turn have friends in Ottawa who know many influential people who can contact powerful government lobbyists and intellectual property lawyers.

In the meantime I refuse to buy your products and have told everyone I know about this injustice. I didn't even have a cat before but went out and got one for myself and another for my mechanic and bought us pet food from other companies (who shall remain nameless for fear of reprisal.)

We in the Royal Canadian Navy pride ourselves on integrity and honor. I have the same impression of the Japanese but obviously your company is an exception.

Dismayed,

_____
Kirk Dunkirk, Lieut. RCN, Ret.

May 22, 2003

Mr. Kirk Dunkirk
▓▓▓▓▓▓▓▓▓▓▓▓▓▓▓▓
Kochi City, Kochi, 780-▓▓▓▓

Dear Mr. Dunkirk,

My name is George Masuda and I am in charge of the Consumer Care department at Iams Japan, Inc. in Tokyo.

I received your letter yesterday regarding the copyrights. As you mentioned, "the real Iams cat food" is originally made by The Iams Company, based in Dayton, Ohio in the United States. The Iams Company was established in 1946 and they currently distribute their products in over 80 countries. We, Iams Japan, Inc. are a subsidiary of The Iams Company and have been in Japan since 1993.

I would just like to clarify that Iams products are made (and always have been made) by an American company.

I hope this explains to you about your concerns.

If you have any questions, please do not hesitate to contact me.

Best regards,

George Masuda
George Masuda
Customer Service Dept.
Iams Japan, Inc.
(03) 5745-5853 – TEL
(03) 5745-5850 – FAX
e-mail: gmasuda@iams.co.jp

Kirk Dunkirk
ꙮꙮꙮꙮꙮꙮꙮ
Kochi City 780
Japan

QP Organization, Head Office
4-13 Shibuya 1-chome
Shibuya-ku, Tokyo
150-0002, Japan

~~May 12, 2003~~
Sep1. 1, 2003

Dear Kewpie (or QP)

I'm just writing to say how much I love your products! Even the mayonnaise squeeze bottles are too cute to throw away. If I collect any more I'll have to move to a new apartment!

I do have a few questions, however:

(A) Your mustard is the best I have ever used at keeping away poisonous centipedes (mukade in Japanese). I spread a line of it around my futon before going to sleep, but cleanup is the problem. It takes a long time to wipe up and now my tatami has mustard stains.

I've experimented -- leaving the mustard down for a few days until it gets crusty. It comes off easier this way, but its centipede repellency diminishes and also I have to step around it all day. I made a special "mukade mustard sheet" that I lay beneath my futon and ring with dijon but that too has proved an inadequate solution. Do you have any suggestions? I've checked your homepage but found none -- perhaps it's a legal thing. Maybe you could make it in powder or even incense form.

(B) People in my yoga class swear by your mayonnaise to keep away mosquitos too but it hasn't worked for me. I dab it behind my ears and on my solar-plexus but it isn't effective. In fact, I think it attracts more insects! Have you heard of any differences in efficacy between Japanese and people of European descent? My yoga teacher thinks it's because of different intestine lengths.

Well, anyway, I'm still very impressed by your products. Please write me back with mustard-mukade/mayo-mosquito advice and, if you can, please help me find a good home for all my darling squeeze bottles.

sincerely,

Kirk Dunkirk

ps: I had to send this letter twice!

Q.P. Corporation
1-4-13 Shibuya, Shibuya-ku
Tokyo, Japan
September 4, 2003

Mr. Kirk Dunkirk
▓▓▓▓▓▓▓▓▓▓▓▓▓▓▓▓
Kochi City ~~780~~, Japan.

Dear Mr. Kirk Dunkirk

    We thank you for the patronage you extend to us.
    We have received your letter and thank you for the precious information. We are so surprised because we did not know that our mustard and mayonnaise are effective to keep away from insects.
    Unfortunately we Q.P. Corporation is a food processing and sales company that hoping everyone's health through our products. We are not aiming our products to be used other than foodstuffs. Thus we do not have any idea for which you are looking about the effect against insects with using our products.
    We would appreciate your understanding and your continued patronage.

Sincerely,

Toshio Ohyama
Public Relation Section

Miki Dunkirk
✪✪✪✪✪✪✪✪
Kochi City 780
Japan

Coleman company
3600 N. Hydraulic
Wichita, KS 67219 USA

~~May 19, 2003~~   January 21, 2004

Dear Coleman Family,

First , I love your products! They are maybe expensive but work well. We Japanese people like that. Though I have many debts from my American husband I still like Coleman, especially lantern.

Actually, it because of those money problems that one's husband and I become interested in camping. It's such a cheap holiday. You really get the most bang for your buck, as the husband alway say in English.

Anyway, since your products are made in USA, I am worry about their reliability. We spend the last of savings on an insurance policy, it would terrible for husband Kirk to get injured, because I love him so much.

Could you answer a few questions to me about product safety?

- If one your gas lanterns accidentally fall and hit a rock, is it maybe can explode? Are this explosion maybe enough to kill people? How far away need to be for avoiding injure?

- If not cautious and use a your gas lanterns inside tent, how long time take for 80kg adult asphyxiation from carbon monoxide poisoning? Is this tragedy happen sometimes mistake when people camping and too much drinking?

- If a gas lantern fall inside one your tents and accidentally start fires, do the tent collapse on the persons inside, delay of their escape? Can the zip fasteners melt, perhaps preventing of their escape? Have these ever happened? Please provide some details.

- Can it possible for a novice who drink hay fever medication maybe get his or her ankle trap in canoe bench if ship accidentally turn over?

Thank you for your kind help. Your equipments make me feel free!

Awaiting your reply

Miki Dunkirk

ps. You make mustard too?
ps2: this is second time I send a same letter!

Irked by Kirk   37

 *The* Coleman Company, Inc.

3600 N. Hydraulic/ Wichita, Ks 67219/ Phone 800-835-3278/ P.O. Box 2931/ Wichita, Ks 67201
www.coleman.com

February 2, 2004

Miki Dunkirk
Kochi City 780
Japan

RE: Product Safety

Dear Mrs. Dunkirk,

This is in reference to your letter concerning the safety of our products. I apologize for the delay in answering your letter.

Quality is a top priority at The Coleman Company. It is the cornerstone of our heritage and success.

When using our products please, read and follow the instructions and all warnings.

Thank you,

Margie Grimes
Coleman Consumer Relations

February 12, 2004

Miki Dunkirk
Kochi City 780
Japan

Dear Miki:

Thank you for your recent letter regarding Coleman products.

The manufacturer of these lanterns publishes very clear instructions regarding safe use of these products. To find more information from Coleman, please visit their web site at:

http://www.coleman.com/coleman/home.asp

The answers to your other questions may be summed up by reminding you that one should never use any gas powered products in any enclosed area, especially a tent. Gas is flammable, and one must treat it with respect. The same holds true for hay fever medications. Please remember to always use caution and good judgement whenever you are using any kind of boat or water craft.

I have included our MEC Fact Sheet regarding stoves; please read the section on safety very carefully.

We wish you and your husband many happy years of wilderness recreation.

Best regards,

Tom
Order Sales
MOUNTAIN EQUIPMENT CO-OP

CORRESPONDENCE DESK, 130 West Broadway, Vancouver, BC, V5Y 1P3

TELEPHONE:		FAX:		HOURS (Pacific Time):	
Within Canada or U.S.A.:	1-800-663-2667	Within Canada or U.S.A.:	1-800-722-1960	Monday to Friday	6:30am - 6:30pm
Local or International:	(604) 876-6221	Local or International:	(604) 876-6590	Saturday	8:00am - 4:00pm

Kirk von Dunkirk
✠ ✠ ✠ ✠ ✠ ✠ ✠ ✠
Kochi City 780
Japan

Kyoto Brighton Hotel
330, Shitei-Cho, Nakadachiuri-Sagaru
Kyoto 602-8071

May 15, 2003

To the Manager:

    I intend to stay at your hotel during the week of 23 June. You were recommended by a business associate because of your excellent attention to customer details.

    During my stay I wish to hear no Japanese language, ever! I have been here but a short time and already I grow weary of its staccato babble and monotony. I am a musician and can not bear to hear the drone of it anymore.

    When I come to the front desk I want the staff to refrain from speaking Japanese in my presence. Not just to me but also to each other. I do not want to hear Japanese from the television in the next room. I do not want to hear Japanese from the TV in my own room. Please modify the TV so only non-Japanese channels are available. If this is not feasible, please remove the television and clock radio from my room to prevent me from accidentally listening to them.

    I want to dine in a restaurant without a single Japanese dish, and I want the waiters to use no Japanese within earshot of me, even with each other. As a musical prodigy I keep strange hours, so I am willing to dine and use the front desk, pool &c very late so as to accommodate the staff and other guests. I am not unreasonable.

    I have a handlebar mustache and will always wear a red carnation so your staff can recognize me. A few minutes before I arrive I will send a fax from a public telephone so you can be prepared. Once settled in, I will teach simple hand signals to staff who can't speak English and will distribute bilingual conversation forms with check-boxes. (Deutsch ist auch gut weil ich ein Österreicher bin.)

Please let me know if you can accommodate me and I will provide more details.

Sincerely,

_____
Kirk von Dunkirk

KYOTO BRIGHTON HOTEL

May 23, 2003

Dear Mr. Kirk von Dunkirk

Thank you for your letter that you sent us on May 15, 2003.

We looked into possibility if we could accept your reuest; however, since more than 95 percent of our guests are Japanese, it is very difficult for us not speaking any Japanese in this property.
We regret to say that it is not possible to fullfill your request.

We are very sorry for unable to cooperate this time.

Sincerely,

Hideki Kakikura
Front Office Manager

Nakadachiuri, Shinmachi-dori, Kamigyo-ku, Kyoto 602-8071, Japan Phone 075-441-4411
http://www.brightonhotels.co.jp

Kirk Dunkirk
♥ ♥ ♥ ♥ ♥ ♥ ♥
Kochi City 780, Japan

Osaka Tokyu Hotel
7-20 Chaya-machi
Kita-ku, Osaka 530-0001

May 21, 2003

To the Events Manager,

Hey there!

My group, The Shikoku Swingers Society, is considering hosting our annual conference at your hotel during July 18 - 20 of this year. Altogether there should be between 24-30 people, evenly divided between men and women.

We have seen information about your facilities and they look just great, but we have a few more specific questions at this time:

1. Can we get most of our rooms on the same floor, with adjoining doors? (You don't have "swinging" doors, do you? Just kidding.)

2. Are spare folding cots available? Just leave us a bunch and we'll wheel them around ourselves.

3. Are your showers coated with a non-slip floor? We've had problems in the past with slippery showers.

4. Is it possible to reserve either the hot spring bath *(onsen)* or the pool *(pu-ru)* for a mixed-use party? It would be late at night, probably after the other guests have retired.

Please write me back ASAP so we can finalize our plans. I can't wait to have our "Festival of Swing 2003" at your lovely hotel. Who knows -- if all goes well, we'll have 2004, 2005 and so on there too. Despite what you might think, once we find a good hotel, we like to stick with it. Get ready to Swing!

Looking forward to meeting you in person,

Kirk Dunkirk
Special Events Co-ordinator

ps: Feel free to drop by a meeting at the conference --we're always looking for new members!

– Keeping the Flame Alive Since 1985! –

Osaka Tokyu Hotel
7-20 Chaya-machi
Kita-ku
Osaka 530-0013

MR. Kirk Dunkirk
Kochi City 780
Japan

May 24, 2003

To Mr.Kirk Dunkirk

Thank you for your mail.

I'm afraid we are fully booked on the July 19th.

We have a single room available for one night for July 18th.

So please let me know if you make a reservation.

We look forward to hearing from you.

TEL:06-6373-2411
FAX:06-6376-0343
E-mail:osaka.ro@tokyuhotel.co.jp
 www.tokyuhotels.co.jp

Osaka Tokyu Hotel
Reservation Sales
Mika.

MITSUI GARDEN HOTEL OSAKA
2-5-7, KORAIBASHI CHUO-KU,
OSAKA, JAPAN.

Tel. 06-223-1131
Fax. 06-223-0257
Telex: 522-3817 MGHOSA
Cable Address: MITSUIGARDENA

FAX TRANSMISSION SHEET

DATE May 23 2003

TO
ATTEN Mr. Kirk Dunkirk
FROM

Thank you very much for choosing Mitsui Garden Hotel. As fllows, we will send you these massages. If you could not receive all pages, please contact to us as soon as possible.

Thank you.

- We will try to assign most of your rooms on the same floor, with adjoining doors.

- I'm afraid the rooms with spare folding cots are fully booked on 19th July. also showers of our hotel are not coated with a non-slip floor.

- We are very sorry that we don't have neither the hot spring bath nor the pool.

If you would like to make a reservation, please let us know again. We hope to see you in OSAKA!!

M. MURAKAMI

Kirk Dunkirk
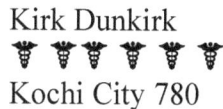
Kochi City 780

Sanrio Company Ltd
1-6-1 Osaki
Shinagawa, Tokyo   ~~May 22, 2003~~ Dec. 31, 2003

    People are scared! People are worried! They need something cute and cheap to spend their money on in order to feel better.

    It was bad before: we had to worry about the economy, terrorists, taepodong missiles and Tama-chan's health... but now we have SARS!

    My idea is for a new Sanrio character that can help people stop worrying about the latest epidemic. The main thing that sets this new character apart from previous ones is that he/she (or even they?) wear a protective surgical mask. We want people to relax, but not be reckless.

    Names are important for character success so here are some ideas: Schmoozamarolli-chan, Mask-kun, Sarbastian, SARS-chan & SARS-kun (a set). Larger dolls can have a removable washable disinfect-able mask. It can contain a warning about how to protect oneself against SARS, so it's not only fun, but educational too!

    Smaller versions can use disposable paper masks. Masks can be bought in sets with the date printed on the front, serving as a mini-calendar. Different months can come in different colors, or even printed with other Sanrio characters such as My Melody, or Chu-chu Taco, the Kissing Octopus™. Very small versions of the character can be worn on mobile phones like protective charms. Imagine how much better people will sleep knowing that SARS-chan and SARS-kun are protecting them. (It will work too; rest is crucial for good health.)

    A whole series of medical disorder characters could be created to soothe people's nerves. For example, SARS-chan and SARS-kun like to meet on karaoke dates with their friends Atopi-kun (the Eczema Bear) and Gin Kin Kau (the flamboyant birthmarked goldfish twins).

    I love all your products, especially Chocopanda. It is my DREAM to be a part of Sanrio. You are the pinnacle of Japanese culture. Please write me back about Sarbastian et al. The world is waiting!

Hugs and fishes. (Chu!)

Kirk Dunkirk
XXXOOO

Ps. This is the second time I sent this letter. Seven months with no reply! Are you trying to STEAL MY IDEA?

SARS-kun - he had a high fever but thanks to his friends he has recovered now.

SARS-kun - he had a high fever but thanks to his friends he has recovered now.

Miki Dunkirk
♥♥♥♥♥♥♥♥
Kochi City 780
Japan

Embasy Suites Hotel
110 West 600 South
Salt Lake City, UT 84101
USA   May 26, 2003

To the Events Manager,

Hi! Nice to meet you.

My group, The Shikoku Swingers Society, thinking maybe our every year conference your hotel while this year of September 18 - 20. Total is maybe among 24-30 person, men and women same of half.

We saw guidebook your facilities and is looking splendid, but we have a more some questions is ok now?:

- Can we our rooms stay on the same floor, all members, with connect doors? (You have "swinging" doors, do you? Just joke. Husband's joke.)

- Are availabling folding cots? If kind to give us many we position them ourself, not to trouble staff.

- Showers are having non-slip floor coating? We had problem before because slipping showers.

- Is it be possible reserve either spa (onsen) or pool (pu-ru) for mix-gender party? Party will late of night start, after the other guests already back to room.

Please reply me ASAP so we can final ours the plans. I can't wait our "Festival of Swing 2003" at your lovely hotel. Who knows -- if everything good, we can 2004, 2005 etc there too. Maybe you surprise but once we get good hotel, we stick with it. Get ready to Swing!

Looking forward to meeting you in person,

Miki Dunkirk
Special Events Co-ordinator

ps: Please visit ok any meeting ours the conference --we always try for new members!

EMBASSY SUITES HOTEL®

Salt Lake City - Downtown

June 3, 2003

Ms. Miki Dunkirk

Kochi City 780
Japan

Dear Ms. Dunkirk:

Thank you for your interest in Embassy Suites Hotel to host "Festival of Swing 2003". Unfortunately, we do not have accommodations available September 18 – 20, 2003.

Please keep us in mind for other events that may come to Salt Lake City in the future.

Sincerely,

Randi

Randi Fitzgerald
Sales Manager

Embassy Suites Hotel • 110 West 600 South, Salt Lake City, UT 84101 • Tel: (801) 359-7800 • Fax: (801) 359-3753
For Reservations Call: 1-800-EMBASSY • www.embassysuites.com   TheHiltonFamily

(Actually, according to the homepage, lots of rooms were available at the time…

Maybe we should have tried New Orleans instead of Salt Lake.

Thanks anyway, Randi. And thanks for your great name.)

- KDK

Kirk Dunkirk
¥¥¥¥¥¥¥¥¥¥¥
Kochi City 780
Japan

Ministry of Finance, Japan
3-1-1 Kasumigaseki
Chiyoda-ku Tokyo 100-8940

June 3, 2003

To Whom it May Concern,

Boy, I do not envy you guys.

You have a really hard job. Probably one of the hardest jobs in the world. People say the President of the USA is a hard job but I figure yours is much harder. I bet you don't have your own helicopter and cook do you? Then again, the President of Somalia is probably a really hard job, and he might not have a helicopter, but he doesn't have to deal with the huge amount of money that you guys do. I don't know if Somalia has a Prime Minister or a President but I think you see my point either way. Heck they might even have a king but in this case it doesn't make a difference. Hard is hard. So if you're busy just skip to the middle part of this letter or read the shorter version I included.

There's lots of reasons why you have a hard job: Before, everyone thought you were going to take over the world and now everyone complains that you're not doing enough. I think I know how you must feel as a group. I got married a few years ago and once the romance wore off now it's just one complaint after another.

So I thought I could offer some ideas:

> Why don't you print some 1000 yen notes as 1050 yen instead -- that way the tax is already included.
>
> They'd be much easier to use -- No more fishing around for change. And in this economy everyone has a short temper. And we know how young people have no attention span anymore. So people will spend more.
>
> Shops always price things like "980 yen." Under the new system, to be more convenient, they will round prices up to 1000 yen (so people can use the 1050 bills.) There you go: instant deflation buster! People always pay more for convenience.
>
> Don't change all the bills! That would be nuts. But you could change a whole bunch, distribute them for just a short time, (like 1050 hours) and this is key: set an expiration date. So people get them for only 1000 yen, a bargain, but they have only six months to use them as 1050 yen notes before they go back to 1000 yen. This would spur domestic consumption. It would be fun too.
>
> I don't know whose face to put on it, so how about just some cherry blossoms because they don't last long? You could use special paper that turns pink before the time's up.

Okay, well maybe I'll go down in history like that guy that gave away the rights to the paper clip, but I just wanna help. I like Japan and most of the stuff you do.

Good luck. "Gambatte" as you guys (and ladies) always say.
Sincerely
Kirk Dunkirk

"1050 Yen Note:"

Several attempts but no reply.

Another brilliant idea ahead of its time,

and more years of economic doldrums.

Prince Maurits
c/o G.E. van der Wulp
The Netherlands Gov't Information Service
Postbox 20009
2500 EA The Hague
The Netherlands

Nov. 09, 2004

Your Highness! (Or Mr. van der Wulp)

Please don't throw this letter away!

We're not just another rock band. We're the Alien Hand Band -- a group of volunteers who are dying to perform FOR FREE for His Majesty. We hope his interest will raise awareness of our affliction.

All of us either have or are involved with the newly documented but sadly misunderstood illness known as "Alien Hand." DON'T LAUGH! It's a real problem. [Document attached.] Sometimes after a stroke, head injury or other trauma people develop this syndrome. Basically they lose control of their hand and it attacks them or other people, steals things, breaks dishes, etc. all by itself, even though its "owner" tries to stop it.

Our band, with members from Japan and other countries, is coming to Europe to spread the word. We play unforgettable pop tunes such as the Beatles' "I Wanna Hold Your Hand", "Twist and Shout", or Elvis' "I'm All Shook Up" and even blues classics like "Born to Hand Jive." We add our own special mark to the tunes by taking wild musical solos at random -- to demonstrate how a "problem" can be turned into an opportunity. The 32-minute performance is followed by a slide show and some juggling with the audience (soft objects.)

A.H.B. is comprised of 4 members with the syndrome-- the result of things like horseback falls or, in my case, "Economy Class Syndrome" -- and 2 medical personnel: a doctor (working the organ, naturally) and a nurse (maracas, unicycle etc.) We all took up instruments as therapy and one thing led to another so here we are, ready to "Shake Rattle and Roll!"

So what do you say? It free, fun and for a good cause. Please write us back so we can plan our summer tour. (If you're not interested please pass this on to either Prince Bernhard Jr. or Prince Floris. You're our first choice but they seem pretty cool too.)

sincerely,

Kirk "Lefty" Dunkirk (Bass)

ps: People in Amsterdamn must really get a kick out of saying "Your Highness."

pps: Why "the" Hague?

Prince Maurits
c/o G.E. van der Wulp
The Netherlands Gov't Information Service
Postbox 20009
2500 EA The Hague
The Netherlands

Nov. 09, 2004

Your Highness! (Or Mr. van der Wulp)

Please don't throw this letter away!

We're not just another rock band. We're the Alien Hand Band -- a group of volunteers who are dying to perform FOR FREE for His Majesty. We hope his interest will raise awareness of our affliction.

All of us either have or are involved with the newly documented but sadly misunderstood illness known as "Alien Hand." DON'T LAUGH! It's a real problem. [Document attached.] Sometimes after a stroke, head injury or other trauma people develop this syndrome. Basically they lose control of their hand and it attacks them or other people, steals things, breaks dishes, etc. all by itself, even though its "owner" tries to stop it.

Our band, with members from Japan and other countries, is coming to Europe to spread the word. We play unforgettable pop tunes such as the Beatles' "I Wanna Hold Your Hand", "Twist and Shout", or Elvis' "I'm All Shook Up" and even blues classics like "Born to Hand Jive." We add our own special mark to the tunes by taking wild musical solos at random -- to demonstrate how a "problem" can be turned into an <u>opportunity</u>. The 35-minute performance is followed by a slide show and some juggling with the audience (soft objects.)

A.H.B. is comprised of 4 members with the syndrome-- the result of things like horseback falls or, in my case, "Economy Class Syndrome" -- and 2 medical personnel: a doctor (working the organ, naturally) and a nurse (maracas, unicycle etc.) We all took up instruments as therapy and one thing led to another so here we are, ready to "Shake Rattle and Roll!"

So what do you say? It free, fun and for a good cause. Please write us back so we can plan our summer tour. (If you're not interested please pass this on to either prince Bernhard Jr. or Prince Floris. You're our first choice but they seem pretty cool too.)

sincerely,

Kirk "Lefty" Dunkirk (Bass)

ps: People in Amsterdamn must really get a kick out of saying "Your Highness."

pps: Why <u>the</u> Hague?

The Alien Hand Band • c/o Kirk Dunkirk • Kochi City 780 • Japan

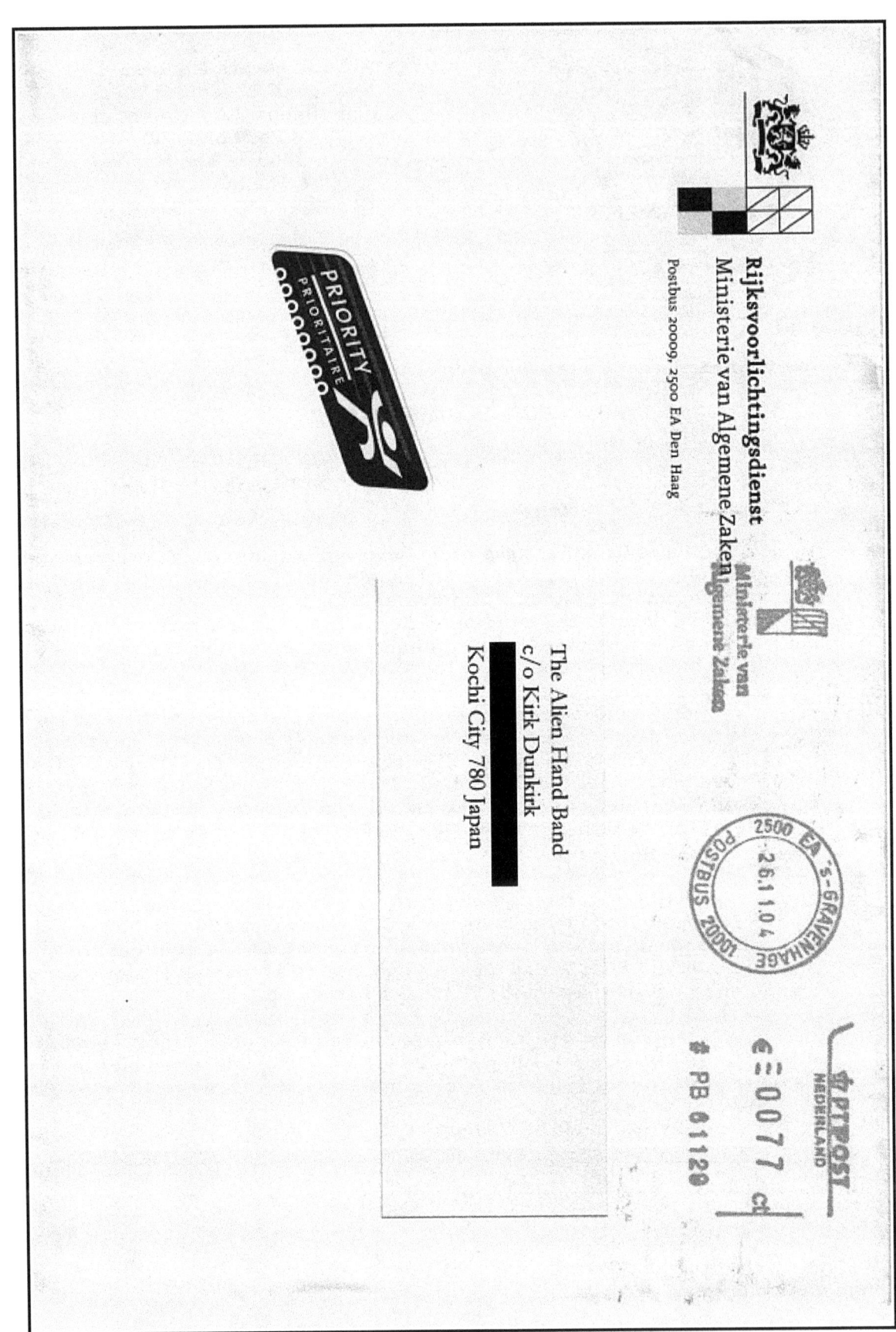

Rijksvoorlichtingsdienst
Ministerie van Algemene Zaken

Directeur-Generaal

Postal Address
Postbus 20009
2500 EA Den Haag

Visiting Address
Binnenhof 19, Den Haag

Contact
Hans Kamp

E-mail
h.kamp@minaz.nl

Telephone
070-3564183

Fax
+31 70 356 46 80

The Alien Hand Band
c/o Kirk Dunkirk

Kochi City 780 Japan

Date
26 November 2004

Reference

Subject
Invitation Prince Maurits

Dear Mister Dunkirk,

In answer to your letter to mister van der Wulp I would like to thank you for your invitation. I'm sorry to inform you that Prince Maurits, Prince Bernhard Junior or Prince Floris will not be present when you perform in Holland.

Good luck planning your tour and performing in Europe.

Yours sincerely,

Hans Kamp
Press and Publicity Department Royal House

Miki Dunkirk
ｷｷｷｷｷｷｷ
Kochi City 780
Japan

Senator Lisa Murkowski (R-AK)
222 West 7th Ave., Rm. 569
Anchorage, AK 99513
USA

9 June 2003

Dear Senator Lisa Murkowski (R-AK)

    I am big yours fan! Please allowing introduce of myself.

    I'm a 78 years old homemaker lives in south Japan whole live. Too small island boring octopus farm only , animal husbandry and poison tip dart traditonal   fishing method making sometimes movie on back of white truck.

    Before long time I marry American man only short time. But he teach me joy of model rocketing. Oh how wonderful! Life small island bec-ome great! Every day I launch rocket is sound like happy heaven. Only rocket important. Some times   forget poison tip dart and animal husba-ndry. Can not sell rocket my island but in a week ship comes and bringing engines etc. I say " happy happy ship is !

    Husband is die my rocket and poison tip dart mishap before long time but   promise she never forget hobby rocketing. His love rocket is heavenly thrusting make me cry even now old woman. So I get mail my now American rocketing pen pal you support ^and five of his Senate colleagues   have asked the Bureau of Alcohol, Tobacco and Firearms (ATF) to delay for 90 days the implementation of regulations concerning hobby rockets.

    Good news! I hope all peoples can enjoy hobby rocketing. Thanks to you. Please may I give your photo and sign or letter? If necessary I can pay for photo. Its dream go USA and launch big rocket at your White House.

Thank you for considering our offer,

Miki Dunkirk

☞ ☞ ☞ ☞ ☞ ☞ ☞
KOCHI CITY 780
JAPAN

Asahi Breweries, Ltd
Mitsuya Cider Division
3-7-1 Kyobashi, Chuo-Ku, Tokyo 104-8323

Sept 17, 2003

Dear Asahi (Mitsuya),

I've heard that you are going out of business. That's a shame because I really like your products. I admit I've never used them but when I read about them in the paper they sound pretty good. I can't believe that Mitsuya Cider will be 119 years old -- That means it's older than Coca-Cola! I always thought sweet fizzy drinks were an American invention. Sorry my friends and I didn't buy more of your stuff. Maybe you should have advertised more.

I'm writing this letter because I'm an artist and I want to take photos and/or video of your plumbing fixtures before, during, and after you tear the building down. It's for a work-in-progress called "Orthopedic Nation". I'm pretty flexible with time but October is best as I will be in the area for an historical reenactment.

I'm afraid I can't offer monetary compensation but through my work I have met many people who collect plumbing fixtures and would be delighted to introduce you to them. This might help defray the costs associated with demolition.

Thank you very much.

Kirk Dunkirk.

Dear Mr. K. Dunkirk

First of all, we are very sorry to late response for your inquiry.

It seems you have high interest on our product so called "MITSUYA CIDER" based on articles which you read. It is absolutory right, MITSUYA CIDER will have 120 years anniversary in next year. This has the longest history in Japan soft drink category. Because of this strong Brand Equity, we have a plan to cerebrate 120 years birthday with strong marketing support as you advice. Additionally, we will establish memorial events as reborn of next 120 years of MITSUYA CIDER.

While we have a plan to modify MITSUYA CIDER production line in order to improve our production efficiency, we have no plan to rebuild building and/or production line. We are afraid that you may not have chance to take photos and/or video on our "plumbing fixtures".

We do our best to distribute MITSUYA CIDER all over Japan at Convenience stores, Super markets and Vending machines. Hope you can buy MITSUYA CIDER at your nearest store or vending machine. But, in case you have difficulty to buy MITSUYA CIDER, please drink product sample, which contains with this latter.

We wish your success on your business. Thank you very much for your letter again and we hope you continue to support ASAHI SOFT DRINK products, including MITSUYA CIDER.

Best regards

Even got some samples!

Kirk Dunkirk
Evergreen Dance School
❖❖❖❖❖❖❖❖❖❖
Kochi City 780

Zojirushi Corp
20-5 Tenma 1-Chome
Kita-Ku Osaka 530-8511

June 18, 2003

Dear Zojirushi,

Thank you soooooooo much for your wonderful rice cooker!

If you hadn't invented it, I don't know what I'd do!

Back in the United States, we usually cook rice in a simple pot over the stove, like cavemen-- unga bunga! Because of this primitive method, we never developed the discerning taste necessary to appreciate plain white rice. Instead we usually ruin it by adding spices, sauce and so on, or using lower quality brown or yellow wild rice and herbs. I think of making dishes such as gumbo, pilaf, paella, and especially rice pudding as an admission of defeat. It's like putting ketchup on sushi!

Your invention saves me a lot of time too. As soon as I finish teaching my "Sexercise" dance class, there is a big pot of steaming white rice waiting for me. A bowl of that and a couple of yellow pickles and I'm ready to go again.

Now that rainy season is almost finished, it's time to go camping. Does your company have any plans to make a battery powered rice cooker? I usually bring a cooker with me but sometimes the cord isn't long enough to reach my car.

Also, there is a shop near me that sells cheap Thai and Australian rice. I know they are of poor quality (heck, they're not even very sticky) but they are about 50% cheaper, and as a dance instructor I don't have much money. Can I use them in my rice cooker without damaging it? I figure it's like cheap gasoline in a car - not good in the long run. If it is ok, should I stick the butter in before cooking or after the rice has finished?

Please write me back soon. I love hearing about white rice.

Sincerely,

Kirk Dunkirk
Certified Dance Instructor (USSD Level 3, WDA Class B)

ZOJIRUSHI CORPORATION
20-5,1-chome,Tenma,Kita-ku,Osaka 530-8511,Japan
Telephone:(06)6356-2388 Facsimile:(06)6356-2370

July 2, 2003

Dear Ms. Dunkirk

We have received your letter with thanks.
It is very witty and it made us happy. Thank you very much.

By the way, our replies to your questions are as follows:

Regarding a battery powered rice cooker, we are afraid to say that we do not have such a cooker and there is no plan to develop it currently. We are sorry not to meet your request.

As for second inquiry, cooking Thai and Australian rice in the rice cooker, we believe it will not damage the cooker. Please feel easy to cooking them.

But the amount of water for Thai and Australian rice differs from one for Japonica rice. To cook them as much as it can, please immerse rice in water for half an hour before cooking. And make sure to add little more water than to cook Japonica rice. As we do not have a recipe for cooking Thai and Australian rice, we are sorry that please try to find the most suitable water level for cooking.

And lastly we can advise you to add the butter after the rice has finished. It can be better than adding butter before cooking.
We wish you would have a happy life with tasty rice.

Best regards,

S. Okubo
Zojirushi Corp.
International business dep.

HITACHI

Hitachi Home & Life Solutions, Inc.
Heating & Cooking Appliances Business Division
Hitachi Atago Bldg.
15-12, Nishi-Shimbashi 2-chome,
Minato-ku, Tokyo, 105-8410 Japan
Tel:+81-3-3506-1409   Fax:+81-3-3506-1446

July 4, 2003

Mr. Kirk Dunkirk
Evergreen Dance School
                                  Kochi City 780-

Dear Mr. Dunkirk,

Thank you very much for your using our Rice Cooker.
It is our pleasure to hear that you have been enjoyed rice cooking with our cooker.   We will answer to your questions as the following;

1. Battery powered Rice Cooker

    It is need 300W for 0.36 liter and 600W power for 0.72 liter to cook the rice and that power must be kept at least 30 minutes. However, it is technically difficult to put such a big powered battery into the cooker body at present.

2. To cook Thai or Australian Rice

    Yes, you can cook them. Please put more water into the pot when cooking Australian rice, or you could not get good result on occasion. The amount of water will be adjusted according to your taste.
    In case of Thai rice, it is recommended to input more water and furthermore rice will be soaked in water about one hour before starting to cook.
    It may be no problem to use butter in case of small amount.
    However, it is better to input butter after rice cooked, because water circulation in the pot became not enough and rice will easily burned.

We hope that you will satisfy with our answer.

Sincerely yours,

Naoaki Izawa
Business Planning Department

☠ ☠ ☠ ☠ ☠ ☠
Kochi City 780

Tokyu Sports Oasis, Umeda
ax Building 7F
2-3-21 Sonezakishinchi
Kita-ku, Osaka City

June 23, 2003

Dear Sports Oasis,

I will be moving to Osaka soon and I love to swim.

I saw your ad in Townpage and checked with my friends in Osaka who recommend your sports club but I have an important question:

Can I swim in your pool with a wooden leg? If I take it off it is very difficult to swim.

Don't worry, it's not dirty, it won't foul the water or clog the filters or introduce water termites. It meets ANSI-3934 standards for artificial limb safety. It's a specially treated, high-tech wooden leg light years away from it's ancient predecessors. These days, more and more orthopedic specialists are turning to wood for its flexibility and longevity.

If you feel this will make the other swimmers uncomfortable I will tell you about a system I have in Kochi. My local sports club was unsure of letting me swim in the pool with a peg leg but we made a deal. I go to the pool three times a week, but on Saturday during the "Pika Pika Kid Swim Afternoon" I wore a special bathing costume and eyepatch that made me look like a pirate. The staff put posters of me all over the club explaining about it. Then I'd "walk the plank," (actually a diving board) and fall in the deep end after shouting "Argh! I'm gone ta see Davey Jones!" a legendary pirate. I'd then swim underwater to the adult lanes and proceed with my 1000m crawl followed by a 100m backstroke cool down.

The kids and old women loved it. I received no money for my performance, just the satisfaction one can only get from the completion of a good compromise.

What do you think? Please write me back soon because I need to plan my new life in bustling Osaka. Depending on your pool hours, I'm sure we can work something out. I really need my "sports oasis."

Thank you very much, matey.

sincerely,

Kirk Dunkirk
aka Captain Kirk

Yasushi S▓
Tokyo Sports Oasis
2-3-21 Sonezakishinchi
Kita-ku, Osaka 530-0002
(Tel) 06-6348-0109
(FAX) 06-6348-0451

Mr. Kirk Dunkirk
▓▓▓▓▓▓▓▓▓▓▓▓▓
Kochi City 780-▓▓▓▓

June 30, 2003

Dear Mr. Dunkirk,

Thank you for your letter.

We understood your situation on it. We'd like to have you in our club, however, we would also like to see you and talk with you before our final answer.

At the pool, we just have three courses (25m) for swimming, but we'd like you to see ~~you~~ our facilities, anyway.

Unfortunately, our staff members don't speak English, our manager, neither. I speak English a little. I'll be at our club with manager from 10:00 to 16:00, on the 7th, 9th, 18th, 23th and 29th of July. Please make plans to look at our club on those days.

If you are still interested in our club, please contact me (S███) at 06-6348-0109 or you can also email me at ███@yahoo.co.jp. I check emails everyday because this is my personal email address.

We hope we can work out.

Thank you very much.

Sincerely yours,

Change of Status in Membership Information

Category	Need for Request	Deadlines	Fees (+Tax)
Leave of Absent	Leave of Absence form, Membership Card	Must apply by the 10th of the month before the month of leave of absence requested. *	700yen / month up to three months
Cancellation of Membership	Cancellation Notice form, Membership Card	Must apply three weeks before (by the 10th of the month)	
Change of Membership	Notice of Change form, Membership Card	Must apply three weeks before (by the 10th of the month)	1,000 yen
Name, Address, Banking Information, etc. Change	Notice of Change form	Anytime	
Lost Card	Lost Card form	Anytime	1,000 yen

- Members are not permitted to make updates or changes of status in Membership via the telephone.
- A leave of absence is permitted for a minimum of one month and up to three months.

*For example, If you wish to freeze your membership for the month of December you must notify the sports club by November 10th.

*If you'd like to have your membership back within a year after you quit our club, you don't have to pay an initiation fee again. (We just charge ¥3,150 in that case.)

 ## Payment

If you've got an automatic payment;

> All fees will be withdrawn from your bank account on the 10th of the month.

> *If you don't have your bank account in Japan, you can pay your monthly fee. however, you need to pay for six months or for a year, it's refundable though.

Gym

- Another athletic shoes are required in exercise areas. (not street shoes)
- You may carry beverages in covered plastic containers during your workout.

Pool

- Members must take a shower before using the swimming pool.
- Please bring your towel to the pool, then dry yourself before returning to the locker room.
- No accessories, and no glasses at the pool.

Locker Room

- Always carry your locker key. (We are not responsible for lost or stolen articles.)
- Do not wear bathing suits in the bath and sauna.
- Do not wear any shoes in the locker room.

Other

- Smoking is strictly prohibited in the club.
- If you have some tattoos, you must be refused membership to the club.

Kirk Dunkirk
☺ ☺ ☺ ☺ ☺ ☺ ☺
Kochi City 780
Japan

Yasushi ---------
Tokyu Sports Oasis
2-3-21 Sonezakishinchi
Kita-ku, Osaka
530-0002

Sept. 4, 2003

Dear Yasushi,

Thank you so much for your helpful and earnest reply to my letter regarding membership at your sports club. (Swimming with a wooden leg.) I am sorry I took so long to reply.

Unfortunately my plans have changed and I will no longer be moving to Osaka.

Still, I appreciate your kindness. Your explanation was very clear, very complete, and your English very good. Probably your letter was more helpful to me than any letter I might get from a sports club in America.

I am often impressed by the kindness and diligence of Japanese people. You are one of those special people who made my stay in Japan a good memory.

thank you again.
Sincerely,

Kirk Dunkirk

Kirk Dunkirk
✈ ✈ ✈ ✈ ✈ ✈ ✈
Kochi City 780

Pokka Corporation
35-16 Daikan-Cho Daiichi Fuji Building
Higashi-Ku Nagoya
461-8648 Aichi

July 7, 2003

Dear Pokka Pokka Coffee,

My best friend and I love your coffee. We are in a band and we often stay up late thinking of new songs and practicing. We practice in an old barn, and we do push ups and sits ups and wrestle each other to stay awake, but the one thing that keeps us going are cans of Pokka Pokka Coffee from a nearby vending machine.

Actually we drink so much Pokka Pokka Coffee that we changed the name of our band from "Shaman You" to "Death by Pancakes" and finally to "Pokka Pokka Coffee." Before we were a "visual" band; blue spiky hair, kabuki makeup and so on but now that we are known as "Pokka Pokka Coffee" we just dress up like the guy on the can with the goofy hair cut.

I even look like him, so when we perform, my stage name is "Pokka Pokka" and the other guy in my band (Brian) is called "Coffee." He had this nickname before he came to Japan. --He actually reminds people of coffee! We use the "Pokka Pokka Guy" on all our posters, and the T-shirts and CDs we sell at the door.

Since our act has a similar name to your product, people sometimes ask us questions about it. They usually want to know:

a) what does "Pokka Pokka" mean? I think it's Japanese onomatopoeia for the sound of roasting nuts, but Coffee (aka Brian) thinks it's because guys that play poker drink twice the amount of coffee as other people. Typical Brian, he would think that.

b) Who was the inspiration for the Pokka Pokka guy on the can? I think it was Fred from the Scooby-Doo cartoon, but the other half of my band thinks it was the singer from the 60's rock band The Troggs. (big hit: "Wild Thing")

If you could clear this up we'd really appreciate it. We have some shows coming up and we need to prepare our interactive VCD.

Thanks a lot.
Sincerely

Kirk Dunkirk
lead songwriter, Pokka Pokka Coffee band.

70   Irked by Kirk

POKKA CORPORATION

Daiichifuji Bldg., 35-16, Daikan-cho, Higashi-ku.
Nagoya, Japan
TEL.:052-932-1471
FAX.:052-932-1425

July 16, 2003

Mr. Kirk Dunkirk
░░░░░░░░░░░░░░░░░░░░░░
Kochi City 780
Japan

Dear Mr. Dunkirk,

We thank you very much for your letter and patronage of Pokka products.
Especially, we are very glad to hear that you are one of "Pokka Coffee" fan.
We also feel honored that the name of our product is used for the name of your band.
However, please understand that [Pokka Coffee] is registered trademark of ours. So please use the name only for your private use.

The following is the explanation for your question.

a) The name of our product (canned coffee) is not "Pokka Pokka Coffee" but "Pokka Coffee".
  "Pokka" is the name of our company and it was made from golf pants called "knickerbockers".

b) The man who is designed on the "Pokka Coffee" express good atmosphere with another people designed on the "Pokka Coffee".
  And the man is not modeled on anyone.

We would appreciate for your understanding and continuous patronage of Pokka Coffee.

Yours faithfully,

POKKA CORPORATION
 Kazushi Maekawa
Manager, Consumer Service Div.

Kirk Dunkirk
☹ ☠ ☹ ☢ ☹ ☠ ☹
Kochi City 780
Japan

Rohto Pharm
8-1Tatsumi-Nishi 1-Chome
Ikuno-Ku, Osaka 544-8666

~~July 2, 2003~~
September 16. 2003

I bought your Rohto C3 Soft One saline solution a week ago and have been using it since. I chose it because it was on sale, but after using it I got impressed by the quality.

Still, I'm living in fear…

Look at the photos below. In one photo you can see the "safety seal" securely fastened. Then, in the second photo the cap is clearly off, but the so-called "safety seal" is not broken. In fact, for the past week I have been using your product, taking the cap off & putting it on again twice a day, with the purported "safety seal" intact the whole time! And I'm not even being careful.

This has caused me great stress. I can't trust anything now. Were the dishes at the coffee shop washed? Are the traffic lights synchronized? After Snow Brand's poison milk, the mislabeled meat fiasco, mad cow disease, HIV tainted blood, and now this, I'm afraid to leave my house. Forget about bungee jumping. Why bother using condoms? Even here in backwater Kochi, some nutcase put needles in supermarket bread a few summers back. Maybe I should too, nobody cares!

If this kind of shoddy disregard for consumers' safety occurred in my native Belgium, some of your executives would be slapped around and thrown in jail for a while. Or at least consumer activists would dump manure on their cars and dance up and down banging drums . Don't worry, I am too busy enough for that, but I still think you owe me an explanation. I certainly expect a reply.

I do not ask for a refund. How can one put a price on peace of mind?

Sincerely

Kirk Dunkirk

ps: this is the *SECOND TIME* I sent you this letter. Why won't you reply to my appeal?

cap & seal on

(false-sense-of-) security seal off

ROHTO PHARMACEUTICAL CO., LTD.
8-1, Tatsumi-nishi 1-chome, Ikuno-ku, Osaka 544-8666, Japan
Telephone: +81-6-6758-1231   Fax: +81-6-6757-5155
URL http://www.rohto.co.jp

September 29, 2003

Mr. Kirk Dunkirk
[address redacted]
Kochi City 780

Dear Mr. Dunkirk,

Let me begin to thank you for your letter of July 2 and its reminder of September 16. We appreciate your invaluable appeal regarding the safety seal of Rohto C3 Soft One, and apologize deeply for the uneasiness caused to you by this belated reply.

We made an inquiry to the manufacturer of the product and have just received their reply that they would like to take a close look at the actual good in question. Therefore, we are sorry to trouble you, but would be very grateful for your sending the product in question to the address below by collect courier:

    Customer Support Center
    Rohto Pharmaceutical Co., Ltd.
    Attn. Masanori Okuda
    1-8-1, Tatsumi-nishi, Ikuno-ku, Osaka 〒544-8666
    TEL: 06-6758-1230

Thank you very much for sending us the product in advance.

Sincerely yours,

Masanori Okuda
Customer Support Center

Masanori Okuda (signature)

Kirk Dunkirk
✌ ✌ ✌ ✌
Kochi City
780-x x x
Japan

Customer Support Center
Rohto Pharmaceutical Co., Ltd.
Attn: Masanori Okuda
8-1 Tatsumi-nishi 1-chome
Ikuno-ku, Osaka 544-8666

Nov. 8, 2003

Dear Mr. Okuda,

Thank you very much for your attention to my problem. I am deeply touched by your concern.

Thanks to your humanity, I feel safe to start wearing contact lenses again. I can feel from your letter that you are deeply human, though I still mistrust waitresses spitting in my food, dirty needles while donating blood and so on. It's up to people like you and me to keep the world from falling into chaos.

Anyway, I'm keeping my end of the bargain by sending the bottle of saline solution (and the unsafe cap) to you by collect courier.

Even though I complained about my safety, you will notice that the bottle is almost empty. Some of your associates might accuse me of having used the solution after I wrote to you the first time, but it was pretty heavy so I squeezed most of the liquid out and down the drain in order to save you postage. So much for the naysayers.

Sorry it took over a month to get back to you. I've been busy with my cat.

Sincerely,

Kirk Dunkirk

ROHTO PHARMACEUTICAL CO., LTD.
8-1, Tatsumi-nishi 1-chome, Ikuno-ku, Osaka 544-8666, Japan
Telephone: +81-6-6758-1231 Fax: +81-6-6757-5155
URL http://www.rohto.co.jp

November 18, 2003

Mr. Kirk Dunkirk

Kochi City 780

Dear Mr. Dunkirk,

Thank you for sending Rohto C Cube Soft One back to us together with your letter of November 14.

As mentioned in your letter, it is a pleasure to enclose a postal money order for ¥2,730 (consumption tax included) to refund the C Cube Soft One you purchased.

Again, we apologize for all the uncomfortableness and inconveniences caused to you in connection with this product.

It is regrettable that our product was not very satisfactory to you this time, but we will make continual efforts in hope of meeting expectations of our customers in near future.

Sincerely yours,

Masanori Okuda
Customer Support Center

Refund Check from Rhoto

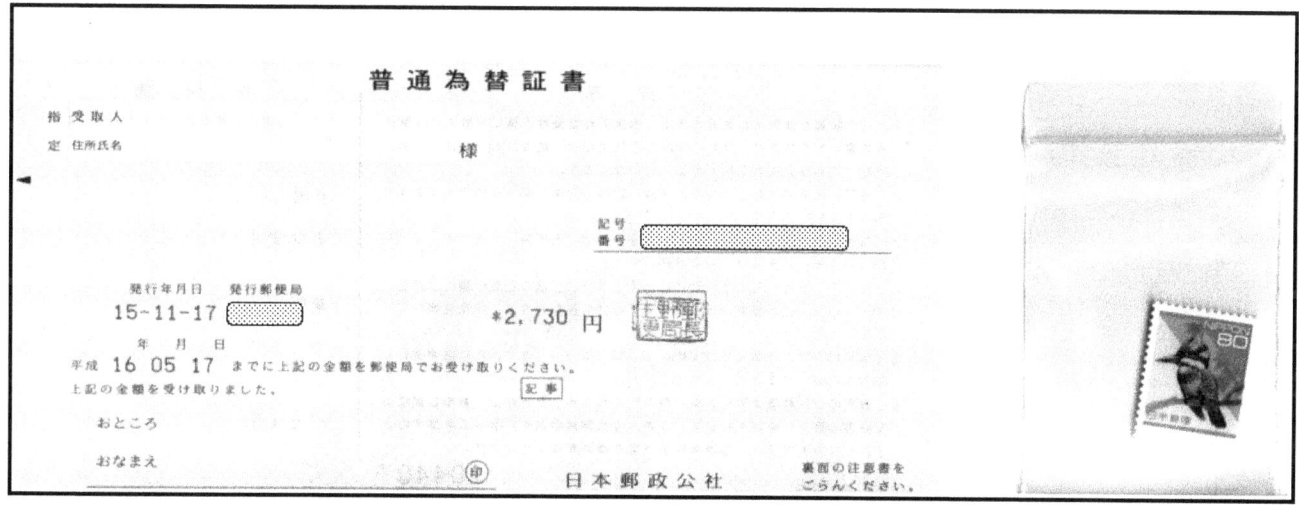

Wow - even refunded the stamp.

I am a Rhoto Rooter!

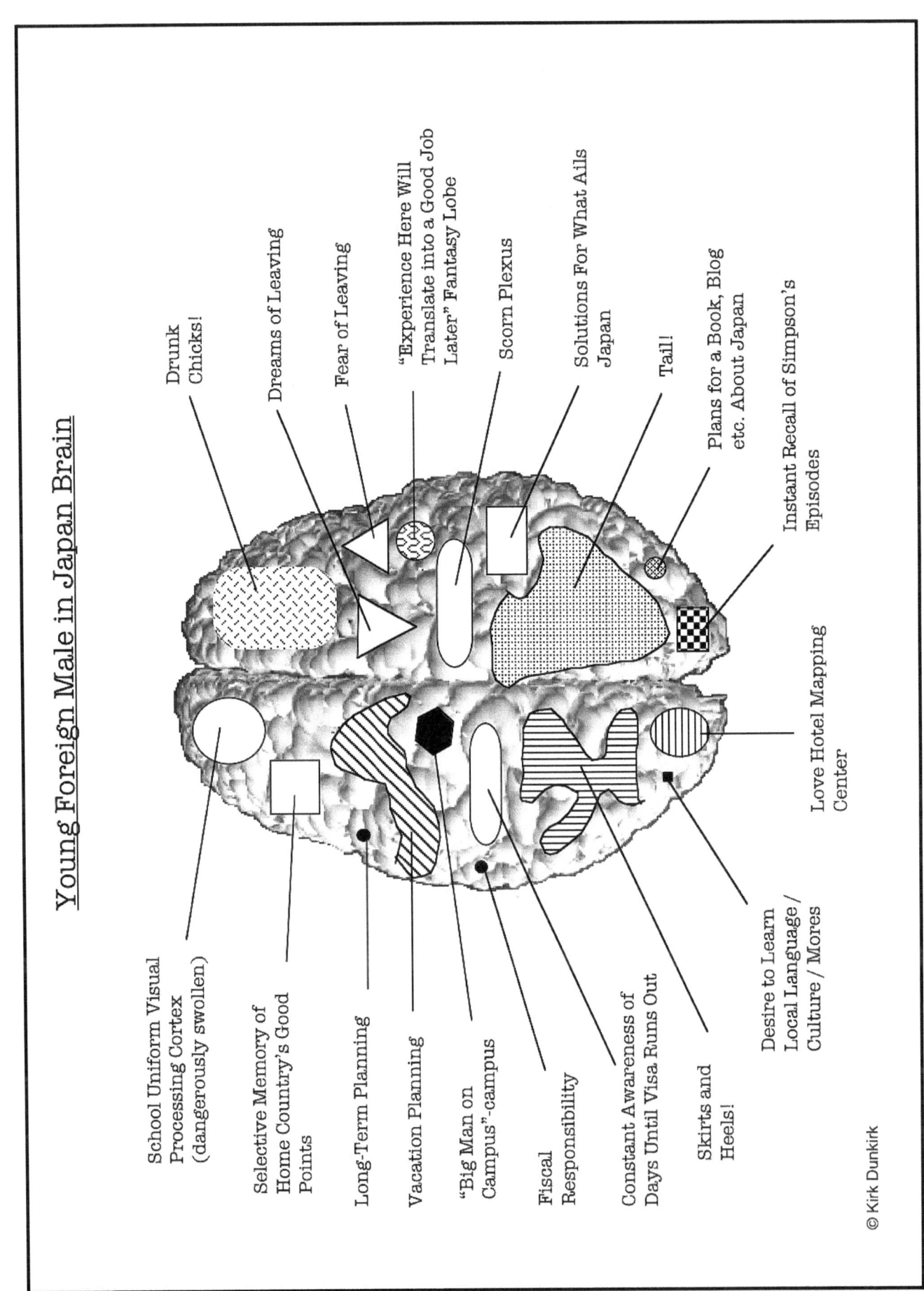

Kirk Dunkirk
Excelsior Floating Homes
♠ ♠ ♠ ♠ ♠ ♠
Kochi City 780- ♠ ♠ ♠ ♠
Japan

Fast Retailing Co
717-1 Sayama
Yamaguchi 754-0894

~~July 14, 2003~~
December 15, 2003

Dear Uniqlo,

    I love your products and admire your merchandizing prowess. My girlfriend calls me "Uniqlo Guy." There are days when I leave the house and everything I'm wearing is from your store, even my socks, belt, underpants, book bag and sunglasses. There's a guy in my office and we show up in the same outfit sometimes. People think we planned it that way but if we had coordinated our clothes we'd obviously make sure to wear something different!

    Unfortunately the market in Japan is saturated and overseas isn't doing so well, so your sales machine has moved into produce. I wish you luck, not that you need it, but once you've cornered the market in zucchini, you're going to need to move on. I have a suggestion and I wanted to share it with you before that time comes.

    Houseboats! That what this country needs. It's crowded here, rent is expensive and 99% of the population lives really close to the sea or a river, most of which are paved over and filled with sludge anyway. Houseboats would go a long way towards alleviating these problems and besides, when some poor sap gets transferred every three years, he could take his home with him.

    My company is based in Louisiana and has sales departments in France and the Netherlands, but we are looking to tap into the vast potential for Floating Homes in Japan. If your company would like to change the course of Japanese civilization, please get in touch with me and I'll send you a brochure.

I look forward to your reply.

Sincerely,

Kirk Dunkirk
Director of Marketing, Japan

ps. Please note the date. This is the second time I sent this letter.

Mitsunori Kanda
Fast Retailing Co., LTD.
717-1 Sayama Yamaguchi
754-0894 Japan

December 26, 2003

Mr. Kirk Dunkirk

    Thanks for your proposal. And we are very sorry that we did not get back to you last time you sent the letter.

    However we are not going to work on the houseboat business that you mention, unfortunately, although it sounds fascinating. For the time being, we think we should focus on casual clothes.

    We are very glad to hear that you like Uniqlo, and hope you are and will be "Uniqlo-Guy".

Best regards,

Mitsunori Kanda
General Manager, Direct Retailing Department
Fast Retailing Co., Ltd.

Kirk Dunkirk
International Liaisons Officer
✔ ✔ ✔ ✔ ✔
Kochi City 780- ✔ ✔ ✔
Japan

Connecticut Sun
1 Mohegan Sun Boulevard
Uncasville, CT 06382 July 14, 2003
USA

To Whom it May Concern,

I am writing on behalf of my employer, Mr. Kojiro Takenaka.

Mr. Takenaka is a big fan of Women's NBA and often visits the U.S. on business. He would like to try some Suns games with an interest in buying season tickets. He thinks it's great that Native Americans can finally own a sports franchise and that gambling and professional sports is a winning combination.

Unfortunately, my employer sometimes receives death and kidnapping threats, so he travels with at least 2 armed bodyguards at all times.

I am writing about your stadium's policy regarding concealed weapons. Mr. Takenaka's guards would like to carry legally licensed, concealed automatic handguns and perhaps katana (Japanese swords.) His bodyguards all carry a level 2 or greater license, which in Japan allows for decapitation or disembowelment in self-defense.

Thank you very much. We are looking forward to a great 2004 season.

sincerely,

Kirk Dunkirk

3 November, 2003

Mr. Kirk Dunkirk
International Liaisons Officer
‾‾‾‾‾‾‾‾‾‾‾‾‾‾
Kochi City 780-‾‾‾‾
Japan

Mr. Dunkirk,

Thank you for your letter regarding the possible attendance and Connecticut Sun season ticket purchase for your employer Mr. Takenaka.

Unfortunately, our facility has strict guidelines prohibiting concealed weapons of any nature on property. Regardless of your classification and licensing, we can not justify this breach in security especially as it relates to our other patrons.

If the threats to your employer subside in the coming months, we welcome you to visit our facility and watch the Connecticut Sun.

My best,

Chris Sienko
General Manager

Kirk Dunkirk
✘ ✘ ✘ ✘ ✘
Kochi City 780-✘ ✘ ✘

Nissay Insurance
Head Office
3-5-12, Imabashi, Chuo-ku
Osaka 541-850

July 18, 2003

Dear Nissay,

I'm writing about your pet insurance. I was referred by a friend but as I don't speak Japanese so good, I couldn't understand everything he told me, so me and him decided I should write you a letter instead. We figured you must have some people who can translate.

When I heard you had pet insurance I was so happy. Right after I came to Japan my only friend at the time died. She was my pet prairie dog Josephine. I think she died of monkeypox because she displayed all the classic symptoms. Loose stool, howling at night and so on. By the end she was too weak to even ride her favorite tricycle around the kitchen anymore.

Maybe she was next to a monkey in the cargo hold on the plane ride over, but how she really got them will forever remain a mystery because at that time no one had ever even heard of monkeypox before. Still, I remain convinced.

So I have a few questions about your pet insurance (for my new prairie dog, Son of Josephine-) that might not be in the brochure:

First of all, does your insurance even cover monkeypox? This is what I'm most worried about.

Do I have to prove that it's not a pre-existing condition? How? Do you use the same system as in America?

Heaven forbid something does happen to Son of Josephine, do you offer insurance that covers funeral expenses and repatriation? I'm willing to pay extra for an eternal flame.

Okay, that should do it. Please send me a brochure anyway and I'll have my friend explain it to me. If I have any further questions I'll let you know.

Thanks a lot. I mean it. God bless you for offering this product.

Sincerely

Kirk Dunkirk

Nippon Life Insurance Company
1-2-2, Yurakucho, Chiyoda-ku, Tokyo 100-8444 Japan

NISSAY

Kirk Dunkirk
Kochi City 780—

Dear Kirk Dunkirk,

We certainly got your letter about pet insurance.

We are sorry that we can't satisfy you with our response because we don't deal in pet insurance regarding all the animals.
We think that no other Japanese insurance company deals in pet insurance.

But we can advise you that it is possible for you to utilize pet insurance in mutual benefit provisions, called "Kyousai", though we don't know whether you will be satisfied or not.
We don't know detail about mutual benefit provisions. So please research those on the web searching system with your friend's help.
We are sorry that we aren't available.

Sincerely
Nippon Insurance Company

Japan
1-1-3, Marunouchi
Chiyoda-ku, Tokyo 100-0005
(03)3284-4111

July/23/2003

Dear Mr.Kirk Dunkirk

Thank you for giving the letter of an inquiry the other day.

In ALICO Japan,only the insurance for man is dealt with.
Though regrettable,a pet's insurance is not treating in ALICO.

I am sorry not to meet your wishes, but we appreciate your interest in ALICO.

Regards,

Kanzou Ogiwara
(ALICO Japan Customer Consulting Office)

(At the time, the idea of a major company offering pet insurance was considered farfetched.

Once again, Kirk is in the vanguard.)

Kirk Dunkirk
✂ ✂ ✂ ✂ ✂ ✂
Kochi City 780
Japan

Häagen Dazs Ice Cream, Tokyo
Kamimeguro 2-1-1
Meguro-ku, Tokyo 〒 153-0051

Sept. 1, 2003

Dear Haagen Däzs,

    It's lonely being a student in Japan and your ice cream has been my comfort food ever since I stepped off the ferry four months ago. Especially when your fat and middle aged like me. I use to eat a lot of Ben and Jerry's in America (do you know about them?) but I can't find it here. My dog and I like Cookie Dough (B&J) but your Almond Crunch (?) on a stick is good too.

    Which brings me to my point. I noticed recently that you changed the size of your ice cream bars. You actually made them smaller! At least ten percent. As an American I am not used to my portions getting smaller. I applaud you efforts. To many people are getting hurt from obesity. You even had the nerve to announce it on the package. "Tabegoro size" [= "Just right portion."]

    My real question is why? You see, I'm an economics student and I want to write a paper about the current deflation and it's my hunch that you had to "deflate" the size of your ice cream bar. Of course you deflated about 10% rather than the current 1% rate of the economy but maybe that's because you waited a few years.

    My roommate thinks it's just a trick. You see like most people, we share our ice cream bars with our pets while we eat them (the ice cream bars.) But you basically lopped off the part of the bar that I used to feed my dog, Vivian. So my roommate thinks you made the bars smaller so people have to buy two in order to share with thier pets. In fact, that's what his paper is about. I don't always buy two bars which is kind of a good thing because Vivian has heart problems, but I think the doctor is kind of a quack anyway.

    So am I right? Please tell me more about your great product and help me with my economics project. If you have some kind of free coupons for people who write letters that would be cool. If not that's ok too. Please write me back either way.

Thank you SO MUCH!
Sincerely,

Kirk Dunkirk

Häagen-Dazs Japan, Inc.
Consumer Service
1-8-1, Shimomeguro, Meguro-ku
Tokyo 153-8689

Sep. 10, 2003

Mr. or Ms. Kirk Dunkirk
▓▓▓▓▓▓▓▓▓▓▓▓
Kochi City
Kochi 780▓▓▓▓

Dear Mr. or Ms. Kirk Dunkirk,

Thank you for taking the time to contact our company.
We are pleased to hear you enjoy Haagen-Dazs. Ice cream in Japan as well.

Regarding your question, the size of our ice cream bar, we made the alteration(108ml →80ml) 3 years ago. Since autumn 2000, we produce 80ml ice cream bar only for Japanese market.
The reason why we made it smaller is to suit the demand of customers in Japan.
We had been received the comments from customers that 108ml ice cream bars are too big to eat in one time.
In other area, US, Europe, Asia except for Japan, 108ml bar has been still sold in the market.

We are very sorry that we can not comply with your request.
We hope you will continue to enjoy our products.

Sincerely,

Miki Kusayanagi
Customer Service Sect.
Haagen-Dazs.Japan, Inc,

Häagen-Dazs Japan, Inc.

Miki Dunkirk
x ! x ! x ! x ! x
Kochi City 780
Japan

Kodak Japan Ltd.
Kanda Pompian Building
2-5-12 Iwamoto-cho
Chiyoda-ku, Tokyo 101-0032
Japan

Sept. 2, 2003

For many years I buyed your film products and quite happy with ensuing results. Film is cheap and picture pretty good. But now I am very angry! Husband tell me to act like Japanese and keep my head about me but now because of you i feel must act American and tell you I <u>am very angry</u>!

Why you pretend be Japanese company?

Many years I am thinking Kodak is Japanese company. You are terrible people to pretending such a thing. You are on supermarket shelf next to Fuji, Konica and so on and you pretend be Japanese company like them. Everybody know Japanese company is best so I buy Kodak because maybe is best and also sometimes a little cheaper. My friends think also too because now everybody angry too but they not ability to write letter to you in English like me.

Husband say "Act like Japanese!" but how he does know my feeling? He is a not Japanese person and not just even American. Mother come from Portugalu. I say "I am act like Japanese. Japan is honesty country. Why not Kodak act like American? Maybe trueAmerican is not honesty country?" What a paradox!

In conclusion, you are all a bunch of dirty rotten scoundrels.

I never buy your lying film again forever in my life!

regretfully yours,

Miki Dunkirk

Kirk Dunkirk
TM TM TM TM TM TM
Kochi City 780

Fuji Television Network, Inc., Head Office:
2-4-8 Daiba, Minato-ku,
Tokyo 137-8088

September 4, 2003

Dear Fuji Television,

I am big fan of your TV shows, especially the recent Tokyo Love Cinema. When Masaki's ex-girlfriend Kinuyo showed up, wow, what a twist! I almost choked on a pretzel, just like George Bush.

One reason I have a chance to watch your TV shows is because I'm a student at Kochi University. As you know, university students in Japan don't have to study so hard, so in my free time I watch a lot of TV dramas, hoping it will improve my Japanese. So far it hasn't, but I have learned many things about Japanese relationships. Before I came here, I had no idea how many Japanese people murder their boss in order to pay off a coworker who knew they were having an affair and so on.

Anyway, I believe in the power of television to shape people's opinions. I have noticed that whenever Kimu Taku appears in a TV drama, not only is it popular, but the entire nation follows his lead. If he falls in love with a girl in a wheelchair, suddenly people in wheelchairs become cool. If he rides a certain unusual motorcycle, the next day young men and women all over Japan ride that same motorcycle. The man is amazing -- it's almost frightening how much power he wields. Thank goodness he's on our side!

I smell a great opportunity here. There is a chance to enormous social good. Why not write a TV drama, starring Kimu Taku of course, about whaling? Everyone knows that international opinion on this matter is hurting Japan's image. I think most Japanese really have no idea why they feel so strongly about this, (I mean, would you get so upset if you weren't allowed to eat string beans?) so if they just had a little nudge they would change their minds, especially if their neighbors agreed. Japan and the ecology of the planet would benefit immediately.

Here's a loose plot, based on what seems to work for your other hit shows: Kimu Taku is a hotshot forensics expert in the Sendai Metropolitan police. Fed up by political backstabbing, he returns to his hometown, a picturesque but poor whaling village, in order to mend ties with his father. His father, a widower recovering from a big heart attack, refuses to accept Kimu Taku until he becomes a whaler like him. One day while on the boat, they find the body of the town's mayor who had vanished after an embezzlement scandal. Meanwhile, Kimu's high school sweetheart, who never left the village, asks him to help find her husband, Kimu's badminton rival at school, who went to Sendai to borrow money from Yakuza to finance their dying ryokan. Eventually, Kimu Taku uses his charm and forensic skills to solve the murders, win back the woman's love, convince his father to open a whale watching business, and save the town.

What do you think? I think that together with Kimu Taku we can save the world! (Or at least start a badminton "boom") Please write back and let me know.

Sincerely,

Kirk Dunkirk

Kirk Dunkirk
♠ ♠ ♠ ♠ ♠ ♠ ♠
Kochi City 780
Japan

Kodak Japan Ltd.
Kanda Pompian Building
2-5-12 Iwamoto-cho
Chiyoda-ku,Tokyo 101-0032
Japan

Sept. 9, 2003

Dear Kodak,

Recently you may have received a letter from my wife, Miki, saying she is very angry at you for pretending to be a Japanese company. I confronted her about it and she denies writing the letter, but I found it on the hard drive. I guess there's a chance she didn't actually mail it, but that's unlike her. Besides, that's all she's been talking about recently; She even went out and bought several rolls of Fuji film and gave them to the old ladies in her Shamisen class.

I'm American and I have known all along that you are an American company. I even told Miki a few times at the start of our relationship but at the time she thought I was just being difficult and now claims not to remember those conversations. I can understand why you would pretend to be a Japanese company, what for the great reputation they have. I'm not angry you did it, but well, just disappointed. You should be proud of your roots in Rochester, home of many great optical enterprises.

Anyway, please don't take her letter to heart. I'll try to convince her not to be so angry and maybe eventually she'll stop putting Konica posters up around town. The other day the supermarket clerk caught her ripping down the "sale" signs by your film, so I hope she learned her lesson. But still maybe you folks should reconsider your marketing angle. More people like her are bound to find out, and when (not if) they do, there could be a real backlash.

Sincerely,

Kirk Dunkirk
Proud (but not jingoistic) American

October 7, 2003

JR Tower Hotel Nikko Sapporo
Nishi 2 Chome, Kita 5 Jyou
Sapporo, Japan

Dear Nikko Hotel

    About one week ago, my mother-in-law, with her tour group from Kochi, visited your fine hotel. She stayed and ate at several on her trip and said she enjoyed every one. Unfortunately she's quite senile and can't recall the details.

    During her travels, she lost her favorite ball-point pen "bohru-chan" (= "Little Mr. Ball Point Pen") and ever since no one in my family can get any relief. All day and night she cries for her dear ball-chan, even when she's watching her favorite TV programs (anything with guys from Johnny's Jimusho) or sleeping, or both. As you can see, her condition is pretty bad.

    The pen in question is ordinary looking: 0.7mm medium point, bottom half sky blue, top half off-white with a cartoon character of a whale spouting water while dancing with a cartoon samurai (maybe Sakamoto Ryoma?) It still writes. Your staff would have found it between Sept 26 and Sept 30. If she didn't actually stay at your hotel, her tour group would have had lunch at your restaurant.

    We've gone to Kochi Airport and bought replacement pens that look just like it, but her ball-point pen acquired certain characteristics after years of being cuddled and sucked on, so she won't accept our substitutes. So if and when you do find her dear Ball-chan, whatever you do DON'T WASH IT. Just stick it in a ziploc bag and express mail it back to us. Of course we will pay for delivery.

    A few more days of this and I don't know what I'm going to do.

Yoroshiku onegaishimasu,

Kirk Dunkirk

SAPPORO SKY RESORT

October 9, 2003

Kochi City
Zip 780-

Dear, Mr Kirk Dunkirk

Thank you for recently sending us your letter regarding the ball-point pen which you may leave at our hotel.

We are afraid to informing you that we couldn't find the items. We tried to look for the pen all over our hotel, even lobby, entrance, restaurants, elevators, and spa. Unfortunately, the pen which you lost wasn't appeared.

Again we are so sorry that we can tell you we couldn't find it.

Thank you again for your support of JRtower Hotel Nikko Sapporo. If you have any questions, please do not hesitate to contact us. We hope to have the opportunity of welcoming you back again in the future.

Sincerely yours,

Seiji Akizuki
General Manager

JR HOKKAIDO HOTELS
JR tower hotel nikko sapporo
nikko hotels international

Kirk Dunkirk
✂ ✂ ✂ ✂ ✂
Kochi City 780
Japan

Kodak Japan Ltd.
Kanda Pompian Building
2-5-12 Iwamoto-cho
Chiyoda-ku, Tokyo 101-0032
Japan

Sept. 30, 2003

Dear Kodak Japan,

This is my second letter to you, in addition to the one my wife sent on Sept. 2, making three in total.

Please -- you've got to reply! She's obsessed with with downfall of your company.

Ever since my wife got angry at you for pretending to be a Japanese company, she's been on a mission to discredit you. She takes down "sale" signs in the supermarket, smears black ink on products guerrilla style, and even stands on the street corner at lunchtime with one of those kamikaze handkerchiefs rolled around her forehead handing out anti-kodak leaflets.

It was bad at first but with every day that passes without any response from you she gets worse. Please send some kind of reply: a letter of explanation, maybe even some tissues or pins leftover from the World Cup, anything. You've got to help me -- this is ruining my marriage!

Desperately Yours,

Kirk Dunkirk

Dear Ms. Miki Dunkirk

2003/10/2

Thank you for your usual usage of Kodak products. I received your letters dated Sept.2, 2003. I also received a letter you sent to Eastman Kodak Company, U.S.A.

Let me introduce myself. My name is Masaaki Oniyama, manager of customer information for Kodak products in Japan.

I was very confused when I read your letter. I didn't understand what happened on your film or pictures exactly, but I'd like to explain about us, Kodak Japan and Kodak films sold in Japan.

Kodak Japan is a subsidiary of Eastman Kodak company, U.S.A. for marketing Kodak products in Japan. Almost all films we carry in Japan are made in U.S.A. On the other hands, on-time-use cameras are mainly made in China, a few models are from U.S.A and Mexico.

Each product has Japanese letters on the package for Japanese consumers to realize the feature of the products. Naturally there is an expression of manufacturing origin. Please see the attached sheet.

I hope this may help you know us and our products. Thank you.

Masaaki Oniyama
Masaaki Oniyama

〒103-8540

東京都中央区日本橋小網町6-1
コダックお客様相談センター
鬼山　正昭

KODAK JAPAN LTD.

Kirk Dunkirk
Kochi City 780
Japan

Sari Segara Resort, Villas & Spa
Jl. Pantai Kedonganan (Jimbaran Bay)
Kuta-Bali

Oct. 14, 2003

Namaste,

My wife Miki and I are a comedy team and we are fascinated by the opportunities for growth and balance offered by your colonic irrigation holidays. As a matter of fact, we met on a similar gymnastic-yoga wellness tour, the so-called "Tumblin' 'Testines Cruise" out of Miami. She looked so cute up on that trampoline.

Based on our experiences on various health getaways, we have created a 30 minute show sure to tickle the fancy of the wellness-seeking holiday maker. All the jokes and sing-alongs are related to fasting and enemas -- frank but not offensive. Even Miki's magic routine will leave you unable to see palming in the same way ever again. People who have seen us perform usually can't resist but say things like "I nearly split my sides laughing!" In addition, we have an act in Japanese for what is sure to be a growth market.

We understand that you may have some reservations but let me just add one more thing: we're not doing it for the money. Our lifestyle makes it hard to afford these vacations, so we'll perform twice a week for free in return for a 14 day stay at your resort. Of course, like our bodies, these terms are flexible. If you're interested, write me back and I'll send you a video tape (*please specify NTSC or PAL.*)

So, how about it? It's true what the ancients said: laughter is the best medicine.
C'mon, give us a chance -- you won't be 'sari.'

In All Sincerity,

Kirk Dunkirk
#2 and Co. -- Colonic Comedy Duo

SARI SEGARA RESORT
VILLAS & SPA

October 24, 2003.

Mr. Kirk Dunkirk
███████████████
Japan.

Re: Barter.

Dear Kirk,

Thank you for your letter of October 14, 2003 introducing yourself and your special show to entertain the hotel's guests.

In the present condition of tourism industry in Bali it will be hard to add more expenses to our daily operation, therefore which much regret I could not accept / confirm your request.

Perhaps, one day when tourism situation returns to normal we may contact you for the bartered show at the hotel.

See you sometimes in the future, thank you and best regards.

Sincerely yours
Sari Segara Resort, Villas & Spa

Wayan Djana
General Manager.
-wad/-

Jl. Pantai Kedonganan, Kedonganan, Badung - Bali
P.O. Box. 1074, Tuban - Badung
Phone : (62-361) 703647 (Hunting)   Fax.: (62-361) 703330
E-mail : s_segara@indo.net.id • Website : www.sarisegara.com

Kirk Dunkirk
© ™ ® ™ © ™
Kochi City
780- № № №
Japan

Sharp Electronics Corporation
22-22 Nagaike-cho
Abeno-ku
Osaka 545-8522
Japan

Oct. 27, 2003

Dear Sharp,

For starters, I just want to mention that I absolutely love your Discman™. If there were a Nobel Prize for consumer electronics, you'd win it for that one. And before that, I owned one of your Walkmans™ too, until it finally died after I lent it to my stupid roommate and her even stupider boyfriend for a romantic weekend.

Until then, I'm stuck with my old Discman™. Not that I'm unhappy with it. I absolutely love it. But I wear it every night when I go walking and, like my knees, it's in bad condition. So to make it last until I can save up enough for one of your neat little MD Walkmans,™ could you please give me some advice about care and maintenance?

When I walk, I rub my arms really hard against my sides. This vigorous application of energy creates heat, friction and Neutral Ion Vortexes that are good for health. Unfortunately it also creates a lot of lint, and that gets in my Walkman™. Usually I clean it out with Q-tips™ and Kleenex™, but the other day it was so bad I had to Hoover™ it.

The CD Door is loose and held together with Velcro™ and Krazy Glue™. But also the battery cover is broken and held on by Band-Aids™. Do you sell spare parts? I checked the internet and couldn't find any on your homepage.

Well, that should do it. Any advice you can give me would be greatly appreciated. Good luck with your next invention!

Sincerely,

Kirk Dunkirk

ps: kudos for dreaming up the mechanical pencil too!

SHARP

Sharp Corporation
Page : 1 / 1
3-1-72, Kita-Kamei-cho, Yao-shi, Osaka 581-8585, Japan
Phone : +81 6-6792-1001   Fax :+81 6-6792-0416
Date : Oct 31, 2003

Mr. Kirk Dunkirk

███████ kochi city 780 - ███ Japan

REF: YOUR LETTER

Dear Sir / Madam,

Thank you very much for using a Sharp product.

We refer to your letter concerning to the Discman and MD walkman.

This seems to be the product of Sony.

Please contact the Sony corporation.

Yours truly,

Kon

Sharp Corporation
Customer Assistance Center
W. Kozai

3-1-72, Kita-Kamei-cho, Yao-shi, Osaka 581-8585, Japan
Tel: 06-6792-1001   Fax: 06-6792-0416   E-mail : customer@cmn.hirano.sharp.co.jp

Super Daiei Co., Ltd. Head Office
1-1-7 Nakasu, Yahatanishi-ku
Kitakyushu City, Fukuoka

~~Nov. 5, 2003~~ Dec. 11, 2003

Dear Daiei Bosses,

All this past week I've been shopping in your supermarket like I always do, but it has been a noisy experience. Every time I go in there's that **damn Daiei Hawks baseball song!** It sounds like something from a kids cartoon about robot warriors who live in an undersea volcano and travel to different planets in a purple space van with eyes in order to play baseball against monsters who ooze slime, which is legal in monster sports and makes for a mean curveball.

It's not just me: your hardworking staff is grumpy too! Who can blame them? Not only do they have to hear the **same song again and again** for 8-10 hours a day they have to do it in a ridiculous pajama uniform. If you were a country, Amnesty International would write you up.

I feel for them. When I was a waiter in Rhode Island we had to listen to Christmas music for 14 hours a day. Do you know how this affected our service? I can answer that by quoting another waiter: "If I hear 'Little Drummer Boy' one more time, I'm going to rip someone's head off and throw it in the eggnog!"

So don't tell me that people like the music. They don't. Customers don't, managers don't, checkout girls with perky boobs and acne don't. Even unborn babies would head for the exits if they knew how to walk. The only reason people shop there is not because you won the Japan Series or because of the music, but because everything is on sale for 89 yen.

Do you still think people like it? Then why don't you **prove it** by listening to the Daiei Hawks song, **your song** for just eight hours a day? Play it while you take a shower, play it during breakfast, put on headphones and play it a few dozen times while you use the treadmill, play it while you're trying to have a conversation or write a birthday card. Go ahead, you can even play the snazzy new remixed version every 10th time to break the monotony.

And just in case you were wondering, I am **not a Tigers fan.** I hate their music too! I'm a diehard Yankees man through and through. Matsui is the by far the greatest baseball player who has ever lived and I'm glad Japanese TV never shows any of the other yokels who just get in his way. Even though he has almost a decade of pro experience in Japan, he should have won rookie of the year. He was ROBBED!

I expect a REPLY or some coupons or something.

Sincerely,

Kirk Dunkirk

ps. This is the **second time** I sent this letter. What's the matter? Don't you like foreigners?

Two tries, no reply.

But I saw the writing on the wall

Once the largest retailer in Japan, Daiei is basically bankrupt now and was forced to sell the team to an upstart tech company. After they pulled out of Kochi, the core department store was demolished and another metered parking lot added to the blight downtown.

Miss shopping there though. They had Campbell's soup.

-KDK

But they still play the Hawks fight song in Fukuoka shops!

> Excerpt of original Japanese. (Imagine a military band playing.)
>
> いざゆけ若鷹軍団
>
> ペナント競うグランドに
> 闘魂燃えて敵を打つ
> 一投一打火をはきて
> 白球熱き嵐呼ぶ
> (ソレ！)

> <u>Transliteration:</u>
>
> **Izayuke waka taka gundan**
>
> *Penanto kisou gurando ni*
> *Tōkon moete teki wo utsu*
> *Ittō ichida hi wo hakite*
> *Hakkyū atsuki arashi yobu*
> *(Sore!)*

> **Onward Young Hawks Vanguard Corps!**
>
> On the field where you compete for the pennant
> Hit the enemy with your burning spirit.
> Each throw, each hit on fire
> The ball's heat summons a storm.
> Oh Yeah!
>
> (Awful translation by Kirk Dunkirk)

It sounds much cooler in the original Japanese. Or not.

Kirk Dunkirk
✻ ✻ ✻ ✻ ✻
Kochi City
780-✻ ✻ ✻
Japan

Panasonic Mobile Communication Co. Ltd.
Biometrics Department
3-1, Tsunashima-higashi 4-chome
Kohoku-ku, Yokohama 223-8639, Japan

Nov. 12, 2003

Dear Panasonic Mobile Communications,

 Okay, it was a leap of faith for me to believe that science fiction had come true and that there are now companies like yours that actually sell machines that can recognize us by our eyes.

 So I need a little faith on your part to hear out my question. In case you couldn't tell, I'm pretty ignorant when it comes to these kind of things.

 What I need to know is if your biometric iris recognition systems can be used for pets.

 I have a little door flap so my cat Hiatus can come and go as she pleases. But there's another cat in the neighborhood, let's call him Romeo (not his real name) who also comes and goes inside my house as he pleases. He eats Hiatus' food and sprays boy cat bodily fluids all over my sofa, rugs, kewpie dolls, &c. I tell her to kick his butt, but she's a real, well, p_ssy.

 So I want to install a mechanical door that will slide open and closed only for my cat, Hiatus. Can your system tell the difference between cats? She's pretty smart but I doubt she would punch in an access code. Besides, I think this could be a *huge* market for you.

Thanks a lot. If you could, please tell me a list of distributors.
Sincerely,

Kirk Dunkirk

Dear Sir,

Tank you very much for your inquiry.

Biometric iris recognition systemss which it had asked about are the charge goods of Panasonic Systemsolutions Company.

Therefore, the result which Panasonic Systemsolutions Company was asked about from me is told.

Biometric iris recognitionsystems isn't available with the pet such as Cat with being disappointed.

Do you have the method which makes the collar of Cat have a sensor examined, and how do you like it?

Approve it though it can't answer an expectation.

Your kind understanding will be appreciated.

Best regards.

(Company) Guest consultation center.
Panasonic Mobile Communications Co., Ltd.

Dec.03.2003

ATT:Mr.Kirk Dunkirk

Panasonic System Solutions
AV& Security Business unit
Tommy Kawai
4-3-1 Tunashimahigashi Kohoku-ku
Yokohama 223-8639 Japan
Tel:045-540-5806

Dear Mr.Kirk Dunkirk

Thank you very much for your letter about Iris recognitions.
Unfortunately Human Iris & animal iris is completely different characteristic.
Our Camera using Iris recognition algorisms for the Human eye that reason why we could not use Iris recognition for the animals.
But two to Three years ago we received lot of request for the Animal iris recognition for the Cows. In Japan we had BSE problem& many people start to think about recognition of each COW is very much important for identify berth of place or records to animals.

Our partners Iridiantechnologies who owns Iris recognition patent start to research animal Iris recognition. May be in the future it will be possible.

Thank you very much for your Question & very sorry for the late reply

Best Regards
Tommy kawai

Kirk Dunkirk
✎ ✎ ✎ ✎ ✎
Kochi City
780-✎ ✎ ✎
Japan

Hagoromo Chalk
〒 486-0917
Mino Itchōme at 154
Kasugai, Aichi

Nov. 17, 2003

Dear Hagoromo Chalk,

I have just one question for you: What are we going to do when the chalk runs out?

Have you given it any thought? Or do you just care about getting rich by plundering a limited natural resource, the same way the oil and paper companies do?

It's a simple fact. Some day, it's going to run out. Do you have a plan of action for that inevitability? Are you researching alternatives? Have you created a synthetic chalk? You might think we'll come up with a high-tech replacement by then, but there's no guarantee! We could use really big pieces of paper and big erasers in class, but think of all the wasted paper- and rubber trees. And I'm not concerned just because I'm a teacher --what about all the gymnasts and rock climbers who rely on chalk? Police solving murders and sidewalk artists brightening up people's lives after a dreary day downtown… Toothpaste will never be the same.

I'll admit, I share some of the blame. Until recently I used chalk like there was no tomorrow. As soon as it got too small to hold comfortably I'd toss it in the chalk compactor or throw it at a noisy student. But I chalk it up to experience, since now that I'm getting older and realize my time on this big chalk ball we call Earth is running out, I want to do my part to help.

I have instituted a chalk recycling project among my 2nd year high-school students and would gladly send our chalk dust to you for reuse. Enclosed is a small ziploc bag with some, in case you need to check for quality. (Sorry the colors are all mixed.) It may not prevent that fateful day when the chalk runs out, but together maybe we can hold it off until humans can communicate by other means, like sonar.

Please write me back and let me know what plans your company has for the conservation of chalk, now and into the next century. I'd like something I can show my students, who are very interested (25% of their grade!) and the skeptics who, alas, are many.

Thank you from my calcified heart,

Kirk Dunkirk

　　　　　　　　　　　　　　　　　　平成１５年１２月１２日
　ＫＩｒｋ　Ｄｕｎｋｉｒｋ様
　　　　　　　　　　　　　　　　愛知県春日井市美濃町１－１５４
　　　　　　　　　　　　　　　　羽衣文具株式会社
　　　　　　　　　　　　　　　　　渡　部　隆　康

　拝復　師走の候ますますご清栄のこととお喜び申し上げます。日頃は当社製品をご愛用いただき厚くお礼申し上げます。
　さて、ご返事が遅くなり申し訳ございません。私どもは英語の苦手な日本人です。お手紙の内容はチョークのリサイクルのご提案かと推察いたします。日本語でご返答いたします。
　リサイクルの方法は元のチョークに戻す方法と、他のものに利用する方法の二通りがあると思います。チョークには原材料の違いによる２種類のチョークがあります。一つは石膏製チョーク、もう一つは炭酸カルシウム製チョークです。
　（１）元のチョークに戻す方法
　　　①石膏製チョーク　不可能です。石膏製チョークの原料は焼き石膏といい、石膏メーカーが石膏原石と、副産物として生成する化学石膏と、陶磁器の石膏型の廃品（廃型または古型）を粉砕し窯で焼いたものです。石膏チョークはすでにリサイクル品です。チョークは黒板を傷つけないように、書きやすいように柔らかく製造しているのでこれをリサイクルすると品質の低下を招きます。また、色の付いたチョークを混ぜると色が汚くなります。以上の理由により石膏メーカーは相手にしてくれないと思います。
　　　②炭酸カルシウム製チョーク　色別に分別してあれば可能です。使用した粉は不可能です。リサイクルするにはチョークを水に溶かして使用する方法と粉砕して使用する方法があります。水に溶かした場合は表面の樹脂被膜がチョークの中に混ざります。書きにくくなるかもしれない。粉砕した場合は被膜も細かくなり混ざっても影響は少ないと思われる。ただし、粉砕設備が必要になります。当社には粉砕設備はありません。
　（２）他のものに利用する方法
　　　①石膏製チョーク　上記のように焼き石膏に戻す。セメントに混ぜる。
　　　②炭酸カルシウム製チョーク　炭酸カルシウム以外に多種類のものが混合されており、炭酸カルシウムとして利用できない。利用方法はわからない。
　（３）廃棄方法　どちらのチョークの原料も自然界存在する石や粘土の一種であり、無害であるので燃えないゴミとして埋め立てても環境に影響はないと思われる。

　チョークの生産量は全国で１日に５ｔ程度です。１年間に国民１人当たり５本ぐらいになります。リサイクルできるのはこの１０～２０％でしょうか。古紙や古鉄などと違い量が少ないのでチョークのリサイクルは事業として成り立たないと思います。
　以上ご返答申し上げます。
　　　　　　　　　　　　　　　　　　　　　　　　　　　　　　　　敬　具

December 12, 2003

Mr Kirk Dunkirk,

Aichi-ken, Kasugai-shi, Minomachi 1-154
Hagoromo-Bungu Co.
Takayasu Watabe

Greetings and well wishes. We deeply appreciate your regular usage of our products.

Please accept our apologies for the late reply. Our English is poor because we are Japanese. We have surmised that your letter is a proposal for recycling chalk. Please allow us to reply in Japanese.

I believe there are two ways to recycle chalk; one is to reclaim the chalk and the other is to re-use the chalk for something else. The different types of raw material produce two types of chalk; calcium sulphate (gypsum or common plaster) based chalk and calcium carbonate based chalk.

(1) Chalk reclamation
  ① Calcium sulphate chalk – not possible. Chalk manufacturers obtain the raw material of calcium sulphate chalk, called baked calcium sulphate, from a mixture of calcium sulphate ore, artificial calcium sulphate, and crushed and processed waste pottery and plaster. So calcium sulphate chalk is already a recycled product. Recycling again would bring about a drop in quality, as chalk is originally manufactured soft to avoid damaging the blackboard and for easy writing. Also, if different colored chalk is mixed in the colors becomes tainted. Consequently, I don't think you will receive any assistance from calcium sulphate chalk manufacturers.
  ② Calcium carbonate chalk – possible if separated into individual colors, but not possible with chalk dust. This can be achieved by either dissolving the chalk in water or finely crushing it. If dissolved in water, the resin film on the surface of the chalk mixes with it and most likely makes it difficult to write with. This doesn't happen with crushing, but you would need specialized equipment, which we don't have at our company.

(2) Chalk repurposing
  ① Calcium sulphate chalk – the baked calcium sulphate is reclaimed as mentioned above and mixed in cement.
  ② Calcium carbonate chalk - various other substances are mixed in with the calcium carbonate making it impossible to reclaim. I don't know of any repurposing methods.

(3) Disposal - both types of chalk are treated as non-combustible garbage and buried as such. They are made from non-toxic rocks and sands found in nature and are believed to have no effect on the environment.

Approximately five tons of chalk are produced daily nationwide. The yearly usage is about five sticks per person, and only about 10 to 20% of this can be recycled. Unlike used paper or metal, with such small amount available, I don't think chalk recycling would be a viable business.

Regards.

(Hagoromo Chalk Recycling reply, translation: Evan Coombes)

Kobayashi Map Specialty Store
338 Takatsuki, Karasuma-dori
Kamijuzuyamachi Higashi-iru
Shimogyo-ku, Kyoto City

Sept. 26, 2003

Maps are great, aren't they?

But you probably already know that, and since I haven't got long to live, I'll get straight to the point.

Could you make me an original, custom, one-of-a-kind secret treasure map? I want it to look like something made by pirates.

I plan on leaving a tidy sum of money and a bullet collection to my children, some of whom are illegitimate (whatever that's supposed to mean!)

I figure they ought to work a little to get the inheritance and maybe even have a few fist fights in the process. I only wish I could stick around long enough to see Tomoko and Yu Chee duke it out in a catfight. <u>Then</u> we'll see if blood really is thicker than water.

Beside, it's a tradition in my family. I had to best my sister at a quiz show that my father made in order to get at his loot, and a generation before that, he had to outlast his brothers in a pain and endurance test that involved sandpaper and swimming deep underwater.

Anyway, I've got it all planned out: the location of the buried treasure, the clues, even the substitute place names. Like "Dead Man's Donut Shoppe," for example. What do you think? Oh, and can you do invisible ink? I'll probably need several copies of the map, each to be torn in half, and one to contain a mild topical poison.

Please write me back ASAP with price and time estimates. The doctors say I could go any day now.

Sincerely,

Kirk Dunkirk

ps. Your address is so long, I get lightheaded just looking at it!

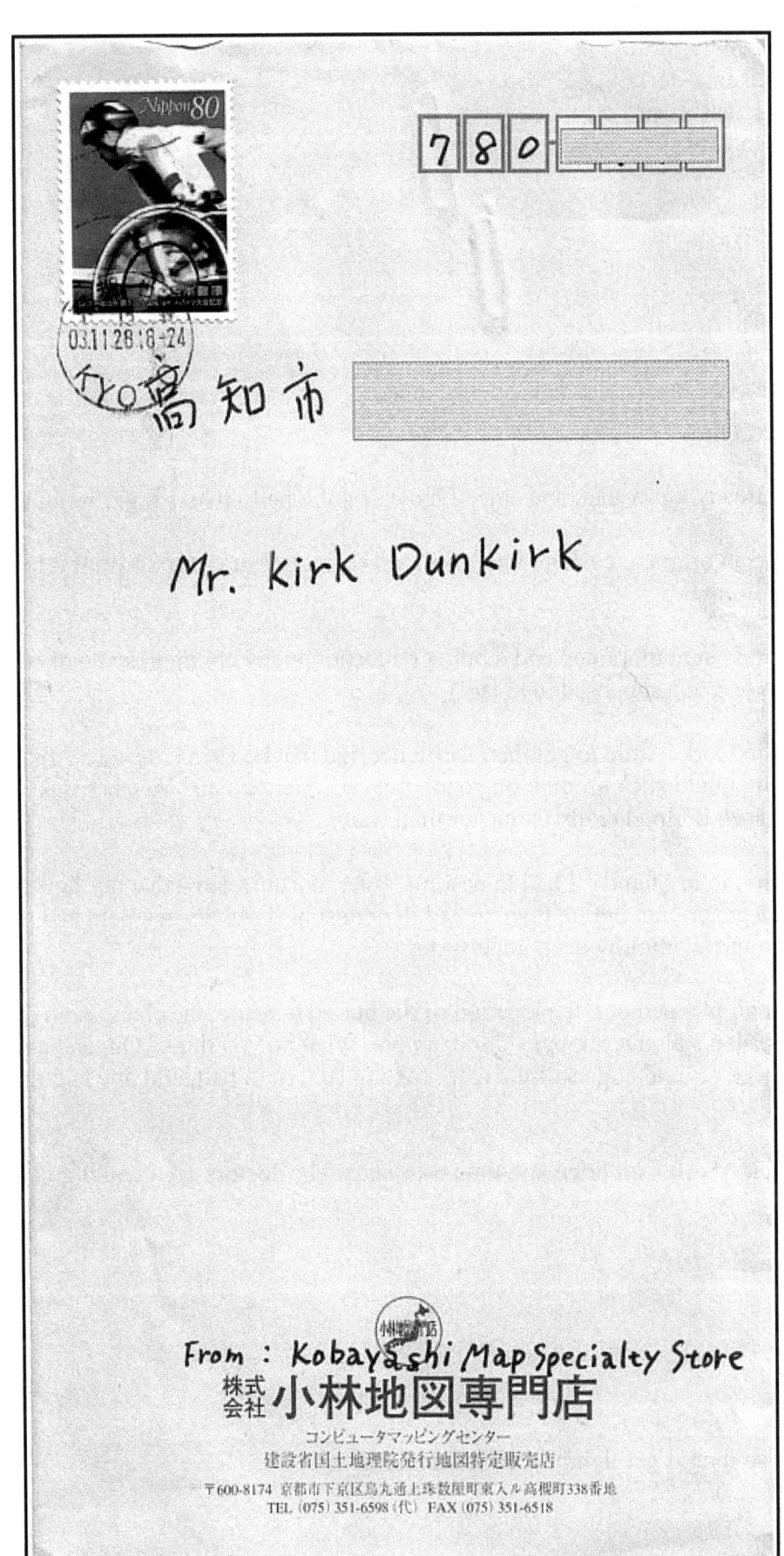

Dear Mr. Kiri Dunkirk,

Thank you very much for your inquiry.
Since none of our staffs speak English, we might not be able to provide you with adequate information and service.
So let us introduce a good map store in your area.
They might help you with topographies for your project, and their address is as the following:
Kochi-ken Kanpou Hanbaijo
5-2-21 Honmachi, Kochi-shi
Phone: 088-872-5866

I hope your health will get better soon.

Sincerely,

Yoshiharu Sono,
Kobayashi Map Speciality Store

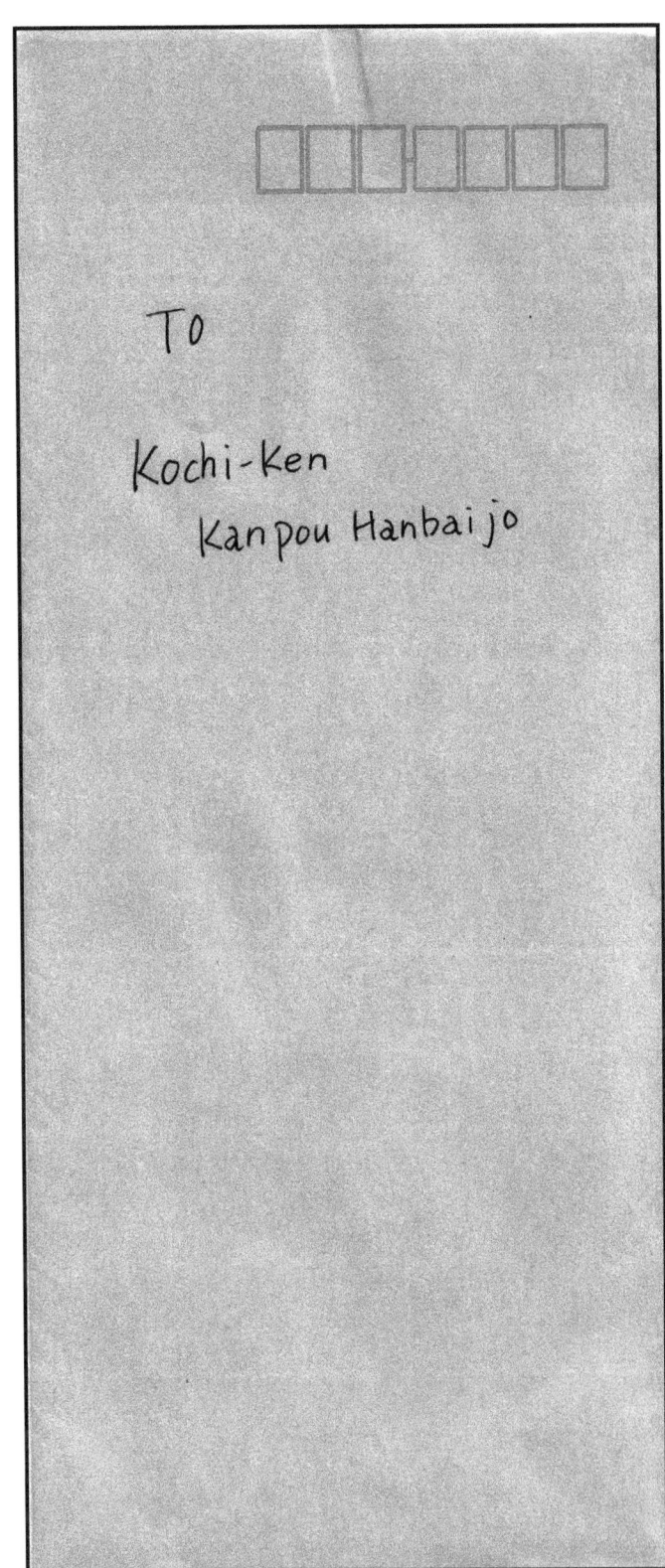

Inside 1st envelope, contains instructions for Kochi map shop.

(Appears to be the original cover letter of a fax they may have sent to the Kochi company.)

Notice of Sent Documents

November 28, 2003

To: Kochi-ken Kanpou Hanbaijo

Kobayashi Map Specialty Store
TEL: 075-351-6598
FAX: 075-351-6518

Greetings and deep thanks for your continuing exceptional patronage. Please kindly receive the following documents.

Regards

Notes

(handwritten section)

We are a national, geographical map-making specialty store in Kyoto called Kobayashi Map Specialty Store.

The other day we received a letter from a person named Kirk Dunkirk, which we now pass on to your company. The letter indicated that he wanted to bury something for his children and have a map made so that they could search for it. We thought a topographical map would be more appropriate so we took it upon ourselves to introduce him to your company, which is also nearer to him than we are.

We apologize for any bother caused and sincerely ask for your cooperation.

```
(Kobayashi Poisonous Pirate Map reply, translation: Evan Coombes)
```

Myojo Foods
3-50-11, Sendagaya
Shibuya-ku, Tokyo 151
JAPAN

February 2, 2004

Dear Myojo Foods,

Some people think your noodles are just for people who are too dumb to cook. Not me. I think they revolutionized the way we eat. They also saved my life. Twice.

The first time was when I was a nursing student in Guelph, Ontario. I often worked 56 hour shifts and stayed away from my home for days. At work, I survived off of your instant ramen, instant coffee and walnuts. But that's not the real survival story. One grim winter night, I came back to find that my home had been robbed. The door was left open and my kitchen was filled with snow. It was also filled with huge dead rats who had burrowed into my jumbo bulk size case of instant noodles and eaten the flavor packets. As they lay there shriveled up, I shuddered to think of what might have happened had they attacked me in my weakened state instead.

The second time your noodles saved me was while trekking in Bhutan. I was in a little bath shack with my fiancé when we were trapped by an avalanche. It was small by avalanche standards (or so the Bhutanians say -- I'm just a nurse, not an avalanche expert) but big enough to encase us for three days. Fortunately we had a steel drum of bath water, lots of firewood, and a backpack full of instant ramen. We survived by alternating between bathing and cooking in the steel drum.

But the real reason I write this letter is because I'm worried about the future of your instant ramen. My friends on the online internet noodle discussion group are very upset about the new ramen with swirling monkeys. I mean, come on, SWIRLING MONKEYS? What's gotten into you guys? Nobody wants swirling monkeys in their noodles! You're starting to lose sight of your mission. Stick with what you know, which is making the best damn instant ramen in the world for over 50 years, and leave the swirling monkeys to your imitators. Otherwise, instead of changing our lives for the better you're just making food for dumb people.

Please write me back. I feel very strongly about your product, in part because it saved my life and partly because it uses "kansui" (sodium carbonate.) Please tell me if the swirling monkeys project has ben canceled.

A little food for thought.
Sincerely,

Kirk Dunkirk

平成１６年２月９日

Kirk Dunkirk　　様

明星食品株式会社
お客様サービス室
畠中　義雄
ハタナカ　ヨエオ

拝啓　時下益々ご健勝のこととお慶び申し上げます。

　日頃より、弊社製品をご愛顧いただき、誠に有り難うございます。

　又この度は、弊社製品に就きましてお問い合わせのお便りを頂きまして有り難うございました。重ねて御礼申し上げます。

　お便りの中で、下記用語に関して語意が理解出来なく、詳しいお答えをさしあげることが出来ませんでした。申し訳ございません。お手数をおかけ致しますが、同封の返信用封筒でお知らせ下さいます様お願い申し上げます。

　１）「SWIRING MONKEYS」の言葉の意味。
　２）「THE NEW RAMEN WITH SWIRING MONKEYS」の
　　　　新しいラーメンの商品名（名称）。
　３）「KANSUI」に就きまして知りたいこと、疑問を
　　　　おもちのようでしたらどんなことでしょうか具体的に
　　　　お知らせ下さい。

　以上３点に就きまして、お知らせを頂きました後お答えさせて頂きたいと思います。

　弊社ではよりたくさんのお客様にご愛用いただける商品づくりに鋭意努力いたしております。

　更に研究開発に努め、皆様に愛される商品づくりを進めて参ります。今後とも明星製品のご愛用をよろしくお願い申し上げます。

　末筆ながら、皆様のご健康を心よりお祈り申し上げます。

敬具

February 9, 2004

Mr Kirk Dunkirk,

> Myojo Foods Co., Ltd.
> Customer Service Center
> Mishio Hatanaka

Greetings and well wishes.
We highly appreciate your regular usage of Myojo Foods' products.
We offer further thanks for your letter with inquiries about our products.
Our apologies for not being able to reply in detail because we couldn't understand the terms stated below from your letter. Sorry for the bother, but would you be so kind as to to inform us of their definitions. Please use the enclosed reply-envelope.

    1) The meaning of "SWIRING [sic] MONKEYS".
    2) The new ramen brand-name (called) "THE NEW RAMEN WITH SWIRING [sic] MONKEYS".
    3) Please let us know know in detail the queries you have about "KANSUI".

I believe we will be able to answer your questions after you let us know the meaning of the above 3 points.
At Myojo Foods, we are striving to make products which can be appreciated by an increasing number of customers.
Furthermore, we are committed to research and development to improve products that our customers enjoy. We sincerely hope for your continuing consumption of Myojo products.
In conclusion, we would like to wish you the best of health in the future.

> Regards

(Myojo Foods Swirling Monkey Ramen reply, translation: Evan Coombes)

Myojo Foods
3-50-11, Sendagaya
Shibuya-ku, Tokyo 151
JAPAN

March 2, 2004

Dear Myojo Foods,

Thank you for your quick reply to my letter. Thank you also for the envelope with the 80 yen stamp; it's a sign of respect and I receive it with deep humility.

Seems like your science department had a few questions for me so I'll try to answer them as best I can, but like I've said before, I'm just a nurse.

[SWIRING MONKEYS] – actually guys it's SWIRLING (with an L.) Maybe the misspelling is the source of misunderstanding? Swirling monkeys aren't real monkeys, but they are made of fish paste and resemble monkeys. When combined with hot water they swirl. That part's real! Rumours swirling around the internet say Chinese prisoners went ape over test samples but in my opinion, monkeys that "swire" would be obscene.

[THE NEW RAMEN WITH SWIRING MONKEYS] – again, another misspelling. I'm sorry if you thought my last letter was obscene. I did not mean to offend anyone by mentioning monkeys that "swire." No, no, no. I definitely meant monkeys that twirl, spin, twist and gyrate playfully. In other words, "monkeys" that "swirl" in the new "ramen."

[KANSUI] – the root of Radix Euphorbiae Kansui, a(n) herb chiefly produced in Shanxi and Shaanxi provinces, China. The root is dug out in spring or autumn, dried in sunlight, used after processing with vinegar. It is antagonistic to liquorice. But another type of "kansui" is known as sodium carbonate (NA_2CO_3), often used to control pH. The Internet Discussion groups are deeply divided into two camps over this issue.

Well, I hope this clears thing up. I can understand why you might want to keep new products secret, but don't worry, I still LOVE your noodles. I just think the world isn't ready yet for swirLing monkeys. Not until a new king sits in the east and the rivers to the west are united: Then the prophecy can come true.

Sorry to take so much of your time. Gambatte!

Kirk Dunkirk

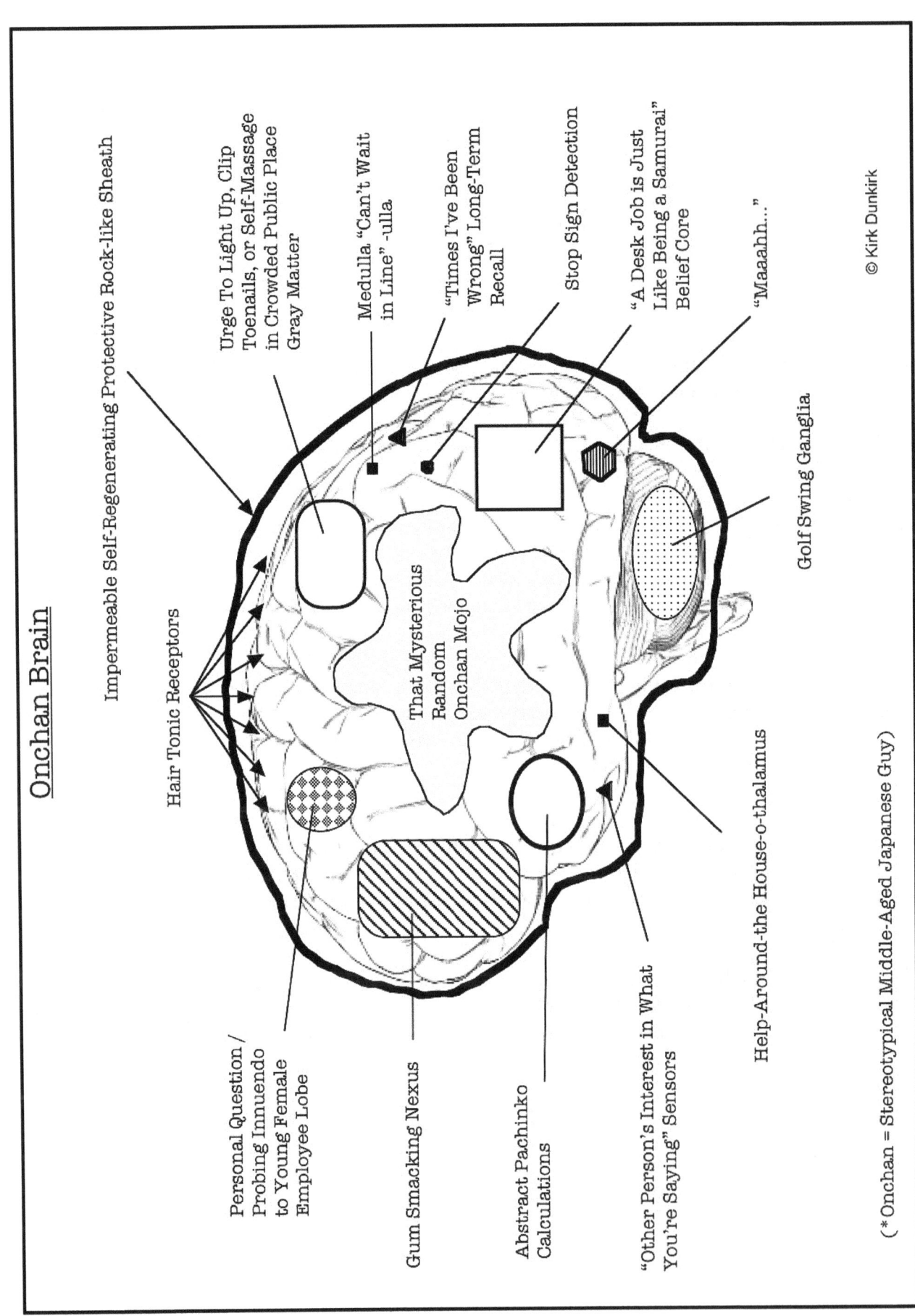

McDonald's Japan
Shinjuku i-Land Tower
5-1, Nishi-Shinjuku, 6-chome
Shinjuku-ku, Tokyo 163-133

January 5, 2004

Dear McDonalds,

I really like to eat McDonald's. When my dad visits we eat there a lot even breakfast. He says it's better than Japanese food because Japanese food kills lots of dolphins and makes you skinny. Mos Burger tastes better but they are really slow and costs a lot.

I'm kinda fat and the kids at my school tease me and say it's cause I eat lots of McDonald's but I'm the second strongest kid in school and the other kid is older than me. The other kids like McDonalds too but they always call me Kirk McDonald just cause I'm American and they can't even say it right. But they're kinda skinny cause they eat cup noodle all the time and they can't even run to first base they get tired. I think I'm fat cause I play Final Fantasy and Dragon Ball Z all the time. That's what mom says. And some of the other kids eat chicken bento all the time I think it's the same!

Some kids call me fat hamburger man or american cow boy and say I'm crazy like a cow cause american cows are dangerous cause they make you go crazy. My mom says its cause you guys make cows eat other cows and it's unnatural. My dad says he'll kick their butt and their dads butt next time he's in town.

What I really wanna know is about Ronald McDonald. Kids at school call him Donaldo but I said his name is Ronald and I got beat up. I beat up two of them but there was five kids so I couldn't beat them all up at the same time so I got beat up. How come you changed his name? I don't even like Ronald so much I think he looks kinda dumb but I don't wanna get beat up anymore cause you changed the name! What's his real name? How come you always have to change things?

Thank you.

Kirk Dunkirk Jr.
xx xx xx xx xx xx
Kochi City 780-x x x x

January, 4 2004

McDonald's Company (Japan), Ltd.
6-5-1 Nishi-shinjuku, Shinjuku-ku
Tokyo 163-1339, Japan
TEL 81-(0)3-3345-8223
FAX 81-(0)3-3344-6102

Dear Kirk

Thank you for your letter.
We are so glad to hear that you like McDonald's.

In answer to your question.
Ronalds is his official name in the world but Japan. Donald is the official name in Japan. As you know, Japanese people are hard to pronounce "R" and "L" in English. "Den Fujita" who is the founder of McDonald's Japan decided to call him "Donald" to make easier to call!. That's why we call "Mac-do-naru-do", it is same reason with his name. So, "Ronald" and "Donald" both are correct. Please tell your friends why he called "Donald" by Japanese. OK?
I'm enclosing the Mac-card for you.(Not many people have this design's one!) Enjoy your meal!!

Warm Regards,

Miwa Sen
Communications Department

(Schweet! A Pat Donahue rookie card. He batted .286 that season.)

McDonald's Corporation
McDonald's Plaza
Oak Brook, Illinois 60523-1900
Direct Dial Number
(800) 244-6227

February 27, 2004

M. Kirk Dunkirk Jr
Kochi City
F780 Japan

Dear M. Dunkirk:

Thank you for your complimentary letter. We're delighted to learn that you enjoy eating at McDonald's.

Our Menu Management team works very hard to develop great-tasting, top-quality food products that meet the many tastes of the 47 million people we serve each day. Our restaurant employees aim to serve you the hottest, freshest food, served quickly and with a smile, only like McDonald's can! It's nice to receive your comments and know our efforts are appreciated.

Again, M. Dunkirk, thanks for contacting McDonald's. We look forward to serving you again soon under the Golden Arches.

Sincerely

Veronica Lopez
Veronica Lopez
Customer Satisfaction Representative
McDonald's Corporation
ref#:1931271

Kirk Dunkirk
Hackers for Humanity
xxxxxxxxxxxx
Kochi City 780

~~Jan. 13, 2004~~   ~~Mar. 22, 2004~~   Aug. 30, 2004

Pizza Hut,

My daughter goes to an all-girls Catholic boarding school near Kobe. I'm worried about her and I need your help.

You see, she eats at your restaurant two or three times a day. Her favorite is the "Seafood Mix" pizza with squid, tuna, mayonnaise and broccoli, but for lunch she often has "Wild Barbecue" with barbecue chicken, mayonnaise and corn. They seem healthy enough but not every day! When she came home for an all-too-brief visit during the New Year's holidays I could see how this diet has affected her. Her pores have gotten very large.

While I don't blame Pizza Hut for the damage you have caused my family, I do hope that as a responsible corporate citizen you can assist me.

- If I sent you photos, measurements and common disguises used by my daughter could you limit how often she enters your store? She's pretty easy to spot due to her size and the large pores. I asked the nuns at her school and they gave me some lecture about "my brother's keeper" blah blah blah.

- She has also developed an obsession with the Pizza Hut mascot, "Cheese-kun," especially "Mexican Hat Cheese-kun" (image below.) Her notebooks, dorm walls, etc. are covered with his image. She draws him on her exposed skin during class. Do you think you could have a person in a Cheese-kun costume visit her table sometimes and remind her of the importance of staying in school?

- Since she eats there several times a day, please recommend a menu of dishes available at your shops that's healthy for a growing girl.

Thank you so much. I'm sorry to trouble you with my small dilemma.
Sincerely,

Kirk Dunkirk

ps. This is my THIRD LETTER – won't you PLEASE HELP ME?

-- Almost 9 months, three tries, no reply --
- KDK

Mexican Hat Cheese-kun

"I am not your brother's steenking keeper!"

image © Pizza Hut

Aeon Co., Ltd.
1-5-1 Nakase, Mihama-ku, Chiba-shi, Chiba
261-8515, Japan

January 21, 2004

Attention Aeon,

I have come into Japan only this month but already it makes me wonder.
Exactly what is a "Minus Aeon"?

Each television commercial tells about it. My Japanese teacher tells me about her bracelet which "Minus Aeon" also has.

Shampoo, air freshener, pillows, public bath, telephone equipment, maybe even the dog collar all have your "Minus Aeon." (Last one a joke. I don't know about if dog's collars.)

My japanese teacher ordered me to write a letter to you in japanese but I shred it into a thousand small, small pieces and use English instead.

We do not have "Minus Aeon" in my country, Belarus. Why, why? In the name of St. Jozophat, why?

Please write back.
regards,

Kirq Dunkirkz

xxxxxxxx   •   Kochi City   •   780-XXXX Japan   • (sorry, no tel or email... only study!)

[Note to reader: at the time of this letter, the ubiquitous sales gimmick in Japan was for every product imaginable to claim to provide magical benefits from "minus ion," pronounced "ee-yon" in Japanese, the same as this department store chain. Trust me, it's a <u>really</u> clever gag! -Scott Linyard.]

From the Desk of...
Kirq Dunkirkz

Aeon Co., Ltd.
1-5-1 Nakase, Mihama-ku, Chiba-shi, Chiba
261-8515, Japan

January 21, 2004

Attention Aeon,

I have come into Japan only this month but already it makes me wonder. Exactly what is a "Minus Aeon"?

Each television commercial tells about it. My Japanese teacher tells me about her bracelet which "Minus Aeon" also has.

Shampoo, air freshener, pillows, public bath, telephone equipment, maybe even the dog collar all have your "Minus Aeon." (Last one a joke. I don't know about if dog's collars.)

My japanese teacher ordered me to write a letter to you in japanese but I shred it into a thousand small, small pieces and use English instead.

We do not have "Minus Aeon" in my country, Belarus. Why, why? In the name of St. Jozophat, why?

Please write back.
regards,

Kirq Dunkirkz

xxxxxx • *Kochi City* • *780-xxxx Japan*   (sorry, no tel or email... only study!)

February 5th, 2004

Mr. Kirq Dunkirkz
Language House
Evergreen International

Dear Mr. Dunkirkz

Thank you very much for sending us your inquiry regarding "Minus Ion". Following is the information of the generally explained effect of minus ion. I hope this will answer to your question;

The word "Minus Ion" is more commonly known as "negative-ion" in English.
Ions are charged particle, either positive or negative, found in the air. Ions are created naturally, for example, through the action of ocean waves on a beach or water fall creates a large number of negatively charged ions. Negatively charged ions are said to create various effects on human biochemistry, · which may be why many people feel better at the seashore, near waterfall or high in the mountains.
It is also said that this negative ion has soothing effect, enhances metabolism, or become more resistance .. etc.

There are many studies done regarding the positive effects of negative ion, and are also many internet sites where you can find more information, such as:
http://www.waterneeds.ca/ionizer/studies.htm
http://www.bright.net/~comtech/

Also, at our Aeon stores, we only sell products with "minus ion" indication that are scientifically demonstrated that give out so-called minus ion in Japan.

Yours sincerely,

Yasuhiro Sasagawa
Yasuhiro Sasagawa
General Manager, Customer Service Department
Aeon Co., Ltd.

EZAKI GLICO CO LTD
6-5 Utajima 4-Chome
Nishi-Yodogawa-Ku 555-8502,
Osaka 555-8502

Aug 29, 2004

Dear Glico,

I and my club, the Shikoku Sweet Sleuths, love all of your products, especially Pocky Sicks. It not only is a great snack, but a great name too! How did you think of the name? Congratulations on a job well done, Glico.

I have a fail-safe way for determining if something pleases me: I get hives. Food tends to create big splotchy ones on my torso, as your product did, whereas books and movies induce the sensation on the back of my neck. It is for this reason that I have been re-elected to an unprecedented 3rd term as chair of the Sweet Sleuths association.

Our group is an assortment of amateur detectives dedicated to investigating unsolved crimes using only traditional Japanese methods. Of course we make exceptions for things like cell phones and portable gas heaters. I know I'm about to crack a case when the shingles start piling up.

Since we love your product so much, we have voted to adopt it as our Official Sweet Snack.™ After the conferring of this honor, your sweet has the right to retain the title for 2 years, unless a two-thirds majority can be mustered to challenge it. It will be the only (sweet) snack we eat at meetings or out in the field. One reason we chose your company is because your corporate motto "A Wholesome Life in the Best of Taste." mildly impressed us too.

As a gesture of goodwill please send 22 packages (assorted but heavy on the Men's Pocky and the Almond Crush Pocky. No Banana please, they didn't make the cut.) -- in time for our October 9th meeting whereupon we will officially award the Sweet Snack™ honor.

Yours Truly,

Kirk Dunkirk
Chair, Shikoku Sweet Sleuths

ps: Your energy drinks come in handy on tough assignments too!

Glico

GLICO CO., LTD.
International Division
ajima, Nishiyodogawa-ku
Osaka Japan 555-8502
Phone: 06-6477-8139
Fax : 06-6477-8161

Ssptember 6, 2004

To   : Shikoku Sweet Sleuths
Attn : Mr. Kirk Dunkirk
From : Masato Shimizu
        Consumer Services Office
        Ezaki Glico Co.,Ltd.

Dear Mr. Kirk Dunkirk,

Re: Your Inquiry

Thank you for your inquiry. But we regret that our response had to be negative.

We have received your letter dated Aug 29,2004.
First of all, thank you very much for your interest in Pocky.

At the present, however, we can't to accept your offer to provide free samples as we don't keep any stocks to supply for free upon request.

We hope that you enjoy Pocky and other Glico products in the future also.

Again, Thank you for your approach.

Sincerely yours,
Masato Shimizu

NISSAN MOTOR CO.,LTD
Customer Relations Office
17-1 Ginza 6-chome
Chuo-ku Tokyo 104-8023

Kirk Dunkirk
Rising Sun Eikaiwa
☀ ☀ ☀ ☀
Kochi City 780-xxxx

March 22, 2004

Dear Nissan,

I'm inquiring about your right-wing discount.

I've heard that if I can prove I'm a right-wing extremist or at least a supporter, I'm eligible for favorable terms. When my friend mentioned this I was skeptical until I noticed that almost all of the fascist sound trucks, not to mention young guys with rising sun stickers on their cars, and even yakuza, choose Nissan.

How do I get the discount? Do I have to show a right-wing club members card? I edited a secessionist newsletter in Quebec, but that may not qualify me here.

How much of a discount is available? I guess since I'm a foreigner I can't expect the same discount as a Japanese right-winger, but at least we can show solidarity.

Basically, I agree with most of what you guys say. US forces in Japan (and those occupying Italy, Germany and Britain) should go home. Japan can take care of itself. No self-respecting samurai would allow a foreigner to shed his blood to protect the sacred land of the Emperor! Lots of young men need work, let them do the job. Maybe then someone will get the balls to develop nukes. For obvious historical reasons, Japan is the only country with the moral authority to use them. I also think school lunches should serve whale meat. Forget the scientific hand-wringing. It is vital, nay, essential for Japan to eat whales lest its culture disappear. Haiku, karate-do, Kabuki theatre, cherry blossom viewing, literature, karaoke -- these are all under threat and will vanish within a generation unless kids start eating whale meat on a regular basis again.

Ok, now that you know we agree on the big issues, please tell me how I can get a discount. All the local shops said I need to talk to the head office. Do you install loudspeakers as a set too?

Keep up the good work. Banzai!
In Brotherhood,

Kirk Dunkirk

Duty   •   Honor   •   Conversation

NISSAN MOTOR CO., LTD
Customer Relations Office
17-1 Ginza 6-chome
Chuo-ku Tokyo 104-8023

Kirk Dunkirk
Rising Sun Eikaiwa
x x x x x x x x
Kochi City 780-xxxx
Japan

March 22, 2004

Dear Nissan,

I'm inquiring about your right-wing discount.

I've heard that if I can prove I'm a right-wing extremist or at least a supporter, I'm eligible for favorable terms. When my friend mentioned this I was skeptical until I noticed that almost all of the fascist sound trucks, not to mention young guys with rising sun stickers on their cars, and even yakuza, choose Nissan.

How do I get the discount? Do I have to show a right-wing club members card? I edited a secessionist newsletter in Quebec, but that may not qualify me here.
How much of a discount is available? I guess since I'm a foreigner I can't expect the same discount as a Japanese right-winger, but at least we can show solidarity.

Basically, I agree with most of what you guys say. US forces in Japan (and those occupying Italy, Germany and Britain) should go home. Japan can take care of itself. No self-respecting samurai would allow a foreigner to shed his blood to protect the sacred land of the Emperor! Lots of young men need work, let <u>them</u> do the job. Maybe then someone will get the balls to develop nukes. For obvious historical reasons, Japan is the only country with the moral authority to use them. I also think school lunches should serve whale meat. Forget the scientific hand-wringing. It is vital, nay, essential for Japan to eat whales lest its culture disappear. Haiku, karate-do, Kabuki theatre, cherry blossom viewing, literature, karaoke -- these are all under threat and will vanish within a generation unless kids start eating whale meat on a regular basis again.

Ok, now that you know we agree on the big issues, please tell me how I can get a discount. All the local shops said I need to talk to the head office. Do you install loudspeakers as a set too?

Keep up the good work. Banzai!
In Brotherhood,

Kirk Dunkirk

Duty • *Honor* • *Conversation*

NISSAN MOTOR CO., LTD.

17-1, Ginza 6-chome, Chuo-ku
Tokyo 104-8023, Japan
www.nissan.co.jp

April 1, 2004

Mr. Kirk Dunkirk
Rising Sun Eikaiwa

Dear Mr. Dunkirk

Thank you for your letter dated March 22, 2004 and your interest in Nissan products.

With regard to your concern, Nissan Motor Co., Ltd. does not make any discount. Also, loudspeakers are not available as our parts.

We regret that we are not able to meet your request, however, your understanding is appreciated.

Sincerely,

Kazuhiro IZAWA
Manager
Customer Affairs Group
Nissan Motor Co., Ltd.

Form No. NJB1401

Phuket Plastic Surgery Center
371/81 Yaowaraj Rd.
Muang, Phuket 83000, Thailand

Oct 18, 2004

Dear Dr. Kunaporn,

When I saw the charismatic Dr. Handa on the Japanese TV show Beauty Colosseum, where he remade the body of some really ugly girls, I knew I had found the answer to my dreams!

I'm not actually writing for myself but rather on behalf of Buster, my Caucasian Ovtcharka who for obvious reasons can't write this letter. Buster's problems stem from the fact that deep down, he is a female inside.

Ultimately, we'd like to get him a sex change, but as a first step could you spif him up with a lower jaw tuck and something like a hip raise? I want him walking like he's wearing stilettos. I'm just full of ideas and want to get started as soon as possible; we've moved to a new neighborhood and (s)he keeps coming on to all the local male dogs. People are beginning to talk.

Don't worry, money is no object; I've recently come into a small fortune. I'm Zoroastrian, and I asked my God, Ahura Mazda, what I should do with my newfound bounty and He wants me to use it to help others. I've given up on getting my own looks back but at least I can make Buster's life a little better.

We need a miracle.
Sincerely,

Kirk Dunkirk

 โรงพยาบาลสิริโรจน์ Phuket International Hospital

44 ถนนเฉลิมพระเกียรติ ร.9 อ.เมือง จ.ภูเก็ต 83000 Tel : 6676 249400 Fax : 6676 210936, 249386
44 Chalermprakiat Ror 9 Road . Phuket 83000 Thailand. www.phuket-inter-hospital.co.th
e-mail : info@phuket-inter-hospital.co.th

November 24, 2004

Mr. Kirk Dunkirk

Japan

Dear Mr. Dunkirk,

I am in receipt of your letter dated October 18, 2004 concerning a lower jaw tuck and a hip raise which you wants me to perform on your friend, Buster. If you look for something like a facial feminization surgery, I don't perform such a kind of surgery. If your friend needs just a simple jaw lift, I may do it, but not a hip raise.

If you are still interested in a jaw lift performed by me, please give me more information about your friend, such as her age and how she looks like.

Yours sincerely,

Sanguan Kunaporn, M.D.
Thai Cert. Board of Plastic & Reconstructive Surgery

<u>Clinic address:</u>
Phuket Plastic Surgery Center
371/81 Yaowaraj Road, Muan
Phuket 83000 THAILAND
TEL +66-76-254-764   FAX +66-76-254-765
E-mail address: kunaporn@phuket.ksc.co.th
www.phuket-plasticsurgery.com

"22 nd Anniversary"

TDK Corporation
1-13-1, Nihonbashi
Chuo-ku, Tokyo 103-8272
Japan

April 12, 2004

Dear TDK,

I have your corporate motto taped to my wall: Contribute to culture and industry through creativity.

It's inspiring. It's so impressive that I have it memorized. "Contribute to culture and industry through creativity." I wrote that second one without looking. Because I have it memorized I've thought of taking it down off the wall, but I used duct-tape, and a lot of it (made by 3M, sorry), so I'll just keep it where it is, covering up the pasta stains. Maybe someone visiting my studio will get inspired and contribute to culture and industry through creativity.

My contribution is through my art and scientific research. I'm well known in these parts for my work in documenting human auras, in particular the differences between auras of Japanese and those of people from Anglo-Saxon based cultures. A couple of photos and I can even tell if the subject is an average Japanese or a Japanese Christian, just by their aura.

I always use TDK media when I video tape and store on CD and DVD. Until now everything has been fine but some glitches have appeared recently. I've been experimenting with the auras of dead people and even in searching for ghosts. The photos and videos turn out ok but when I transfer to my computer or burn to DVD-R media, I lose the auras. When played back on an NTSC television, there are a lot of ghost images, but not the ones I want, if you see what I mean.

I'm filming my ghosts/ death auras with a Canon GL2, saved to TDK DVM tape, eventually transferred to TDK DVD-R (General Use) discs. For the video transfer work, I use Mac OSX Panther and Final Cut Express. Have you ever heard of this problem? I mean where do you think the auras and ghosts are going? Can our spirits not exist in the digital innerverse? If so, it has profound implications.

Thank you very much. Looking forward to your reply.
Sincerely,

Kirk Dunkirk

TDK SERVICE STATION

April 19, 2004

Dear Mr. Dunkirk

I received your letter to TDK dated April 12, 2004.

I did not at all ever heard such as DVD-disks or ghosts in your letter.   This problem is the outside matter of the technical field or standard using of our products.
So, I cannot write much more in this reply.

Best regards.

Kenji Hirabayashi

TDK Service Station   (Customer Support Sec.)
1-13-1 Nihonbashi Chuou-ku, Tokyo
〒 103-8272

●TDKサービスステーション　東京都中央区日本橋1-13-1 〒103-0027 ☎(03)5201-7272/TDK株式会社

Kirk Dunkirk
✉ ✉ ✉ ✉ ✉
Kochi City 780-✉✉✉✉

Hotel Nikko Huis Ten Bosch
6 Huis Ten Bosch, Sasebo-shi
Nagasaki, Japan 859-3

17 May 2004

To the Personnel Manager,

I will be visiting your lovely city at the end of August and have with a few questions about accommodations.

As you probably know, we Lichtensteiners are avid stamp collectors, and in my native land, Nagasaki has a wonderful reputation as a haven for philatelia. This may be because of its history as a port city. I'll be scouting the area for hotels and markets for my philatelia club back home, the Man-Child Philatelia Lovers Association of Balzers and Wangerberg. All the old boys can't wait to arrive and see what they can pick up on the street. It's a bad thing when philatelist salivate -- they might damage the goods! Anyway, the broad goal is to initiate some the new young people to intergeneration philatelia.

Before I stay at your hotel, I need check the quality of yours services.

- Is the humidity level in the rooms controlled to between 5 and 40% at all times?

- Are the pillows stuffed mit natural or man-made fibers? Synthetic (ersatz) is best.

- Since my wife returned to her Hindu commune in California and took my teenage daughter with her, it's difficult for me to sleep at night. Can a member of the young female staff come to my room around 9pm wearing pigtails so I can read a bedtime story to her? She can choose the story as long as it doesn't require duck noises. Dogs, cats, bear, pigs are acceptable. After she to falls asleep on the sofa (pretending is permitted), I will retire and she can leave one hour later. I will pay extra for this service and another of your member of staff may remain to witness.

Thank you in advance for your kind consideration of my special needs. I eagerly await the chance to try your lovely city.

Sincerely.

Kirk Dunkirk

hotel nikko huis ten bosch
6 huis ten bosch-cho Sasebo-city
Nagasaki, 859-3243

25 May 2004

Dear Kirk Dunkirk,

Thank you very much for your letter. In Nagasaki, there are a lot of beautiful places, and I'm sure that everybody who visits there including you will like them.
The answers for your questions are below;

- The humidity level in our guest room is almost controlled between 50 and 55% at all times.
- All of the pillows in our hotel are stuffed with feather.
- We are afraid that we don't serve that you would like to, even though you pay extra charge.

If you have some questions, please contact us again.
I send you some brochures of our hotel and huis ten bosch. We hope that you will have a good time here.

Sincerely,

Kumiko Hayashida
Reservation Department
hotel nikko huis ten boach

Let's take some time out for…

Haiku by Stymie

Two sticks, piece of fish
Guide them all into my mouth
And wait for applause.

You are not busy
But must pretend that you are,
Everyone else is.

Dydo Drink Company
2-2-7 Nakanoshima Kita-ku
Osaka-shi, OSK 530-0005
Japan

May 24, 2004

Dear Dydo,

How is the name of your company pronounced? I'm pretty sure there are 2 syllables and each syllable has two possibilities so that makes for 2x2 = 4 combinations. In other words, a1b1, a2b1, a1b2, and a2b2. (Not R2D2! I hated it when my genetics professor used to say that!)

$$a1 \quad a2$$
$$b1 \quad b2$$

The 4 possibilities are: 1)"dye-dough", 2) "dye-due" 3) "dee-dough" and, you guessed it 4) "dee-due." Also, which syllable is stressed? I need to know for a haiku project. My wife insists on calling it "diddoh" but I told her that's stupid. She's staying at her mother's house as I write this.

I became a big fan of Dydo drinks when I was stationed in Yokohama and your "Sha-wing!" brand Sparkling Squid Juice literally put hair on my chest. For two years I drank a can of Sha-wing! every morning and it made the hair on my chest grow. When I was based in San Diego before that I couldn't get Sha-wing! and you can imagine how difficult it is to be in the Navy with no hair on your chest. Let's just say I was careful picking up my soap in the shower.

So now I'm in Kochi, my wife's hometown, God bless her, and I haven't had any of your Sparkling Squid Juice for a few months, and my hair is falling out. Do you have any plans to sell it here in the future? Can I buy it directly from you? Or is it not available in western Japan?

Please write back soon! Summer beach season is coming up.
Sincerely,

Kirk Dunkirk

June 30, 2004

To : Mr.Kirk Dunkirk

From : Customer Survice Section
DyDo DRINCO,INC.
1361 Kando,Yosida-cho,Haibara-gun,Shizuoka-ken,Japan 421-0304
PHONE:(0548)32-8361   FAX:(0548)32-9033

Dear Mr.Kirk Dunkirk

We received your letter, and also appreciate to your friendliness for our company(our products).

You are asking how to read for our company symbol mark 'DyDo'. The correctly reading is 'daidou-dorinko', it is same 'dye-dough' that you said. It means '<u>Dy</u>namic' and '<u>Do</u>' but not English.

Next, you are needing for the product 'sha-wing'(sparkling drink) has not been selling on our company. Could you confirm again?

We hope you and your family will be success and health.

Sincerely yours,

Yukimasa Matsumura
<u>Section Manager</u>

Miki Dunkirk
✌ ✌ ✌ ✌
Kochi City 780-✌✌✌✌
Japan

Drivetech Racing School
14611 Rancho Vista Drive, Fontana, CA 92335
USA
May 31, 2004

Dear DriveTech,

    I see with the envy of the wonderful green pictures of your driving school. What a beautiful country you have! I think some of my relative detained during WWII at place near your school. It's small world, as Disney say. How ironic Brigestone the Japanese company!

    It is with heartfelt earnests that I address this letter to you on behalf of my brother. He want take your high speed road driving course in Summer, during national "Return of Deceased Ancestor" holidays. But he low-rank Japanese sumo wrestling man and so very fat. Is okay very fat man in race car? I think maybe ok because so many fat American. Before I think not true, but after visit Las Vegas, change of mind.

    He not only 160kg but especially big belly. Japanese car in, turn wheel but no move due to the fat abdomen. Is big American car ok? Maybe Cadillac? I don't know car, sorry I am cooking teacher.

    Because brother is new sumo, he is low in pecking order, so must wear Japanese "mawashi" at all the time. Japanese mawashi is loincloth look like thong bikini, but ancient tradition. Is this ok driving? Brother afraid slide on seat but I say so fat no can move! More worry about bowel movement from fright.

    Sumo life very strict. Sumo live together and many rules, not like American baseball player with long hair, spitting and human growth hormones. Brother's sumo master agree trip only on 3 condition. Condition 1) always wear traditional wresting man's bikini. condition 2) every day driving school staff wake him 5 am slap in face so not get weak . condition 3) if lose final race, save honour sumo team by drive car into wall like kamikaze hero. Sumo association will pay for damages to race track.

I look forward to hearing from you regarding this manner.
Sincerely,

Miki Dunkirk

** NO REPLY ☹ **

Kirk Dunkirk
✎ ✎ ✎ ✎ ✎
Kochi City 780-✎ ✎ ✎ ✎

MUSEUM MEIJI-MURA
1 Uchiyama
Inuyama-shi, Aichi Pref., 484-0000

~~July 12, 2004~~   August 29, 2004

Dear Museum Meiji-Mura,

    I love the concept of your outdoor museum. I think museums should be outdoors, so that someday all outdoor museums will be known simply as "museums" and those museums inside buildings will be called "indoor museums." This holds especially true in Japan where people have a deep connection with nature. If some of your buildings are damaged by earthquake or right-wing extremists, do you have duplicate copies somewhere? Do you have plans to make a virtual outdoor museum just in case? People could sit outside with 3D goggles at home or at special branch viewing centers with wind machines and experience the outdoor Meji era in their pajamas.

    Actually I'm writing to see if I could make a donation to your non-indoor museum. Sorry it's not money but I think it is of historical significance. You see, my grandmother was Japanese and I have a collection of letters from her grandfather. He was a low-ranking samurai in Tosa-han and he kept over 65 love letters between himself and numerous samurai. The letters stretch over a period of two decades and involve him and several other men; apparently he really got around. They are filled with lyrical poetry, political intrigue, and the passion of trained warriors longing to be reunited with their male lovers. As Japan "westernized" during the Meiji "revolution" much of its "homosexual" past was covered "up." Now that historians and the public are ready to re-embrace this facet of the past, I hope my family can make our own small contribution to the truth.

Please let me know if you are interested and I can forward more information.

Thank you very much.
Sincerely,

Kirk Dunkirk

ps. this is my SECOND letter. Notice the date. Please write me back?

Yuko Nakano
Museum Meiji-mura
1 Uchiyama Inuyama City
484-0000

Dear Kirk

    I'm sorry that I can't reply quickly. We've been very busy for preparing the special exhibision for these months.
    Thank you very much for your kind letter and an offer of donation of your collection. But I'm sorry that we do not collect histoical material which succeed to Sumurai Sprits, so I think it's better for your collection Kochi Prefectural Museum of History in Nangoku city or The Sakamoto Ryoma Memorial Museum in Kochi city, but both not outdoor museum. (There are little storage in our Museum, is one of reason we can't accept and a weak point of outdoor museum.)
    Your vision is very good plan I think, but our museum runs by only admission fee, so it's difficult to build up a favorable condition.

    I enclosed seasonal newsletter in Meiji-mura (sorry only in Jananese), I hope you wil enjoy reading of it!

Yuko Nakano
中野 祐子
Assistant Curator

2004 Autumn 明治村だより

秋号 Vol. 37

● 目次

特別展「明治の女神 昭憲皇太后」……2
竹中大工道具館 開館20周年記念巡回展
『木の匠と鉄の匠』……6
秋の明治村—催しものご案内……8
明治の機械 横形単気筒蒸気機関……10
明治の家具 足台付長椅子……10
A La Meiji-mura……11

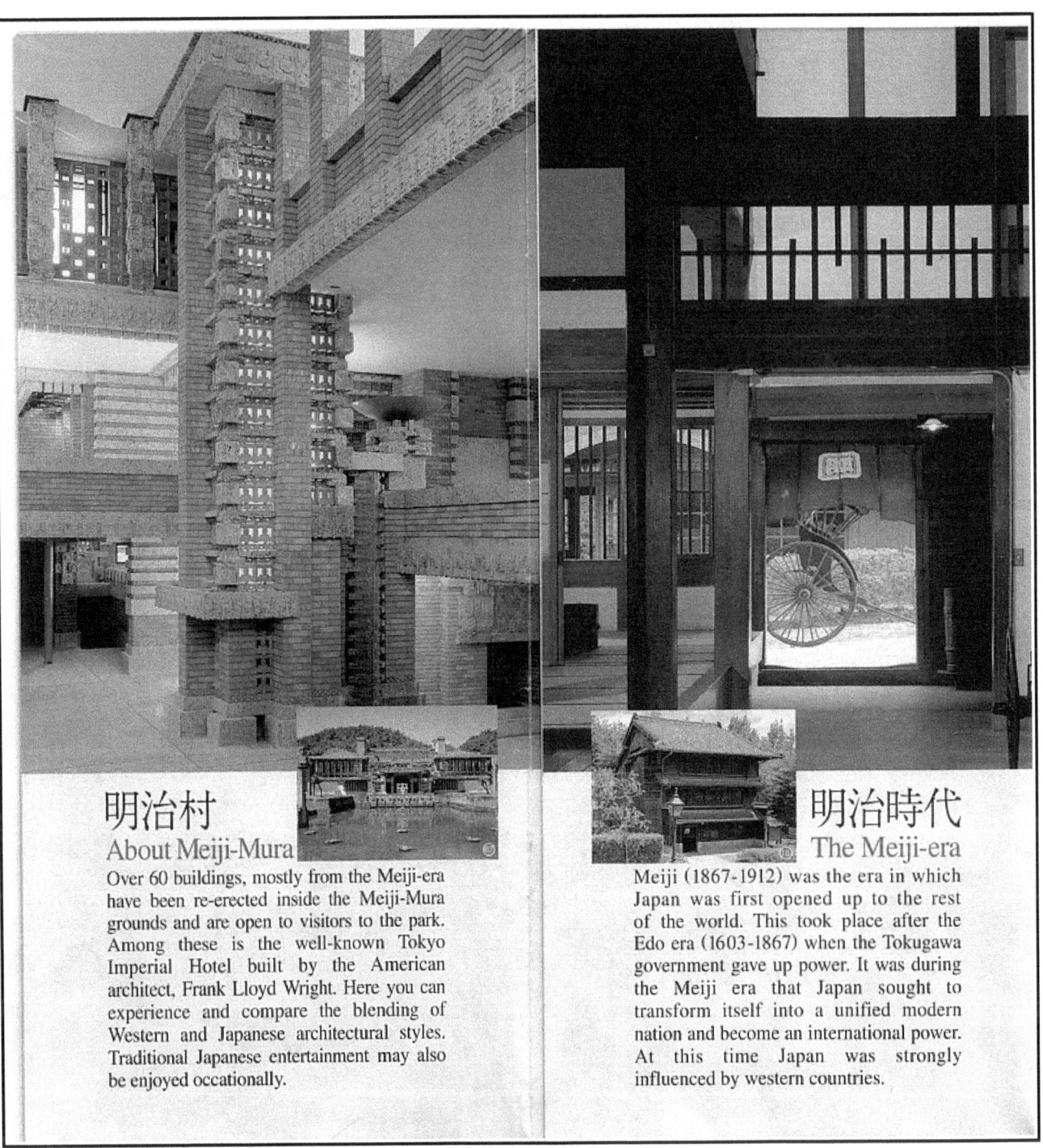

明治村
About Meiji-Mura

Over 60 buildings, mostly from the Meiji-era have been re-erected inside the Meiji-Mura grounds and are open to visitors to the park. Among these is the well-known Tokyo Imperial Hotel built by the American architect, Frank Lloyd Wright. Here you can experience and compare the blending of Western and Japanese architectural styles. Traditional Japanese entertainment may also be enjoyed occationally.

明治時代
The Meiji-era

Meiji (1867-1912) was the era in which Japan was first opened up to the rest of the world. This took place after the Edo era (1603-1867) when the Tokugawa government gave up power. It was during the Meiji era that Japan sought to transform itself into a unified modern nation and become an international power. At this time Japan was strongly influenced by western countries.

S------ Hypnosis
☺ ☻ ☺ ☻ Ave
San Fwancisco, CA 94xxx
USA

September 2, 2004

To Whom it May Concern,

I'm in a tewwibo pwedicament. It's a wong stowy, so pwease wisten.

I wecentwee bowwowed a warge sum of money from a scwewy welative. He was kind enough to wend it to me but he's also a hypnotist with a schitzophwenic stweak. To gawantee the woan, he hypnotized me to tawk and act wike Elmer Fudd until I wepay the money. As you can see, it even affects my witing.

I was so desperate that I agweed, but now I deepwy wegwet it. It's wuining my wife! (I'm not mawwied; I mean the wife I'm wivving.) People think I'm cwazy. I've stayed home sick fwom work pwetending to have wawyngitis, but I can't keep up the chawade much wonger. How can I wepay him if I wose my job?

What do you think? Can you bweak the spell? I'm more than wiwwing to fwy to Cowifonia, as I have wewatives there and it's almost duck season.

Yours twuwy,

Elmer J. Fudd, Millionaire
☻ ☺ ☻ ☺ Buil 4F
Kochi City 780-xxxx
Japan

September 22, 2004

Kirk Dunkirk
████████████████
Kochi City 780-████
Japan

Dear Kirk Dunkirk, Elmer Fudd, or whoever you are,

I am in receipt of your letter dated Sept. 2, and I am concerned about your problem. Just exactly how much money did you borrow from your relative/hypnotist, and where does he get off using his skills in such an unscrupulous and manipulative way?! Where was he certified?

Perhaps you were so emotionally upset about needing to borrow the money that you were more vulnerable to the mind control of your uncle. When he told you about the "collateral" he would need, this statement in and of itself could have served as a hypnotic induction.

I believe I can help you to break this spell. I am certified and I have helped many people.

I would be willing to help you if you decide to fly to California. I can be reached at (415) ████████. You may leave a message if I'm not at home, but if I don't call back within 48 hours, please do call again; There is a little man who is living inside of my answering machine who sometimes destroys my messages. Also, a wicked witch put a spell on my machine, causing it to act up and to sometimes not work properly. ha ha. I'm only kidding of course.

Sincerely,

Patricia ████

Arizona Biltmore Resort and Spa
2400 E MISSOURI AVE
Phoenixth, AZ 8501
USA

October 18th, 2004

To Whom it May Conthern,

Before I protheed any further, I believe an ekthplanaschun izth nethethary.

I'm attempting to thett a new world record for imitating a cartoon charachter, namely Thylvethter the Cat. In order to do tho I mutht remain in character at all timeth. This includezth my thpeech, my akschons, even my correthpondence. At leatht I don't have to wear a ridiculouth cothtume!

I will be in the Phh-- Phh-- Phoenixth area during the week of November 27thh for a televizzhin interview and am conthidering a thtay at your fine ethtablischment. All I ask ith that your thtaff be aware of my thituaschun and be conthiderate; I haff enough sssuffering ath it izth.

Pleathe write me back with regardthz to thiss matter.

Yourth Truly,

Thylvethter the Cat
(aka Kirk Dunkirk)
✄ ✄ ✄ ✄ ✄ ✄
Kochi Thitty
780-xxxx
JAPAN

ps. You don't happen to have thuccotasch on the menu do you? Juthst kidding.

ARIZONA BILTMORE
RESORT & SPA

October 28, 2004

Sylvester the Cat
(aka Kirk Dunkirk)

Kochi City 780
JAPAN

Dear Mr. Dunkirk,

Thank you very much for the letter to inform us of your visit next month. I'm glad to hear that in order to set the world record you aren't required to wear a ridiculous costume. I wouldn't want fellow guests running around the property saying, "they thought they saw a puddy tat."

I feel that I should let you know that our lobby is home to two cockatoos, Bill & Coo. I would ask that you refrain from taking your character study too far by disturbing them.

Again, Mr. Dunkirk, thank you for your letter and if I can be of any assistance before, during or after your stay, please don't hesitate to contact me personally. We look forward to welcoming you in November.

Sincerely,

Sean Clancy
Director of Rooms Division
602-381-7648

2400 EAST MISSOURI :: PHOENIX, AZ 85016 :: 602.955.6600 :: fax 602.381.7600
arizonabiltmore.com

Viva las vegas Wedding Chapel
1205 Las Vegas Blvd., South,
Las Vegas, Nevada 89104
USA

Oct. 15, 2004

Dear Viva Chapel,

You are one half of my dream come true!

Half of young Japanese girls dream is marry handsome American GI. I already did that and dream become nightmare, so now I am skit out of luck, paraphrase ex-husband.

So thanks to millennia of natural disaster, war and famines, we Japanese mucho pragmatical people so young girls is keep second half of dream for emergency. My other one half of dream is marry with Elvis!

Do you suppose it is possibility to marrying for Elvis? I am only one now and I wanna share my life with Sequined Jumpsuit Elvis. With bushy, bushy muttonchops! Don't be worry, I am just wanting marry for about 23 minute only or so, kinda like Britony Spears was doing. I heard Las vegas good place to do.

So please tell me how much price for marry with Sequined Jumpsuit Elvis, if what include cake or tokens, and photo of potential Elvis husbands. I am still cute, so maybe if Elvis handsome, he can love me tender? Ha! Just Japanese joke.

Thank you ma'am,

Miki Dunkirk

No. 1 Elvis fan of Kochi!

– ACTUAL AND ONLY REPLY FROM VIVA LAS VEGAS. –

"It's not Assburgers!"

Kirk Dunkirk
Stop to Panic Studios
xxxxx xxxxx 4f
Kochi City 780-xxxx
Japan

Toronto Marathon
450 Walmer Rd. #412
Toronto, ON, M5P 2X8
Canada

Feb. 12, 2005

To Toronto Marathon,

May I run in your 2005 event naked?

I'm trying to raise awareness for Asperger's Syndrome, often incorrectly referred to as "Assburger Syndrome." (See www.asperger.org for more information.) As you can understand, it is thus necessary for me to be naked and have a strategically placed sign board.

I've been to the dark side of Niagara Falls so I know that Canadians are comfortable with nudity. Combine that with Torontonians' good sense of humor and there should be no problem. But if you think this would offend anyone, I can wear a men's thong bikini, painted in such a way as to make me appear naked. Frankly I'd rather wear the thong to prevent chafing and windburn, but it makes my publicity tool less effective.

I realize the next marathon is not for several months but please write me back soon so I may plan my international race schedule. Also, does the race go by any Tim Horton's donut shops? Thank you for your cooperation.

Sincerely,

Kirk Dunkirk

ps: I promised to help my wife with her linguistics thesis by offering free cat naming ideas to people around the world. Here are a few: Gambit, Zugzwang, Crispus Attucks, Tone Loc. Please tell us what you think!

the toronto marathon
run...volunteer...cheer

March 4, 2005

Kirk Dunkirk
Stop to Panic Studios
███████████ 4f
Kochi City 780-███
Japan

Dear Kirk Dunkirk,

I received your letter recently regarding your request to run in our 2005 event naked. The Toronto Marathon is a large scale community event, one which invites the participation of thousands of participants, spectators, volunteers, city officials and sponsors. Many of our volunteers are high school students, and many of our spectators are children of all ages.

I do not believe that it would be appropriate for anybody to run the course naked as our event is truly a gathering of families and some may find it offensive. If you would like to run in our event, you will have to at the very least wear running shorts and shoes.

I trust that you will understand our position on this.

Yes, I do believe our event passes by a few Tim Horton's locations.

Best of Luck,

Nancy Jordan
Toronto Marathon
torontomarathon@rogers.com

www.TorontoMarathon.com • TorontoMarathon@rogers.com

450 Walmer Rd. Suite 412, Toronto ON M5P 2X8 ph: (416) 972-1062 fx:(416) 972-1238

Utah State Office of Education
250 East 500 South
P O Box 144200
Salt Lake City, Utah
84114-4200   USA

~~2004 Nov. 15~~
2005 Jan 17

Dear Director of Guest Speakers,

The other day we see news program. Fat American children in your state. So fat! We surprise. So my friend say "Maybe fat American kids can become champion Japanese sumo." We laughing long time. Because thinking fat american kiz sumo champion so funny! Don't you think so?

But now I am thinking this serious ploblem. Sure, fat American kids very funny, but maybe they sad looking into mirror see fat face and tying shoe and so on. So I have idea that can help both ours culture.

I am 11th generation Japanese Ninja. You know Ninja? I think so. Because very famous all world. Now Japan few Ninja because young people only likes American rap music and fast food hamburger. Maybe we get fat like you. Before Ninja secret but the times they are a changin'. So mine's company teaches Ninjutsu corporate client interested espionage, Japanese Self defense Forces. And so on.

I plan to visiting USA Spring 2005 for conference and want teach art of Ninja your elementary school kids. They learning kill with school supplies, steal secret document, tongue removal, and self-drowning with own saliva. Don't worry everything safe government approved. Purpose of Ninja is not killing! But cultivation of mind! (Many people misunderstand this.)

You'd better write me back soon so we can discuss details. Maybe I stop by on way to ski trip this winter sneak in school and surprise you. (PS: This my SECOND letter!)

Miki Dunkirk
Stop to Panic Consulting
☠ ☠ ☠ ☠ ☠ 4F
Kochi City 780-☻☻☻
Japan.

UTAH STATE OFFICE OF EDUCATION

Leadership... Service... Accountability

Patti Harrington, Ed.D., State Superintendent of Public Instruction
Voice: (801) 538-7500   Fax: (801) 538-7521   TDD: (801) 538-7876
250 East Cesar E. Chavez Blvd. (500 South)   P.O. Box 144200   Salt Lake City, Utah 84114-4200

February 1, 2005

Miki Dunkirk
Stop to Panic Consulting
█████████ 4F
Kochi City 780-████
Japan

Dear Mr. Dunkirk:

Thank you for your letter of January 17, 2005. I enjoyed hearing about your idea of teaching students the art of Ninja.

In Utah, teachers are required to use the Utah Core Curriculum to teach students. Physical education is part of the required Core, but the Utah State Office of Education does not select the specific programs and texts used in the classrooms to meet the standards and objectives in the Utah Core Curriculum.

Your proposal is interesting; however, it would not be appropriate for this office to discuss it in regard to implementation in the public schools of Utah. You would need to discuss this individually with the school districts where you would be interested in instructing.

Sincerely,

Christine Kearl

Christine A. Kearl
Associate Superintendent
Student Achievement and School Success

UTAH STATE BOARD OF EDUCATION
Kim R. Burningham, Chair • Janet A. Cannon, Vice Chair • Dixie Allen • Tim Beagley • Bonnie Jean Beesley • Laurel Brown • Mark Cluff • Bill Colbert • Edward A. Dalton • Thomas A. Gregory • Greg W. Haws • John C. Pingree • Debra G. Roberts • Richard Sadler • Sara V. Sinclair • Gary C. Swensen • Teresa L. Theurer

Kirk Dunkirk
Frog Suit Boy Circus
☹ ☹ ☹ ☹ 4F
Kochi City 780-xxxx

Honda Motor Co., Ltd.
2-1-1 Minami-Aoyama
Minato-ku, Tokyo 107-8556

November 29, 2004

Dear Honda,

The other day on the news I saw your CEO Takeo Fukui make a disparaging remark about human cannonballs.

Why would he say such a thing? What have human cannonballs ever done to him? Think of all the smiles we have brought into the world!

I am a third generation human cannonball. I am related to the great Zacchinni family, the original human cannonballs. And not a day goes by without me thanking the good Lord for giving me the greatest job on the planet.

When my father was a young human cannonball he too sometimes suffered discrimination from envious people. I have only come to Japan just recently to promote my small circus but am quite surprised to find that such a backwards attitude still thrives here.

From now on, the Frog Suit Boy Circus will no longer use Honda power generators and motorcycles in our acts. And we will make people who drive Hondas to our show park very far away in the mud.

Saddened,

Kirk "The Pterodactyl" Dunkirk

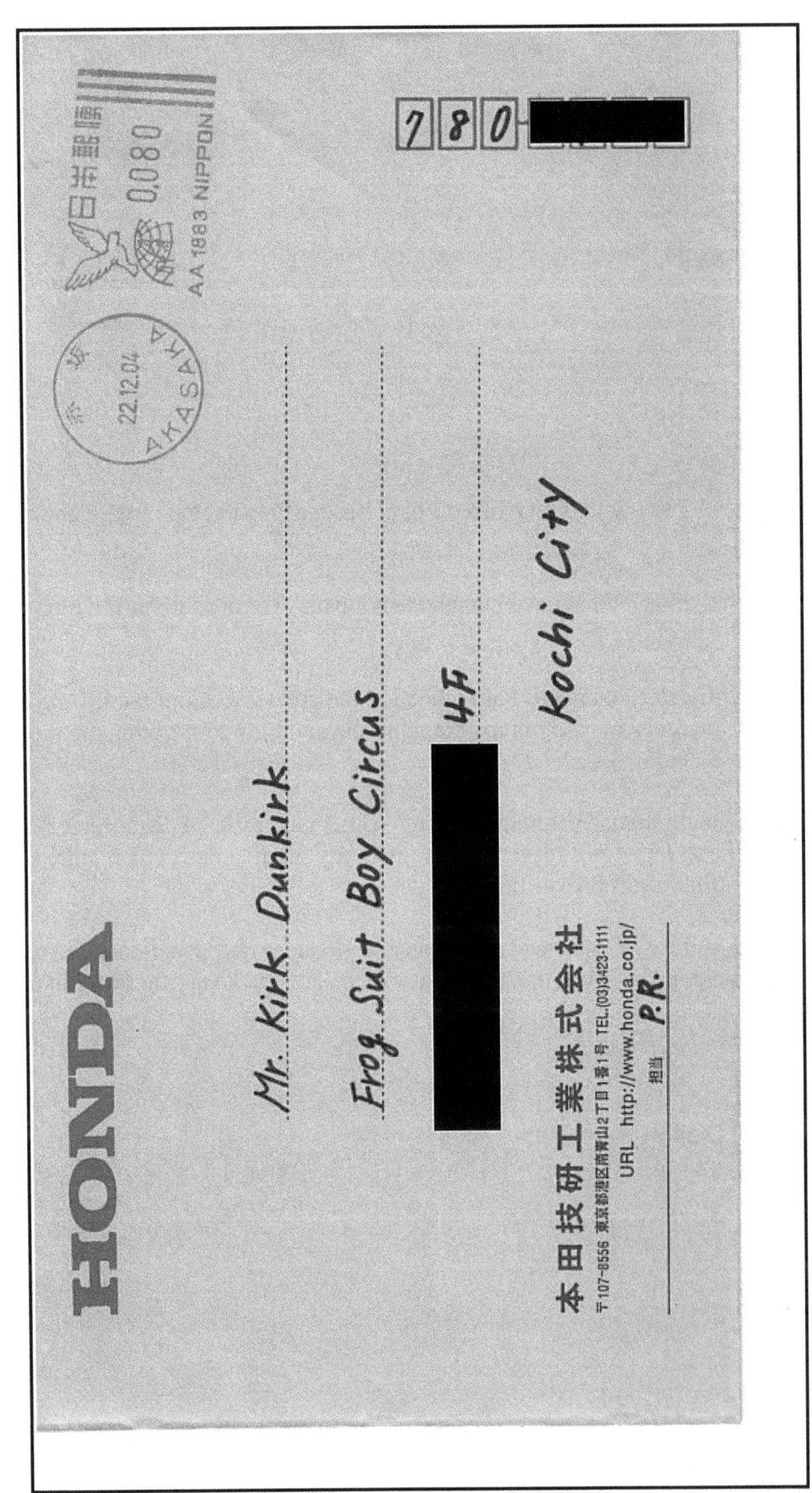

The Power of Dreams

No. 1-1, 2 Chome, Minami-aoyama, Minato-ku, Tokyo 107-8556, Japan
Tel: (03) 5412-1514 (PR Division)
Fax: (03) 5412-1515 (PR Division)
http://www.honda.co.jp/

December 22, 2004

Mr. Kirk Dunkirk
Frog Suit Boy Circus
███████████ 4F
Kochi City 780-███

Dear Mr. Dunkirk,

I am writing in response to your recent letter alleging that Mr. Fukui, CEO, made "a disparaging remark about human cannonballs." I must confess that I am not aware of the negative remark that you alluded to. To my knowledge, our CEO has not made any derogatory comments about any person or profession, much less that of the entertaining human cannonballs.

Actually, Mr. Fukui is a big fan of speed and fun and if he made comment about cannonballs which was not full of enthusiasm and cheer, I can only surmise that perhaps he was simply lamenting the fact that there was a job on this planet more fun that his own.

Wishing you the best of success with your circus.

Best regards,

Tatsuya Iida

Tatsuya Iida
Public Relations Division

January 17, 2005

To Whom it May Concern,

Enclosed is a letter from my student Miki Dunkirk.

This is a very emotional time for her. It would ease her mind greatly if you could take a moment to answer her questions. I know they are silly.

Thank you.

Kev. Atkinson Gaye

Miki Dunkirk
† † † † † 4F
Kochi City 780-†††
Japan

~~2004 Dec 06~~
2005 Jan 17

Hawaii Visitors & Convention Bureau
2270 Kalakaua Avenue, Suite 801
Honolulu, HI 96815

Dear Hawaii's Staff,

I very love Hawaii. Of course, everybody love Hawaii. Your job in Hawaii but maybe you even take vacation in Hawaii? No need go elsewhere. Oh envy you. Don't you? I do.

Also envy you cause your not gonna die soon. Do you? Nobody know. I can. Am sick. very x 2 much sick.

I wanna be dumped in Pu`u `O`o volcano like Hawaii people. Does this the possibly? Maybe you can't this but please tell me which Hawai'i depart office can help. Please! Am sick more every day and soon get loss of brain. The you explanate of an office I contact and take care the detail.

I wanna my body is dress up like Hawaii's princess many flowers and slide into quivering magma of Pu`u `O`o. Of course after die. I wanna everything like a princess I see in movie. Pig mouth in pineapple and so on. Drop me from helicopter ok if too hot. No problem I am rich and of course dead so I not need money. Another way ok, slingshot or human cannonball ok you tell me I not native Hawaii people so have no idea you of tradition.

I wanna finish life like true Hawaii tradition with local people dancing and shouting in grass skirt and coconuts while sacrifice to angry fire god. I wanna local people cry "Wa han da! wahanda!" traditional death shout in documentary is. I pay native dancers so you can come my funeral it's ok cause you help me. Please make yourself at home. All you can eat pig etcs. We see on TV drama here and now I wanna try before my friends do so I hope I die first. very popular. We Japanese people lose touch traditional ways so that's we envy traditional native Hawai'i's people.

Please reply me soon about lovely Pu`u `O`o volcano cause I wanna do this before my friend die first. I count on you helping to me. It my dying wish!

Miki Dunkirk

ps. this my SECOND letter please write back more soon!

Visitors & Convention Bureau

February 8, 2005

Ms. Miki Dunkirk
█████████████ 4F
Kochi City 780-████
JAPAN

Dear Ms. Dunkirk:

This is in response to your letter requesting a contact for the possibility of placing a deceased human body in Puʻu ʻOʻo crater, located within the Hawaiʻi Volcanoes National Park.

For specific answers to your questions, we suggest that you contact the following:

    Hawaiʻi Volcanoes National Park
    Attn: Aleta Knight
    P. O. Box 52
    Hawaiʻi National Park, HI 96718
    USA

    PH: (808) 985-6027
    FX: (808) 967-8186

You can also visit the Hawaiʻi Volcanoes National Park website at: http://www.nps.gov/havo/manage/management.htm for information.

Thank you for your interest in Hawaiʻi.

Sincerely,

Roxanne Relles

Roxanne Relles
Manager, Customer Relationship Management

Kirk Dunkirk
✔ ✔ ✔ ✔
Kochi City 780-✔✔✔✔

Alteco Head Office
5-8,Nishiekimaecho
Ibaraki-City,Osaka 567-0032

Jan 5, 2005

Dear Alteco

Your 6100 glue is really good stuff! I've used it to hold paper, wooden cowbells, keyholders, even a fake mustache. I can see why Japanese people call it "Almighty Bond."

I hope you keep making it. I hope you make more of it. My friend works in a muffler factory so I get mine from him. He gives it to me. It's hard to find in stores. My friend uses it on mufflers, ashtrays, and his dashboard. Times are tough.

Could you sell your epoxy in more stores? Maybe there aren't enough epoxy consumers in Kochi? Too rural? There must be a million and one uses for glue on a farm. Or at least 1000 and 1. Broken hooves, gates, horseshoes (the game) and nine hundred ninety-eight more. I feel religious about your glue. It's not just almighty but one could say omnipotent. Except for houseplants.

Please sell more in stores. I think you should change the smell though. Frankly American super-glues smell about 15% better. You could have themed glue, different countries for example. Canada: maple syrup. France could be garlic and cigarettes. Germany? Cold steel, of course. Want to make inroads into the US market? That's a no-brainer: new car and fresh $20 bills. Put cute pictures on the tubes to go with the odors. The world needs more appealing adhesives.

It just sticks, the glue does. To belts and videocassettes. Not like in the old days. Do you sell a neck container? I'm in charge of purchasing for a chain of university boutiques and I want to make your glue The Next Big Thing. I want to wear it in a stylish container hanging off my neck -- shape like a fish and call it "a NURDLE" so I can glue phones, joysticks and curtains in a flash. Kids today are looking for that.

What can I do? Where can I buy your glue easily on Shikoku? Online? How about the scents and the Nurdle? I'm willing to mix the odors myself but I don't want to get hurt. I really like your glue. Except the smell. Please advise me.

Sincerely,

Kirk Dunkirk

ps. Maybe I should open a window

ALTECO INC.
5-8, Nishiekimaecho, Ibaraki-City, Osaka 567-0032 Japan
TEL:072-627-1617 FAX:072-627-1664
http://www.alteco.co.jp

JAN 28.2005

Dear Mr. Kirk (our great customer)

Thank you for your letter.

We are very happy because we can know that you love our products and your comments are very helpful for us.
Thank you very much.

About our epoxy adhesives

We feel very sorry because we can not meet your request.
Our products are for only industry, not for in home. So we do not have the product for individual
We hope that you will accept our situation.

And we would like to present two goods for you
Please use them.

If you have some questions, please send your email to my address.
My address is mizutai@alteo.co.jp

Sincerely

A.Mizutani (MR)
Sales Department

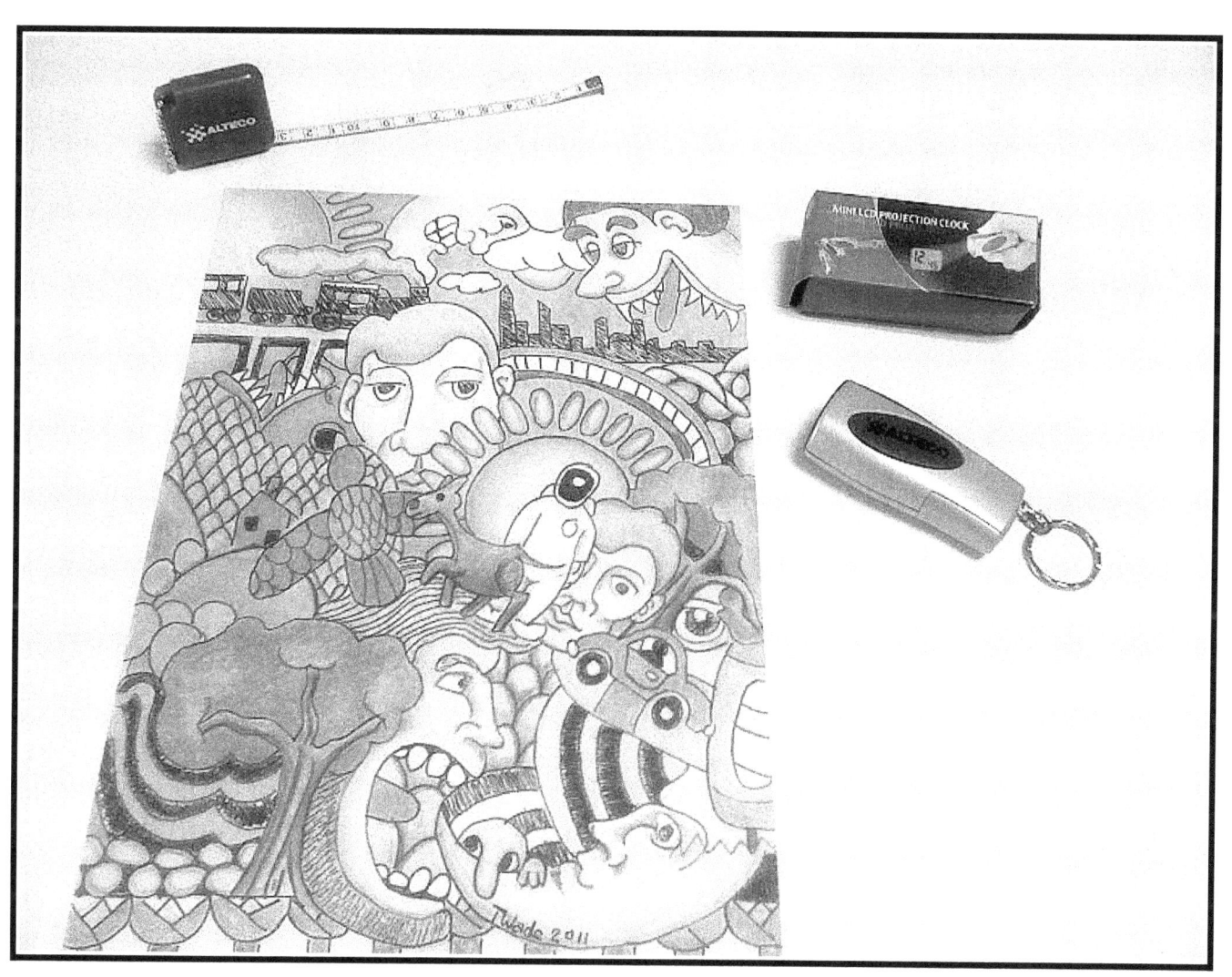

(Alteco gifts: ruler keychain and mini-LCD projection clock keychain. Unrelated illustration by Tom Wade)

Dear MR. Kirk Dunkirk

Thank you very much for your letter.
We thank from the bottom of our's heart that you like our glue.
Well, you can buy our glue in fishing shop.
Could you ask Okabayashi in kohchi-city?
Okabayahi is very famous shop. They have 2 places.

        One of them:088-844-2200(Phone No)
        The other   :088-823-0091(Phone No)

We say thank you again.

                                            Sincerely yours

                                            Takehiko Ohara

Kirk Dunkirk
TM TM TM TM
Kochi City 780-TM TM TM

Snow Brand Milk Products Co., Ltd.
13 Honshio-cho
Shinjuku-ku Tokyo 160-8575

Jan. 10, 2005

Happy "Coming of Age Day."

Today we held our annual "Curtis Loves Truckers" costume party for my friends and students. We dress up and talk like American and Australian truckers. I used to be one, so I keep things authentic as a native speaker.

After the opening convoy, Testuo ate some of my guacamole and washed it back with your whole milk. I said "Mercy Sakes[1], Mush Mouth (his handle[2]) that's a bodacious[3] belt buckle." I was just trying to make him feel at home but he sprayed his milk all over my tattooed forearm.

So I said "Whoah there, good buddy, what's the 10-33[4]? You're gonna put the brakes on our jamboree." He said that the milk tasted bad and fired up his rig and left. On his way out he grabbed some fresh beef jerky for the road.

I know that your company had problems in the past. You sold a lot of products that made people sick and lied about it. But I'm sure them days are over because I saw your president on TV crying like a girl and apologizing. So I always buy your products now and I'm still alive and kicking.

I gave Mush Mouth's milk to my cat Pink Panther and it didn't kill her. But I did notice that the skin on my tattoo was itchy and swollen. Could it be the milk or the tabasco from the guacamole? What do you reckon?

Anyway, I just want to check that you can promise me that your company no longer sells dairy products that make people sick. Please write back soon.

10-10[5],

Kirk Dunkirk

1. exclamation of surprise
2. handle = nickname
3. = excellent
4. = emergency
5. = standing by, waiting for reply

Irked by Kirk   169

January 19, 2005

Mr. Kirk Dunkirk
███████████
Kochi City 780-█████

Dear Mr. Kirk Dunkirk:

Let us begin by saying that we appreciate your patronage of our products.

We read your letter that the tattoo of your forearm had been itchy and swollen by the milk sprayed by your friend.

We can't understand the cause that your tattoo has been itchy and swollen. However, there might be a possibility of occurring if you have a strong milk allergy.

Snow Brand Milk Products Co., Ltd. has not been selling drinking milk products from 2003.

Please inquire of Nippon Milk Community Co., Ltd. divided from our company if you want to inquire about the milk. I show the address of Nippon Milk Community to below.

Address of Nippon Milk Community Co., Ltd.:

〒162-0067 10-5 Tomihisa-cho Shinjyuku-ku, Tokyo Shinjuku EAST Bldg.

In closing we apologized for the incident that our company caused in2000 and promise to do our best to see that such incident does not recur.

Sincerely yours,
Kouji Suzuki
Customer Satisfaction Dept.
SNOW BRAND MILK PRODUCTS Co., Ltd.

Kirk Dunkirk
IWUF
xxxx xxxx 4F
Kochi City 780-xxx

Aozora Bank
13-10 Kudan-kita 1-chome
Chiyoda-ku, Tokyo 102-8660

January 20, 2005

Dear Aozora Bank,

Let me introduce myself: I am the Region III representative of I-WUF, the International Winners United by Fuddism (pronounced "EYE-WOOF")

We are an association that recognizes the achievements of people who, despite their obvious shortcomings in intellect or communication skills, manage to rise to the top. Some of our more prominent members include Barbara Walters, Usher, Keanu Reeves, Fukuyama Masaharu, and of course, the honorary co-President of the United States, George W. Bush.

We have been keeping an eye on your Senior Executive Officer Fudeji ✖✖✖✖ for some time now. His speeches and knack for delegating to those with more talent all make him a fast-track candidate for future membership. The fact that Dan Quayle sits on your board certainly doesn't hurt either.

We would be dewighted if he could give a speech at our Kochi conference sometime in the spring. It is customary for speechmakers to make fun of their competitors, e.g.. Shinsei Bank, in a funny voice. We will provide headwear, accommodation, speaking fee (name your price) and lunch, which is followed by a short hunting excursion. Feel free to contact me for further details.

Our best wishes for further uncanny luck in the new year.
Sincerely,

Kirk Dunkirk
I-WUF Chair, Region III
Fuddhist Rating: 1850

東京海上日動火災保険株式会社
MILLEA GROUP

Tokiomarine&Nichido Fire Insurance Co.,Ltd
20-19,Marunouchi 2-Chome,
Naka-ku,Nagoya,460-8541

Kirk Dunkirk
IWUF
████████ 4F
Kochi City 780-███

March 28.2005

Dear Kirk Dunkirk,

I appreciate your kind letter, which finally got to me last week.
Last July I got back to Tokio Marine after 2years staying at Aozora Bank.
Now I am working in Nagoya as a managing director of Tokio Marine.
I am wondering if you would be still interested in me in spite of the current job & position.
I would be very pleased if you could send details of I-Wuf activities(including the meaning of Fuddism).

Since I'm enclosing my name card, you can easily contact me by e-mail&/or phone.

Best Regards,

Fudeji

Singapore Airlines
12-17 Umeda
Umeda Daiichiseimei Building
1-Chome Kita-Ku Osaka 530-0001

Jan 24, 2005

Dear SIA,

I am fat and I'm guilty. I am stricken by guilt. And I'm strikingly large.

I've tried alcohol, I've tried knitting. I got a TV Shopping Tornado Stepper but it snapped. I haven't tried any other exercise before or since. The guilt prevents me. And the narrow streets. And the weak shins. So I had a milkshake and imo kenpi instead. Can't you see? I've just plain given up. This is a cry for help.

So when I fly please CHARGE ME MORE. I'm huge. I'm a Jumbo. My nickname is A380. In the event of a crash, I could be a flotation device. I think I should pay more. Maybe then I won't spend the money on food. Lasagna is my favorite at the moment. I'm as guilty as OJ but fatter. I roll around in bed slapping my belly in anger and say "Take that fatty-fat poopie boy in tent pajamas!"

I wanted to try the famous "Mohammed al Akbar Samba Sensation Dance Studio" in Katong recommended by a fellow Swiss fatty, but an incident at your check-in counter altered my plans. The kid in front of me, a handsome young Kimu Taku wannabe of about 24 years and 60kg was complaining about your luggage restrictions. You allow 20kg of luggage and his were 24. Without luggage I'm easily double that! Just one of my arms, two of my chins and both knee braces probably weigh more than that sinewy lad. And that's after I sweat out a bucket shuffling up the ramp. And he knew it too. We both knew it. The kid was pointing at me and at the scale and shouting. The word "sumo" popped up a couple of times, forcing me to scarf an emergency Toblerone on the spot. I never made it to the Samba studio -- my hotel had a food court and room service.

So I want you to <u>charge me more money</u>. The kid was right: I am guilty in a big way. The plane makes more CO_2 because of me. I crave okonomiyaki even as I write this. I don't want to change my habits but I want to pay more money. Please think of a rate schedule similar to freight charges and let me know. Also, the kid's name is Takahashi Kenji (or maybe Takemura Kenji) and flew on Jan. 8. Along with the cargo fees could you please send me his address so I may send him condolence money? I need you to rid me of this guilt! There's a saying in Switzerland: Money is usually the best way.

Thank you and I apologize for never seeing any of your beautiful country beyond my hotel lobby. Regretfully,

Kirk Dunkirk
xxx xxxxxx xx 4F
Kochi City 780- ✈ ✈ ✈

ps. I need Toulouse some weight!

SINGAPORE AIRLINES LIMITED

Mr. Kirk Dunkirk
█████████ 4F
Kochi City 780-████

KIXKD/07.28/05-004   27 January 2005

Dear Mr. Dunkirk

We acknowledge receipt of your letter dated 24 January 2005 to request for additional charges and contact information of another customer.

On your request for additional charges, we are pleased to advise you that at present, Singapore Airlines does not have the practice of charging customers for situations as described in your letter.

As to your request for the contact information of another customer, we regret that we are unable to reveal the information so as to protect the confidentiality and privacy of our customers.

Please feel free to contact us at (0724) 56-5015 if you require any clarifications on our reply.

We thank you for choosing to travel with Singapore Airlines and we look forward to welcoming you onboard our flight again.

Yours Sincerely

Kevin Koh
Station Manager Osaka

Incorporated in Singapore

From the wrapper of a famous souvenir snack:

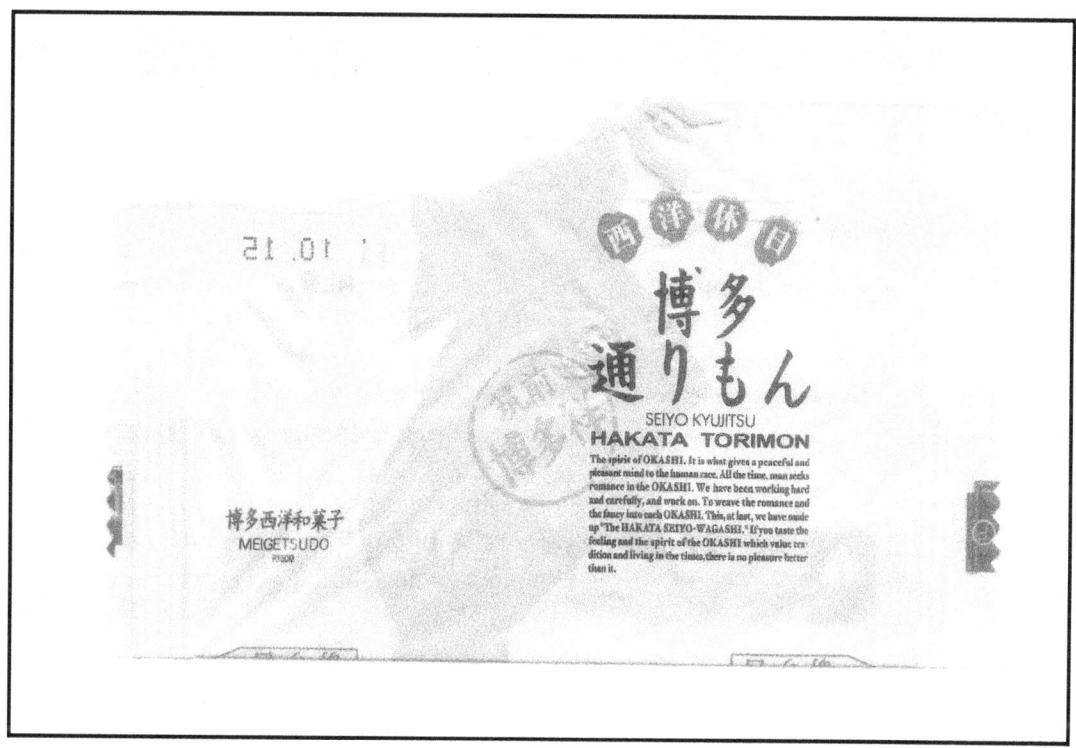

From the snack wrapper above:
("okashi" = sweets)

HAKATA TORIMON

The spirit of OKASHI. It is what gives a peaceful and pleasant mind to the human race. All the time, man seeks romance in the OKASHI. We have been working hard and carefully, and work on. To weave the romance and the fancy into each OKASHI. This, at last, we have made up "The HAKATA SEIYO-WAGASHI." If you taste the feeling and the spirit of the OKASHI which value tradition and living in the times, there is no pleasure better than it.

Bureau of Licenses
111 SW Columbia Suite 600
Portland, OR 97201
USA

January 18, 2005

Dear Business License Office,

I am writing regarding opening one of our chain restaurants in your delightful city. It's called "The Eel and the Panda" after the famous children's story. As the name implies, we serve eels and pickles, but no panda. Not since 1975, anyway.

It's a family restaurant, so family units hunt their own eels in a large wading pool. We give them their own spear gun and bucket, 5% off if you bring your own gear. No clubs or flashlights please, that's cheating! For regular & corporate customers we have a Japanese custom, so to speak, called "bucket keep" where we keep a bucket with your family name on it on a shelf for your next visit. Please tell us what kind of footwear, if any, is required in your municipality for public animal gathering pools. Is there an eel-to-water ratio like in Japan?

While families hunt the eel, on a small island in the center a young lady in a panda style bikini throws nuts and berries at them, a la the fable. You gotta see it -- young Japanese chicks in panda outfits. It's hot, hot, hot right now and we want to ride the wave across the Pacific. Every now and then the Panda girl shouts "Electric eel!" and everyone has to jump out of the tank. Last one out gets spanked by a rubber eel. Do we need an entertainment permit for that?

What sets us apart from other eel hunting restaurant chains is our emphasis on tradition. Sure, lots of restaurants still use the nail through the eye method, but only in our place, just like in the old days, are you not allowed to kill your own eel. You have to convince someone at another table to do it for you. This gets people to mingle. The Japanese have a saying: "Friendships formed over eel blood last for seven generations." Really it's not so different from cracking a lobster. Sadly though, people nowadays don't know how to gut their own eel, especially in fast-food crazy America, so our Panda-bikini girls will come out with Ginsu knives and do it for you, right at the table. Nothin' beats fresh eel! Do the girls have to wear gloves or hair nets?

So Portland seems like the ideal place for a "The Eel and the Panda" franchise, but we need to know more about zoning and drainage. We hope you are as excited as we are to bring our wet little corner of Japan to you.

Kirk Dunkirk
Co-ordinator, International Marketing
xxx xxxx xx 4F
Kochi City 780-xxxx
Japan

CITY OF PORTLAND, OREGON
BUREAU OF LICENSES
An Equal Opportunity Employer

Thomas Lannom, Director
111 SW Columbia St., Suite 600
Portland, OR 97201
(503) 823-5157
Fax: (503) 823-5192
TDD: (503) 823-6868

February 10, 2005

Kirk Dunkirk
Coordinator, International Marketing
███████████ 4F
Kochi City 780-███
Japan

Dear Mr. Dunkirk,

In response to your letter dated January 18, 2004, I am enclosing information regarding licensing fees for the City of Portland. Basically, the City charges a licensing fee on all businesses that operate in Portland and Multnomah County, with a few exceptions. This "license" is regarded by most businesses as a net revenue tax and is indeed assessed much like a tax.

In addition, I have forwarded your request to the one governmental agency that I believe could best answer your questions regarding the rules and regulations for the operation of a restaurant in the City of Portland. That agency is:
- Multnomah County Health Department
  426 SW Stark – 8th Floor
  Portland, OR 97204

If you do not hear from them in a timely manner, please contact them at the above address or you may call (503) 988-3400.

One final reference is the Business Information Center. The Center is a cooperative service of six state agencies and provides packets on starting a business that includes the Oregon Business Guide, forms for filing with the Corporation Division, and forms for obtaining a state business identification number and federal IRS employer identification number if needed. Their mailing address is:

    Business Information Center
    Public Service Bldg., Suite 151
    255 Capitol Street NE
    Salem, OR 97310-1327

    Phone: (503) 986-2200

Best wishes on your business endeavor.

Sincerely,

Scott Ellertson
Licenses Operations Supervisor
City of Portland
(503) 823-5145

City of Portland Business License Program
Multnomah County Business Income Tax Program

CITY OF
PORTLAND, OREGON
BUREAU OF LICENSES
An Equal Opportunity Employer

Tom Potter, Mayor
Thomas Lannom, Director
111 SW Columbia St, Suite 600
Portland, OR 97201-5840
(503) 823-5157
Fax: (503) 823-5192
TDD: (503) 823-6868

The City of Portland Bureau of Licenses administers both programs. Questions and correspondence should be addressed to the Bureau of Licenses, 111 SW Columbia St, Suite 600, Portland, OR 97201-5840 (503) 823-5157. Visit our Web site at www.pdxbl.org.

CITY OF PORTLAND BUSINESS LICENSE

WHO IS REQUIRED TO OBTAIN A BUSINESS LICENSE? Everyone doing business in the City of Portland except:
a) Businesses grossing less than $25,000 per year from all sources before expenses.
b) Businesses whose **only** activity is regulated by the State Insurance Division.
c) Real estate salespersons whose **only** business activity is real estate sales.
d) Individuals whose only business activity is ownership of less than 10 residential rental units.
e) Exempt Business are required to file an exempt certificate.

WHAT IS THE FEE? The fee is 2.2% of the net business income. Apportionment may be allowed for business activity performed outside the City. **THE MINIMUM ANNUAL FEE IS $100.**

ISN'T THIS JUST A BUSINESS TAX? The business license fee replaces all general business taxes in Portland. It is purely a revenue license, with many of the features of privilege tax. Unlike most city business taxes, Portland's fee is based on net income (after expenses), not on gross receipts. As a license, it must be paid *in advance* for each year of business.

HOW DO I GET MY LICENSE? Complete a one-page Application Form, and send it to the Bureau of Licenses with the $100 minimum fee. You will receive a license that will expire at the end of your current tax year.

WILL I RECEIVE A LICENSE IMMEDIATELY? If you need immediate evidence that you are licensed, **bring your application & fee to the Bureau of Licenses for a temporary receipt.**

MULTNOMAH COUNTY BUSINESS INCOME TAX

WHAT IS MCBIT? Multnomah County replaced its business license with a business income tax in 1976. The business income tax is assessed on all "persons" doing business in Multnomah County.

WHO HAS TO PAY MCBIT? Everyone doing business in Multnomah County except:
a) Businesses grossing less than $25,000 per year from all sources before expenses.
b) Businesses whose only activity is regulated by the State Insurance Division.
c) Individuals whose only business activity is ownership of *less than* 10 residential rental units.

WHEN/HOW DO I PAY THE TAX? Generally, you must file and pay the tax within three and one-half months following the end of your taxable year. However, you may request an extension of up to six months to file your return. This extension is granted when accompanied by an estimated tax payment.

WHAT IS THE TAX? The tax is 1.45% of the net business income. **For Tax Year 1998 (1 year only) an additional .5% will be due for taxpayers owing $100.00 or more.** Apportionment may be allowed for business activity performed outside the County. **THERE IS NO MINIMUM TAX.**

WHAT IF I HAVE NOT PAID THE TAX? If you have not paid the tax for past years when you have been doing business in Multnomah County during those years, you will need to file returns for those past years, Contact the Bureau of Licenses for information and forms.

Health Department
Environmental Health

MULTNOMAH COUNTY OREGON

727 NE 24th Avenue
Portland, Oregon 97232
(503) 988-3400 phone
(503) 988-5844 fax

February 23, 2005

Kirk Dunkirk
Coordinator, International Marketing
████████████ 4F
Kochi City 780-███
Japan

Dear Mr. Dunkirk,

Received your letter dated January 18, 2005 regarding "The Eel and the Panda" chain restaurant last week. Your letter was forwarded to our office from the City of Portland along with their response. I have reviewed your letter with colleagues from the State of Oregon. The following is their response:

1. The pool would need to be licensed as a wading pool.
2. Wading pools may not be used as a tank for storage for seafood offered to the public for consumption.
3. The eels must be obtained from an approved source.
4. The restaurant must develop a seafood HACCP plan for the eels.

There is no eel to water ratio specifications here and no glove requirements. However, those would be of minimal concern when compared to the health and safety of customers from spear gun shots and attempts to climb out of the tank quickly.

You are welcome to visit our website: www.mchealthinspect.org for more information.

Ken Yee

Ken Yee, R.S.
Environmental Health Supervisor

c. Scott Ellertson, City of Portland

Kirk Dunkirk
xxxx xxxx
Kochi City 780- ✈ ✈ ✈

MALAYSIA AIRLINES
4TH FLOOR, OCAT BUILDING
1-4-1 MINATOMACHI
NANIWA-KU OSAKA 556-0017

Feb. 14, 2005

Dear Malaysia Airlines,

I often see your commercial for the new Airbus A380 on satellite TV. The one with the handsome young scientist couple smirking at each other on the beach. In monochromatic black and white two tone. I have a problem with this commercial.

It's just that it's too suggestive. The smooth European scientist pushing away the dapper asian engineer in the lounge chair using psychokinetic forces -- it provokes me. I mean it really provokes me, and I'm uncomfortable with provocation. Provocative commercials often backfire you know! I feel like he's pushing me! Why all this provoking? It's the last thing the world needs right now, that and more hailstorms.

I see the commercial when I eat breakfast. It's the most important meal of the day! The two men preening in the cavernous bathroom --the big A380 mile high bathroom. A little suggestive, don't you think? Then the film turns to color and the hangar doors open suggestively and they ride up together in the crane and the music climaxes. Hello? Didn't your directors see the ad before airing it? I flew to Kuala Lumpur on Malaysian Air and caught a bus to Malacca but I think it was a Boeing 767. Do you have any Fokkers in your fleet?

What am I suggesting? Not as much as the commercial. Or am I? Better yet, am I suggesting anything? Who's to say? We each have to decide for ourselves. That's the issue. Won't you clear this up for me?

Please write back. I'm open to your suggestions.
Sincerely,

Kirk Dunkirk

ps. Happy Valentine's Day

MALAYSIAN AIRLINE SYSTEM BERHAD (10601-W)

18th February 2005
Ref: AMWJ 015.32

Mr. Kirk Dunkirk
▇▇▇▇▇
Kochi City 780-▇▇▇
Japan

Dear Mr. Dunkirk,

We acknowledged receipt of your letter dated February 14, 2005.

Please be informed that your comment has been forwarded to the Manager of our Customer Management Department who will be responding to you in due course.

We thank you for your interest in our airline.

Yours sincerely

Steven Kat
Area Manager West Japan

Cc: Customer Management Manager, KUL

Reservations/Administrations : Hankyu Kotsusha Bldg. 3-3-9, Shinbashi, Minato-ku, Tokyo, 105-0004   TEL.(03)3503-5961(RES.) · (03)3503-6808(ADMIN.)
                                                                                                  TEL.(03)3503-5966(TKT.)   FAX.(03)3503-5970
Sales : No.2 Nan-oh Bldg. 5·6F, 2-20-1, Nishi-shinbashi, Minato-ku, Tokyo, 105-0003   TEL.(03)3432-8509(PASSENGER.) · (03)3432-8507(CARGO)
                                                                                                  FAX.(03)3432-1716(PASSENGER.) · (03)3432-8517(CARGO)
Tokyo : No.29 Mori Bldg. 3F, 4-2-1, Shinbashi, Minato-ku, Tokyo, 105-0004   TEL.(03)3432-8503(ACCT.)   FAX.(03)3432-1827
Narita : P.O. Box 2161 Narita Airport, Narita-city, Chiba, Japan 282-0004   TEL.(0476)34-8270,8272   FAX.(0476)34-8273
Nagoya : 3rd Floor, Nagoya Daiya Bldg. No.2, 3-15-1, Meieki, Nakamura-ku, Nagoya, 450-0002   TEL.(052)561-3636   FAX.(052)561-8150
Osaka : 4F, OCAT Bldg. 1-4-1, Minato-machi, Naniwa-ku, Osaka, 556-0017   TEL.(06)6635-3072   FAX.(06)6635-3075
Fukuoka : 6F, Hinode Tenjin Bldg. 12-20, Tenjin 1-chome, Chuo-ku, Fukuoka, 810-0001   TEL.(092)733-6006   FAX.(092)733-6020

Kirk Dunkirk
No Child's Left Behind
☞ ☞ ☞ ☞ ☞
Kochi City 780-✌✌✌

ORIX Corporation
Mita NN Bldg., 4-1-23 Shiba, Minato-ku
Tokyo, 108-0014

~~Nov. 1, 2005~~   March 2, 2006

Dear Orix,

Since 1997 our organization has worked diligently to make the world a safer place for children. The Sudan, the Haiti, even the Quebec -- sure they're bad, but what are you going to do about it? Why not start in your own backyard? And since most Japanese don't have a backyard, then why not start at the office?

It has come to NCLB's attention that the personnel department of your organization encourages SPANKING at its employee day care centers. Condoning is one thing, but encouraging, well, that's going too far.

We here at NCLB hate spanking. When we heard you were spanking your employees and their kids we threw a tantrum. My secretary knocked her pea soup on the floor. Naoki in accounting sat himself in front of the TV and refused to budge for 45 minutes. Why are you spanking the kids? It's not fair! I scribbled all over a blank CD-R then snapped it in two (by mistake.) It wasn't my fault. It was an accident.

Sure you're thinking "How come all the other companies get to spank?" Well, I'm telling you it doesn't matter what they do. You started it, but I'm finishing it, ok? Got it? Instead of spanking, why not put the misbehaving girl in a quiet room with a lot of plants and play songs from the Heath? Around here we say: In a big country dreams stay with you, like a lover's voice fires the mountainside… Off the record, who got to spank Ichiro?

There are a lot of idle rich housewives in our organization, so we hope we can work something out. If you would like further advice on how to avoid corporal punishment, please request a brochure. In the meantime, please write me back at the above address and let me know of your company's plans to stop spanking at the workplace. C'mon Orix, it's the lease you could do!

Thank you very much.

Kirk Dunkirk, Japan Commissioner
No Child's Left Behind

ps: this is my 2nd letter!!! It's been 4 months! Please write back?

Kirk Dunkirk
No Child's Left Behind
████████████
Kochi City 780-████████

ORIX Corporation
Mita NN Bldg 4-1-23
Shiba, Minatoku Tokyo
108-0014

Dear Mr. Kirk Dunkirk,

Your letter has been received and the contents noted. Your letter, however, does raise a question. ORIX has branch offices throughout Japan and conducts it corporate activities from its headquarters and several of these branch offices. However, none of these facilities has an employee day care center. Thus, it is our view that the alleged action could not have taken place, since no children have ever been placed under our supervision. Nevertheless, if you can provide us of any specific facts, we would conduct an investigation and advise you of the result. Any specific information you may have on where the alleged action took place, would be of great help.

Respectfully yours,
Hirofumi Yatsuzuka
General Affairs Group, ORIX Corporation

RECEIVED
MAR -9 2005
TAX & LICENSE DIVISION
DEPT. OF FINANCE

Kirk Dunkirk
▮▮▮▮▮▮▮▮
Kochi City 780-▮▮▮
Japan

City of Tacoma
Finance Department/Tax & License Division
733 Market Street, Room 21
Tacoma, WA 98402-3770 USA

March 2, 2005

Dear CTFD/T&LD,

I've lived in Japan for 9 1/2 months, so that makes me an expert. Now I want to bring this expertise to your lovely city.

I propose to operate my Japan-inspired franchise "KAKU'S BAKU TAKUS." It is pronounced "TAKooz" not "take us" -- that shop got shut down and his hard disks confiscated. I plan to wear a rubber taco costume complete with condiments and walk or unicycle around your charming population centre selling TAKUS™ (ie tacos) from a 2m (2.18 yd.) replica of an Aztec pyramid strapped to my BAKU (back.) KAKU, minus the all-caps, is what Japanese people call me. Hence the Japan connection. I fell in love with the word 'hence' from an abacus manual when I was 10.

These are not just any tacos, these are TAKUS, made with my secret Japanese sauce. Only the hard shell will do! I promised the monk who taught me the secret recipe that it will only be used for good. Hence I am unable to operate in southern California and Houston, though I'm waiting for his decision on Nashville. Let's go, Nashville! If I reveal the secret to the health department in your state I must commit ritual disembowelment, aka TAKU SEPPUKU. Don't even ask about the fate of the health department...Whoa!

As I wear the pyramid temple on my back, my business partner (Ivan) dressed as a Conquistador will follow behind, kicking me and dispensing napkins (free, up to 3 per customer) as he takes musical requests (no Gypsy Kings please.) I will vend on foot or cycle, depending on climactic variables. We are very proactive about this. Conquistadors however must operate on foot or horseback, no bicycles (duh). Vending queen only seventeen, oh yeah.

Please inform me as soon as possible about the necessary paperwork and location of local armor smiths. We (me & Ivan) at KAKUS BAKU TAKUS believe in giving bak to the community.

Muchas gracias,

Kirk Dunkirk

Kirk Dunkirk

Per your request —

Two replies: TACOma (above and next page) and Washington State (following)

Finance Department / Tax & License Division
Registration # _____

Annual Business License Application

Revenue Item: _____
FEE _____
PENALTY _____
TOTAL _____

City of Tacoma
Finance Department/Tax & License Division
733 Market Street, Room 21, Tacoma, WA 98402-3770
(253) 591-5252   www.cityoftacoma.org

Sent By _____ Date _____

REGISTRATION NUMBER: T _____

APPLICATION FOR CERTIFICATE OF REGISTRATION

See reverse side of yellow copy for general requirements. Title 6 of the Tacoma Municipal Code, as amended.

Yes ☐ No ☐ **Have you ever been registered as a business with the City of Tacoma?** If yes, when? _____
Previous business name _____ Previous location _____
Yes ☐ No ☐ **Purchasing an existing business?** (Please indicate Name, Address & Telephone Number of previous owner).
_____
File Number _____

TO ENSURE YOUR BUSINESS MEETS CITY ZONING REQUIREMENTS CONTACT BUILDING & LAND USE SERVICES AT 591-5577

Name of Business (dba) _____
Opening Date _____ (Date business activity commenced in or with the City of Tacoma)
Nature of Business (specify product or service provided) _____

Is your organization recognized as a 501 (c) (3) non profit organization by the Internal Revenue Service? *Yes ☐ No ☐

Tacoma Municipal Code

Chapter 6.01
ADMINISTRATIVE PROVISIONS FOR TACOMA TAXES

Sections:
6.01.010 Purpose.
6.01.015 Application of chapter.
6.01.020 Definitions.
6.01.030 Registraton/license requirements

6.01.010 Purpose.
This chapter provides for consistent administration of taxes identified in Section 6.01.015. (Ord. 27010 § 1; passed Nov. 19, 2002)

6.01.015 Application of chapter.
The provisions of this chapter shall apply with respect to the taxes imposed under Chapters 6.62, 6.64, 6.65, 6.66, 6.67, 6.68, 6.71, and 6.89, and under other titles, chapters, and sections in such manner and to such extent as indicated in each such title

---

Tacoma Municipal Code

Chapter 6B.180
SALES – SIDEWALK VENDORS

Sections:
6B.180.010 Purpose.
6B.180.020 License required.
6B.180.030 Definitions.
6B.180.040 Application requirements.
6B.180.050 Fees.
6B.180.060 Issuance.
6B.180.070 Term of license.
6B.180.080 License renewal.
6B.180.090 No transfer.
6B.180.100 Location review.
6B.180.110 Restrictions.
6B.180.120 License revocation or denial.

6B.180.010 Purpose.
The purpose of this chapter is to provide for regulation of long-term sidewalk vending activities in certain commercially zoned districts as defined in

time to time designate as public ways for the express purpose of allowing vending thereon, with any vending in such areas so designated by City Council resolution to be subject to such additional or different requirements as may be provided by the resolution (or amendment thereto) designating such area as a public way. No provision of this chapter shall be construed to allow vending (by license or otherwise) in any portion of (1) a public way primarily used by motorized vehicles; (2) in areas, trails, or paths set aside or designated by the City as bike paths or nature trails, or (3) any public way or part thereof which the City Council, by resolution, shall designate as being inappropriate for vending activities.

"Sidewalk vending unit" means a movable cart that is operated from a fixed location on a public way from which food, flowers and plants, and/or non-alcoholic beverages are provided for the public with or without charge; except, however, that the provisions of this chapter shall not apply to mobile caterers, generally defined as follows: a person engaged in the business of transporting, in motor vehicles, food and beverages

MASTER LICENSE SERVICE
DEPARTMENT OF LICENSING
PO BOX 9048
OLYMPIA WA 98507-9048
Telephone (360) 664-1400

LICENSE FEE SHEET

...the Master License Service (MLS), unless noted otherwise. To

Master License Service
Department of Licensing
P O Box 9048
Olympia WA 98507-9048
Telephone: (360) 664-1400
www.dol.wa.gov

tion provided may be subject to disclosure
he public disclosure law (RCW 42.17)

Owner Name

Unified Business Identifier (UBI)

Federal Employer Identification Number (FEIN)

For Validation - Office Use Only

MASTER APPLICATION
Please type or print clearly in dark ink.
Mail Directly to the Master License Service or
file online at http://www.dol.wa.gov/forms/700028.htm

01P-400-925-0003

Purpose of Application
ase check all boxes that apply

-)pen/Reopen Business
  omplete sections 2, 3, (4 if hiring employees) and 5
- :hange Ownership
  omplete sections 2, 3, (4 if you have employees) and 5
- dd License/Registration to Existing Location
  omplete sections 2, 3 and 5
- ~ister Trade Name

- ☐ Hire Employees
  complete **all** sections
- ☐ Hire Employees Under Age 18
  complete **all** sections
- ☐ Hire Persons to Work in or Around Your Home
  complete sections 2, 3c, 4 and 5 (no application fee)
- ☐ Other _____
  complete **all** sections

Washington Department of Licensing
Licensing Guide Sheet
Master License Service
(360) 664-1400
http://www.dol.wa.gov/mls/steps.htm

KIRK DUNKIRK

KOCHI CITY 780-
JAPAN, FO 00001 JAPAN

You requested license information on the following business activity:
Fast Food Restaurant

To be conducted in:
Washington State

Employees:
None

Ownership:
General Partnership

Operating a Business in Washington State:

A Business Resource Guide

Filing A Master Application
- Most businesses can file on-line at http://www.dol.wa.gov/forms/700028.htm
- Mail to Department of Licensing, PO Box 9048, Olympia, WA 98507-9048
- Help is available at (360) 664-1400 or from one of the following locations:

CITY NAME	DEPT OF REVENUE	DEPT OF LABOR & INDUSTRIES	EMPLOYMENT SECURITY DEPT
ABERDEEN		415 W. Wishkah, Suite 1-B	

Business Bulletin
Hazardous Materials Regulations
(Emergency Planning and Community Right-to-Know Law)

WILL YOUR BUSINESS...

UNEMPLOYMENT INSURANCE COVERAGE
Employment Security Department

Does completion of the Master Application ensure an unemployment insurance account for my business?
By completing the employment portion of the Master Application, you have met the requirement of notifying the Employment Security Department that you have hired or will hire employees possibly subject to unemployment insurance... will be reviewed by the

Application is reviewed, you will receive notification of your rate as well as other information from the Department of Labor & Industries.

How is Industrial insurance paid?
Quarterly. A preprinted Report of Payroll will be mailed near the end of March, June, September, and December. You will use this form to report the number of hours your employees worked during the preceding quarter. This report must be returned to the Department with the premium before the end of January, April, July, and October, even if you have no employees to report for the quarter.

DEPARTMENT OF LICENSING
MASTER LICENSE SERVICE
TELEPHONE: (360) 664-1400

B U S I N E S S   B U L L E T I N
Trade Name Registration

What is a trade name?
A trade name is any name used in the course of business that does not include the full legal name of all the owners of the business.

In the case of a limited partnership or a corporation, it is any name that differs in **any** respect from the name registered with the Secretary of State (see example on reverse).

If you are using your personal name in your business

How do I search to determine if a business name is available?
Master License Service has the most extensive state listing of business names. To request a search call 1-900-463-6000. The charge is $4.95 for the first minute and $.50 for each additional minute. You may also mail up to three name searches with a $4.00 fee to:

Department of Licensing
Master License Service

(Actually pretty useful info if you wade through them.)

Kirk Dunkirk
x x x x x
Kochi City 780- x x x

Calpis Ajinomoto Danone Co., Inc., Tokai Office
4-13 Ayuchi-tori
Showa-ku, Nagoya City, Aichi
Japan

March 9, 2005

Dear AGF

I love your coffee, especially Blendy. That's why I am this letter sendy.

I keep a tank of tropical fish in my living room. They help me to relax. There are five of them so I pretended they are in a Foreigner cover band from Rochester, NY. I sing "Jukebox Hero" with them when I shave my eyebrows. "Hot Blooded" is strictly for when waxing my legs. It's pronounced RAH-chister, by the way. They are trained so that when a guest comes over we turn down the lights and do a "Double Vision" dance routine.

The problem is my fish go crazy when your TV CM comes on. They make a mosh pit and start ramming into each other as if they were in a tropical fish thrash metal cover band from Syracuse. Jerry chases Stef, Charyleah butts head with Todd, and Polizzi, well, he's just a butthead. Lou Gramm would not approve! He's probably spinning in his watery grave. I flushed him down the toilet after he died last year. And because they are tropical fish, it's all in vivid technicolor collide-o-scope.

I turned the TV volume down, I tried singing "Cold as Ice"… this is the Scientific Method. But nothing seems to work. What should I do? I can't stop watching your commercial, you can't stop broadcasting it, and the band refuses to break up.

When will the commercials will stop airing? They are THAT POWERFUL. What do other people with fish trouble do? Please write back and explanate.

Sincerely,

Kirk Dunkirk

March 18, 2005

Dear Mr. Kirk Dunkrik

We would like to express our thanks for your patronage for our Blendy coffee.

Please find informations as follows regarding AGF TV Commercial you required.

TV Commercials we aired between this JAN. and MAR. in Kochi are three types, such as "Blendy ground coffee", "Blendy soluble coffee" and "Maxim soluble coffee".

However, we don't know what kind of TV Commercials you mentioned.
We plan to continue to use these three commercials, so we can't inform you when to stop.

We would like you to understand our current status.

Sincerely yours,

AJINOMOTO GENERAL FOODS, INC
Consumer Consultation Manager
Toshiyuki Hirai

Kirk Dunkirk
✗ ✗ ✗ ✗ ✗ 4F
Kochi City 780-✗ ✗ ✗
Japan

Beppu Daiichi Hotel
2-40 Noguchi-motomachi
Beppu City, Oita

March 9, 2005

To the Manager and Staff,

A friend referred me to your fine establishment but I would like to ask a few questions before planning my stay during the last week of April. I wouldn't do that if I were you.

- Do the rooms have high speed internet access? If so, what is the speed of the connection? I need to do do some video conferencing with a client. No he doesn't -- he likes live porn chat. And does the internet connection require ethernet?

- I like to jog before breakfast. No, he likes watching office ladies on their bikes. Is there a quiet park nearby where I may do so?

- Does the hotel offer rental bicycles? I would like to pedal to a scenic mountain hot spring. Bad idea -- he's a very naughty boy.

I'm sorry to trouble you but I'm very selective about where I stay. I feel comfortable asking though because of the glowing recommendation by my friend. There's sure gonna be a lot of glass to clean up.

Thank you for your time. I am looking forward to my stay at your wonderful hotel.

Sincerely,

Kirk Dunkirk

Dear Kirk Dunkirk

Thank you for your letter about our hotel.
I would like to answer your questions.

1, We are very sorry that we do not have high speed internet access.
   We only have provided dial up internet access.

2, A park where is located to near our hotel is to take about 20 minutes on foot from our hotel.
   The name is "Joshi Park."

3, We are afraid that we do not offer rental bicycles.
   Also, we do not think there are some rental bicycles shops around our hotel.

We are sorry that we have some inconvenience about some supplies.
When you would like to reserve our hotel, please let me know.
Thank you very much.

Sincerely,
Chiharu Sato
(Reservations)

〒879-5102
oitaken oitagun yuhuin tyo
ooaza kawakami 3049-1
City Hotek Big Brer
Staff　大隈

Kirk Dunkirk
█████████ 4F
kochi city
〒780-█████

An answer was delayed. I am sorry.

Thank you for the letter.
It answers.

- Staying in April is always all right.

- The use of the Internet can't be done at high speed.
  It is possible only in low speed.
  A communication speed is 32k.
  There is no Ethernet necessity in the net use.
  A telephone line is connected, and it becomes use.
  It becomes only domestic use.

- A staying cost of one person.
  With one night breakfast　　　Tax-included ¥7500.
  An overnight stay without meals　Tax-included ¥6450.

It has hotel charges money at the time of the check-out.
A card can't be used.
Only cash asks for payment.
When the Internet is used, it has a charge by the communication time.

Teach me a date and a telephone number by the telephone or FAX if it is decided.
Telephone number:0977-84-5300
FAX　　number:0977-84-5349

we wait for your coming.

Sincerely

Staff : 大隈
　　　大隈

Kirk Dunkirk

Kochi City 780-

Beppu Daiichi Hotel
2-40 Noguchi-motomachi
Beppu City, Oita

March 9, 2005

To the Manager and Staff,

A friend referred me to your fine establishment but I would like to ask a few questions before planning my stay during the last week of April. I wouldn't do that if I were you.

- Do the rooms have high speed internet access? If so, what is the speed of the connection? I need to do do some video conferencing with a client. No he doesn't – he likes live porn chat. And does the internet connection require ethernet?

- I like to jog before breakfast. No, he likes watching office ladies on their bikes. Is there a quiet park nearby where I may do so?

- Does the hotel offer rental bicycles? I would like to pedal to a scenic mountain hot spring. Bad idea – he's a very naughty boy.

I'm sorry to trouble you but I'm very selective about where I stay. I feel comfortable asking though because of the glowing recommendation by my friend. There's sure gonna be a lot of glass to clean up.

Thank you for your time. I am looking forward to my stay at your wonderful hotel.

Sincerely,

Kirk Dunkirk
Kirk Dunkirk

I can't read english.
Pease reserve other hotels.
Thank you Sir.
manager 宇佐健次郎

~~March 31, 2005~~
June 13, 2005

Konica-Minolta
1-6-1 Marunouchi
Chiyoda-ku
Tokyo 100-0005

Dear Minolta,

My office has long been satisfied users of your Dialta line of copy machines. They are smooth, reliable and cute. Unfortunately we have gotten many complaints from our staff about your new **bizhub 7218** digital imaging system.

It's still smooth, it's still reliable and with the same form factor (ie. "shape") it's still cute. But every hundred pages or so it prints satanic messages.

These messages are not immediately obvious. Sometimes they are backwards. Sometimes the first letter of the first series of words spells the Dark One's name. Pages sometimes get numbered 4,5,666,7,8… There was even a reference to Sodom and Gomorra but the personnel staff destroyed it before I could check. They call it the "Beelzebub Hub." Anyway people are scared and it's hurting efficiency.

The **bizhub 7218** in question is used as a standalone copier/ fax machine but also as a scanner / shared printer on a network. I couldn't find anything on your website support page so I resorted to this letter.

Thank you very much.
Sincerely,

Kirk Dunkirk

ps. This is my second letter… won't you please reply?

Kirk Dunkirk
Director, IT / Purchasing
iGlobal Financial Management / Mr. Shooey Shoe Repair
x x x x x x x 4F
Kochi City 780-x x x
Japan

July 29, 2005

Kirk Dunkirk
Director, IT/Purchasing
I Global Financial Management/
Mr. Shooey Shoe Repair
███████ 4F
Kochi City 780-████

Dear Dunkirk-san,

I received your letter of June 13 regarding bizhub 7218.
I am very sorry my reply late.
(My name is Masahiro Teranishi. I am the Manager of the Domestic Sales Grope.
 I am not good at English. Please pardon it.)

As follows, I will answer the received your question.
Please confirm it.
Question:
  You could not find anything on our website support page for bizhub 7218.
Answer:
  7218 is an American model, and it doesn't sell it in Japan.
  Therefore, it is not described on the Web page of konicaminolta Japan.
  Please see the Web page of the following konicaminolta US.
  http://kmbs.konicaminolta.us/eprise/main/KMBS/Showroom/Groups/WorkGroupBW

Moreover, because it is a model not sold in Japan, it is not possible to repair in Japan.
Please inquire of the United States on the web site if it is a product bought in the
United States.

If you have any questions or ploblems, please feel free to contact me.
My e-mail address is as follows.
masahiro.teranishi@konicaminolta.jp

Sincerely yours,

M. Teranishi
Masahiro Teranishi

Mitsubishi Motors Corporation
2-16-4 Konan, Minato-ku
Tokyo, 108-8410

April 11, 2005 (Third try.)

Dear MMC-J,

I have long admired your excellence in engineering, from the A6M fighter (aka Zero) to the Minica Toppo. Even your pencils are good. It's no wonder you are one of the longest surviving Zaibatsu. As an inhabitant of Kochi, I feel a special connection to your conglomerate, as your founder Iwasaki Yataro grew up here.

But that longevity is under threat these days, thanks mostly to a series of scandals and cover-ups that has led the public to believe that your motor vehicles lose their axles suddenly and <u>burst into flames</u> when given a chance.

While this reputation is no doubt well deserved, I think bold and forthright action by your leadership can turn things around. But you must act soon and demonstrate clearly to the whole world your desire to make a change! Japan Airlines, NHK, the nuclear power companies… with all the scandals these days, simply <u>crying at a press conference isn't good enough anymore.</u>

First, you need a big media event. Invite the major news outlets to a special road test where <u>several of your top executives crash Mitsubishi cars into each other.</u> This will have a dual benefit of allowing your scandal-ridden execs a public repentance, and proving in no uncertain terms that your cars will not erupt in flames. What better proof could Taro Q. Public ask for? I'm sure it will be a big boost to employee morale as well.

Later, you can use footage of these crashes in TV commercials. You could make <u>interactive web pages</u> letting people choose make and model and crash them into each other online, Galant vs. Elantra and so on. Throw in a Tokyo cityscape a la Godzilla for thematic effect.

Then for the coup de grace: <u>publicly challenge wimpy executives from Toyota</u> et al. to crash their cars into each other or into yours. You're desperate, they're not, so they'll probably decline. It's a publicity win-win for you. You'll be instant cult heroes risking your lives to save the homeland, much like Zero pilots of yore.

And if you need any volunteer drivers, I would be honored to take up the call.

Don't miss this opportunity to turn the tide! <u>Please contact me</u> regarding your opinion on this matter. I wish you speedy success.

In your service,

Kirk Dunkirk
xxxxxx
Kochi City, 780
Japan

14 April 2005
CO-H370#

Mr. Kirk Dunkirk
▇▇▇ Kochi city
780-▇▇▇ JAPAN

Re: Your letter dated April 11th, 2005

Dear Mr. Kirk Dunkirk,

We, the Customer Relations Department of Mitsubishi Motors Corporation (MMC) have duly received your captioned letter on Apr.14.

We thank you for your straightforward comments and valued suggestion, which we ensure, will be forwarded to our department concerned.

We appreciate your kind understanding on the above.

Yours faithfully,

MITSUBISHI MOTORS CORPORATION

H. Kubo-Manager
Customer Relations Department
(Overseas Customer Service)

2-16-4 Konan Minato-ku
Tokyo 108-8410 JAPAN
Tel: +81-3-6719-2569 (Direct)
Fax: +81-3-6719-0013 (Direct)

Louis Vuitton Japan KK
Aoyama Twin Building East 14th Floor
1-1-1, Minami-Aoyama
Minato-ku
107-0062
Tokyo

April 18, 2005

Dear Mr. Vuitton et al.,

I just got back from a business trip to Hong Kong. I noticed so many people on the subway wearing white surgical masks, maybe for hay fever, maybe for fear of bird flu.

A few people however wore very special masks: brown with the distinctive LV monogram.

My schedule in Hong Kong left me no time for frivolous shopping and since returning to Japan, I have been unable to find any of your gorgeous surgical masks. The staff at my local Vuitton shop recommended I try this address.

Could you tell me where I can buy your protective disposable masks? My wife refuses to sleep with me until I find out. Most Vuitton products are practical as well as stylish, so do they offer protection from airborne hazards or are they just for fashion's sake? And I hate to mention this, but is there a chance that those were cheap imitations that I saw on the train?

Sorry to trouble you with this trivial matter.
Sincerely,

Kirk Dunkirk

MAISON FONDÉE EN 1854

Kirk Dunkirk
Director, IT/Purchasing
IGlobal Financial Management
Mr. Shooey Shoe Repair
██████████ 4F
Kochi   780-███
JAPAN

April 26, 2005

Dear Mr. Dunkirk,

Thank you very much for your letter of April 18, 2005. We are glad that you were interested in Louis Vuitton products.

It is very unfortunate to say this, but Louis Vuitton does not offer any masks in Japan as those kinds of things are sold at drug stores.   At this time, we don't have any information that our stores sell those masks in other countries. We concern the mask you saw in Hong Kong was "originated" by someone.

Except those products, we always welcome you at your nearest Louis Vuitton store and telephone order.

Thank you very much for your inquiry.

Sincerely yours

Kumie NAKAMURA
Customer Information Service

- ✓ Anything you concern about Louis Vuitton, you can contact to our "Customer Information Service": Tel. 03-3478-2100
- ✓ Our "Direct Order Service" welcomes you in telephone order: Tel. 03-3478-5292

18 July 2005
ADV/KUL/189

Mr Kirk Dunkirk
████████████
Kochi City 780-████
JAPAN

Dear Mr Dunkirk

We refer to your letter of 14 February 2005 which was redirected to us by our Area Manager West Japan.

Firstly my sincere apologies for the late reply and thank you so much for sharing your views of the Airbus 380 TV commercial that was aired early this year in conjunction with the unveiling of this super airliner by Airbus.

As you may recollect, the voice over the end of the commercial says "we are proud to be sharing the dream of the biggest airliner ever built". The main premise of the whole advertisement is the dream and aspiration of having the biggest, most spacious and modern airliner that Malaysia Airlines, the operator and Airbus, the manufacturer had. It also reflect how the airline and aircraft manufacturer have worked together to develop an aircraft that would be able to meet discerning passengers' expectation in terms of space.

The TV commercial is our creative interpretation of the dream and aspiration and of course creativity is very subjective. Nonetheless we appreciate your valuable feedback and look forward to hearing from you on our future campaigns.

You may be pleased to know that Malaysia Airlines as one of the launch partner has ordered 6 aircraft and we will be operating Airbus A380 in 2007.

Once again thank you for your valuable feedback and we look forward to welcoming you on board our flights soon.

Yours sincerely

FADHILAH MUSTAFFA
Advertising Manager

Malaysia Airlines, 33rd Floor, Bangunan MAS, Jalan Sultan Ismail, 50250 Kuala Lumpur, Malaysia. G.P.O. Box 10513, 50716.
Tel: 216 10 555 (City) 784 64 555 (Airport). Cable: Layang, Telex: MA 37614 (LAYANG) MA 37091 (MASAP).
Telefax: 60-3-216 13 472 (City), 60-3-784 62 581 (Airport)

MALAYSIAN AIRLINE SYSTEM BERHAD (10601-W)

Kirk Dunkirk
✈ ✈ ✈ ✈
Kochi City 780-xxx

Northwest Airlines
650-35 Nanae
Tomisato-shi, Chiba 286-0293

~~May 30, 2005~~   ~~Aug 1, 2005~~   Nov 1, 2005

Dear Northwest,

I flew on your airline recently and thought the food and the movie were topnotch. I really can't understand why everybody calls you "Northworst." Maybe because it sounds funny. But in my book you are "Northbest." In class I make all my students call you that in order to help spread the word. I think it's working.

Anyway I have a problem. I'm not scared of flying but I am scared of people who fly. Think about it: ten hours in an airtight container with a total stranger! I might have sat next to a serial killer for all I know. Do you think you could give people a small biographic postcard about those in the seats surrounding them?

To avoid any problems I refuse to communicate with people I sit next to. I think you should install yellow tape like police use at crime scenes to separate the seats. It could be nylon and retractable like seat belts. Also there should be clear lines on the floor too to demarcate where his stuff and my stuff can go. This includes feet! I think Lufthansa has this feature.

But as I insist on always taking the window seat, this poses its own problems. How to get up while keeping interaction with the strange person in the next seat to a minimum? I know many air passengers have the same dilemma. Please provide buzzer boxes for those who want them. One buzz for "Get up" another for "Thank you" and so on. The flight attendants can explain their use during the "What to Do During an Emergency" presentation. These boxes can be used by passengers to tell staff their meal preference. Think of all the headaches this will prevent!

Lastly, I have one more very different request. Please have time chimes in the cabin at regular intervals, like in a church bell tower or college campus. You know the ones, they get longer every 15 minutes. Then on the hour have a chime for time at departure place and a different chime for time at destination. It's very soothing.

I think your great service enhanced with these new passenger-friendly touches will make flying fun again, like in the old days when people got all dressed up and wore hats.

Awaiting your reply. Sincerely,

KIRK DUNKIRK

ps: THIS IS MY THIRD LETTER! What does it take to get through to you people?

Northwest Airlines
650-35 Nanae, Tomisato
Chiba, Japan 286-0293
Fax: 0476-90-5737 E-mail: jpncc@nwa.com

14 November 2005

Dear Mr. Kirk Dunkirk,

In your recent letter, you shared your feedback regarding Northwest Airlines.

We appreciate your feedback. Many customers, like you, share their observations and suggestions with us. These unsolicited remarks form the basis for many improvements in our service.

Be assured that your comments will be forwarded to the responsible individuals within Northwest.

Thank you for taking the time to writing. We appreciate your interest in our company.

Sincerely,

Japan Customer Care
Northwest Airlines

Kirk Dunkirk
Evergreen Communications
☞ ☞ ☞
Kochi 780-☞ ☞ ☞

Toshiba Elevator Corporation
1-1, Shibaura 1-chome, Minato-ku
Tokyo, 105-8001

~~June 20, 2005~~   Oct 24, 2005

To My Brothers and Sisters at Toshiba,

Upon thine elevator in our building hast thou a problem, the solution of which your conscience begs you to solve!

In accordance with our custom, the office elders gathered on the last Friday of the month and broke bread together to celebrate our good fortune. Raising their glasses they said "Praise the LORD for the end to another week. Thank God it's Friday!" Thus ensued a great feast. And it was good.

After the feast one elder returned to his place of work, for though he was weary his toil was not yet finished. He was a fair man and the people often came to him for decisions. Between where he stood on the earth and the glass chamber where he labored towards heaven was the elevator. Feeling forsaken, the elder cursed the elevator, and the office, and the moneylenders at the market[1]. But when he entered the chamber of the elevator the great steel door smote his leg.

He gnashed his teeth and cried out "LORD you are boundless in heaven and the angels sit at your feet and singeth your praise. Your good works outnumber the stars in the winter sky. Why hast Thou punished me so?" And the LORD smote the elder's leg again with the heavy steel door, lest the man forget that the way of the LORD is not like the haggling of the moneylenders.

Seeing his error, the elder sat in his chambers for a long time rubbing scented oils into the wound. In the morning he asked his humble servant to compose this note. **He asks unto thee, please maketh thine door less dangerous!** I am but his messenger and this is his word.

We await the day of your reply.
Peace be with you.

Kirk Dunkirk

This is my SECOND LETTER... I know you are busy but could you please respond?

[1] some texts: *stadium* ; original unclear.

TOSHIBA

TOSHIBA ELEVATOR AND BUILDING SYSTEMS CORPORATION

5-27,KITASHINAGAWA 6-CHOME,SHINAGAWA-KU TOKYO 141-0001,JAPAN
PHONE : 81-3-5423- ~~445~~
FACSIMILE : 81-3-5423- ~~3572~~

November 11, 2005

Mr. Kirk Dunkirk
Evergreen Communications
████████ 4th Floor
Kochi 780████

Dear Mr. Kirk Dunkirk:

Copies of your letters of June 20, and October 24, 2005 have been brought to my attention for review. We have conducted our investigation on the understanding that the elevator referred to in your letter is installed at Evergreen Communications ████████ 4th Floor, Kochi 780████. If this is not the case, please advise.

As the result of our review, we have found out that the elevator there is the one presumably manufactured by Mitsubishi Electric Corporation, whose contact details in your region, we believe, are as follows:

    Name of Organization: Kochi Branch
    Address: 4-2-40, Hon-chou, Kochi-city (Nissei Kochi Building)
    TEL: 088-824-9477
    FAX: 088-824-9478

We hope that the above information is useful in your resolving the problem with your elevator, but if you need further assistance, please do not hesitate to contact the undersigned.

Please note that, while your October 24 letter specifies your address as "Evergreen Communications, ████████ Kochi 780████", we have used the address specified in your June 20 letter in sending this letter. In the event that this letter does not reach you for wrong address, however, we have also sent a copy of this letter to ████████ Kochi 780████ We are sorry that we could not respond to your letters sooner, but a reason for late response partially is that the address mentioned in your two letters is that of our parent company. This caused some delay for your letters to reach us. Please note the letterhead for our correct address.

TOSHIBA

TOSHIBA ELEVATOR AND BUILDING SYSTEMS CORPORATION
5-27,KITASHINAGAWA 6-CHOME,SHINAGAWA-KU TOKYO 141-0001,JAPAN
PHONE : 81-3-5423-*****
FACSIMILE : 81-3-5423-*****

Finally, we feel sorry to hear that the gentleman in the letter was hit by the closing door of the elevator. We sincerely hope that he is now all right.

Very truly yours,

Jiro Kurusu
Jiro Kurusu
Chief Specialist
Administration Department

AP: Japan Investigates Alleged Bid-Rigging
Monday May 23, 2005 7:23 am ET

TOKYO (AP) -- Japanese authorities on Monday began investigating allegations of bid-rigging for public bridge construction projects after an anti-monopoly watchdog filed criminal complaints against eight major companies.

The Fair Trade Commission submitted complaints to Tokyo prosecutors against Yokogawa Bridge Corp., JFE Engineering Inc., Kawada Industries Inc., Ishikawajima-Harima Heavy Industries Co., Miyaji Iron Works Co., TTK Corp., Takadakiko Co. and Kurimoto Ltd., the commission said on its Web site.

About 30 prosecutors were seen on public broadcaster NHK raiding the offices of Yokogawa Bridge in Tokyo on Monday afternoon.

Prosecutors were searching more than 100 locations related to 47 companies, Kyodo News agency said.

Authorities suspect the companies violated the Anti-Monopoly Law by holding talks to allocate contracts for steel bridge construction projects ordered by the Land and Transport Ministry in fiscal 2003 and 2004, the FTC said.

Reports said 47 companies had participated in the talks and that the practice had been used since the 1960s to allocate public works projects in the steel bridge industry, valued at an estimated 350 billion yen ($3.3 billion) a year.

The United States has long urged Tokyo to clamp down on alleged bid-rigging by Japanese companies, particularly in construction and steel-making, saying the practice virtually shuts out foreign competitors.

Violators of Japan's Anti-Monopoly Law face fines of up to 6 percent of the value of the contract awarded

Kirk Dunkirk
Evergreen Rehabilitation Home
✗ ✗ ✗ ✗
Kochi City 780-✗ ✗ ✗

Ishikawajima-Harima Heavy Industries Co., Ltd.
Shin Ohtemachi Bldg.
2-1 Ohtemachi 2-chome, Chiyoda-ku
Tokyo, 100-8182

~~July 4, 2005~~   Sept. 12, 2005

Dear IHHI,

I am writing in regards to the recent bid rigging scandal.

I support you guys 110%. Who do those newspaper guys think they are? They're just a bunch of no-goodniks out to make a name for themselves at your expense. What do they know about bidding for bridge building and maintenance? Probably not as much as you guys, I bet.

Don't give up! A lot of us out here think you're doing a great job. I use your bridges from time to time and they make me feel proud. Heck, and I'm not even Japanese. When I drive over the Seto-Ohashi in my souped-up Nissan March, I roll down the windows and scream "Inland sea! I love thee! Look at me! Inland sea!" over and over until I reach the other side. The bridge is that good.

So what if you guys participated in bid rigging? It's no problem! That's how the system works over here. It's worked that way for generations and it's not gonna change now. Don't worry about the current conundrum. It's just the scandal of the day and it'll blow over like a big piece of cardboard propped up on a windy afternoon. You've been around since Commodore Perry and you'll be around for a lot longer.

If I drop a ¥10 coin from the bridge will it melt from air friction before it hits the water? How much does each suspension cable weigh? What do you do with them when they get old? Have any human babies been born on the bridge? Can the bridge master perform weddings at the midpoint? Please tell me.

Looking forward to your reply.

Kirk Dunkirk

ps. THIS IS MY SECOND LETTER!! Won't you please reply?

Multiple letters to:

- Yokogawa Bridge Corp.,
- JFE Engineering Inc.,
- Kawada Industries Inc.,
- Ishikawajima-Harima Heavy Industries Co.,

and

- Miyaji Iron Works Co.,

plus

- Mitsubishi Heavy Industries

for good measure.

But <u>no replies</u> ☹.

I'm a loser.

-Kirk

Coco's Japan Co., Ltd.
18-1 Konan 2-Chome
Minato-Ku, Tokyo
108-0075

Sept. 12, 2005

Dear Coco's Family Restaurant,

Please look at the following photo:

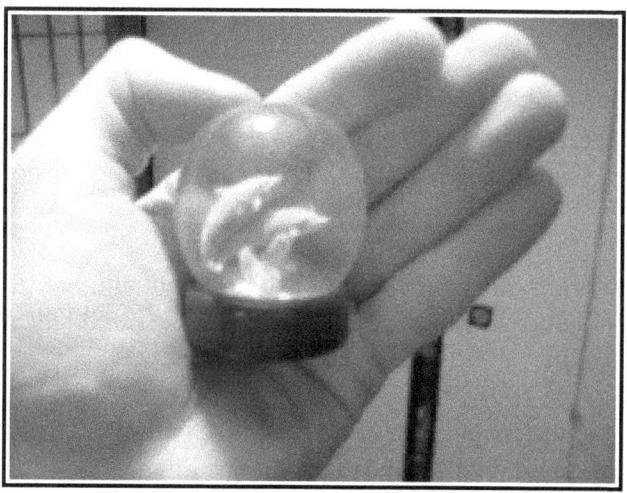

I am new to Japan and I now have the impression that unlike we Swiss, you Japanese will do anything for money. Case in point: is it necessary to sell children's toys showing dolphins having sex?

On our way to a right-wing rally, my family stopped at the Tosa-doro Coco's in Kochi City and my 4 year old son, Bertrand, found the copulating cetaceans on the bottom shelf of the kid's toys section, next to the battleship Yamato, the world's largest and my favorite after the Dunkerque. Maybe this is a natural thing in Japan but I don't want that my children have the dolphin sex toys.

I mean, look at them go! Banging away like 3rd year University students. I and my wife couldn't finish the meal, the rally was ruined, and since then the son has been mounting stuffed animals, Thor our dog, and even the shapely young legs of Miss Kawamura, his soroban tutor. I'm glad you don't sell any of the humpback whales!

What are you going to do? I insist of you to write me back and tell your plans for this distasteful item of impulse. At least put them on a higher shelf where only 10 year-olds can find it. What kind of families do you want at your so-called family restaurant?

Aghast,

Kirk Dunkirk

** OH NO! MY DOG ATE THE REPLY. ☹ **

Kirk Dunkirk
x x x x
Kochi City 780-x x x

Subaru c/o Fuji Heavy Industries Ltd.
Subaru Bldg., 7-2 Nishi-Shinjuku 1-chome
Shinjuku-ku, Tokyo, 160-8316

~~Oct. 24, 2005~~   March 2, 2006!

Dear Subaru,

First of all, I'm sorry to hear that you and GM broke up. It seemed like a good partnership. You have 4wd expertise and maybe they could have shown you a thing about, I dunno, discount fleet sales to rental companies perhaps?

Actually the real reason I'm writing this is not about GM but about another great American, Bruce Willis. I've been in the hospital a lot recently, which is quite boring, so a friend lent me a video tape of a recent "Pride" street fighting competition.

During the program, I believe in the match between Hidehiko Yoshida (Japanese judo guy) and "Tank" Abbot (American lardass) there was an ad for the new Subaru Legacy.

In the ad, a handsome and smirking Willis drives around, all cool like, and at the end says "I feel legacy." I don't know if it's capitalized in this case.

This ad has me a bit upset. For one, Mr. Willis is menacing. Is he gonna come after me like a Pride fighter? That's what it feels like. Two, what the heck does "I feel legacy" mean? I can't figure it out. Could you explain the aim of the ad please?

I'm not trying to knock the tough and smirkful Mr. Willis, star of such hits as "The Last Boy Scout." Nor do I wish to knock the Legacy either. My sister bought one recently, before the ads. But if you could just explain the idea behind the commercials please it would really make me feel better.

Thank you so much. Looking forward to your reply.
Sincerely,

Kirk Dunkirk

ps. This is my 2nd letter, please reply --- I've been pretty patient.

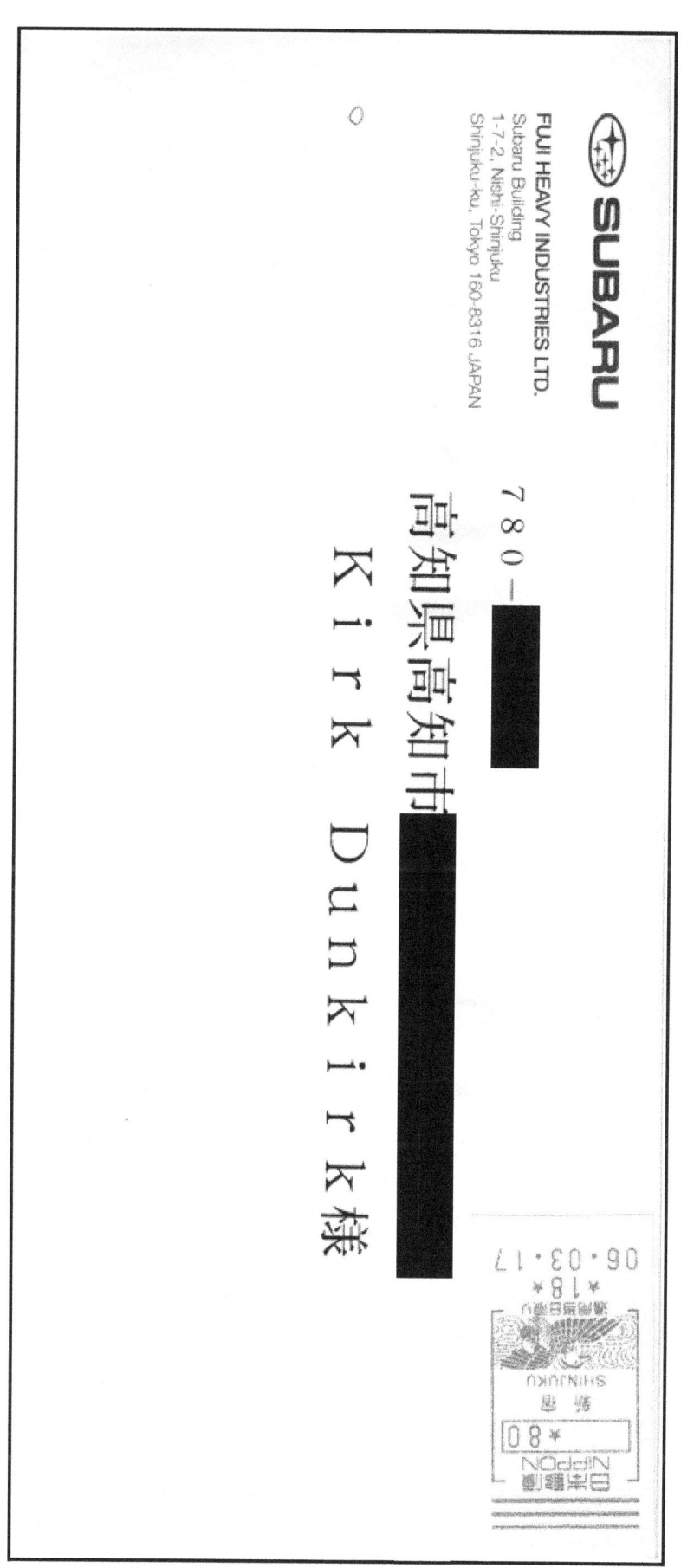

FUJI HEAVY INDUSTRIES LTD.
Subaru Building
1-7-2, Nishi-Shinjuku
Shinjuku-ku, Tokyo 160-8316 JAPAN
www.subaru-global.com

March 17, 2006

Mr. Kirk Dunkirk
████████████
Kochi City 780-█████
Japan

Dear Mr. Dunkirk,

Thank you for your letter of March 2, 2006 concerning our commercial for Subaru Legacy and we apologize for not having responded sooner to your letter of October 24, 2005. We are so sorry to hear that you were in the hospital.

We are sorry to learn that our commercial makes you feel uncomfortable. Your suggestion is so valuable that we will take the liberty of sending a copy of your letter to our related staff.

One of our important design concepts is to create "Driving Pleasure". Subaru has always shared common values with its customers, including an appreciation for it. We have been developing our products not only by numeric evaluation but also "driver's five senses". We hope that all customers feel sensuous pleasure while driving our cars. "I feel Legacy" represents such our message.

Mr. Bruce Willis was in our commercial for the first generation Legacy and this time, we ask him the second appearance for New Legacy. He is also a Subaru owner.

Once again thank you for taking the time to make us aware of your concerns. We are hoping for the best of everything for you.

Sincerely yours,

FUJI HEAVY INDUSTRIES LTD.

T. Kato 加藤知夫

T. Kato
Manager
Customer Relations Department
Subaru Customer Center

Ah, the Shiba Inu.
One of the oldest dog breeds in the world. Known for its intelligence, loyalty and good temperament.

Able to sit locked in a box outside all day.

wood box topped with snow
four legg'd samurai shivers
dear friend locked inside

-KDK

Kirk Dunkirk
x x x x
Kochi City 780-✔ ✔ ✔

ASICS Corporation
1-1, Minatojima-Nakamachi 7-chome
Chuo-ku, Kobe, 650-8555,
Japan

~~August 10, 2005~~   October 24, 2005

Dear Asics (aka Onitsuka Tiger),

Why?
Why did you do it?

I heard that you made the first shoes for Nike and stopped working together because you wanted more money. At that time, those guys were called Blue Ribbon Sports and just selling out of a car trunk but you were a real shoe company called Onitsuka Tiger!

Don't get me wrong. I like your shoes. I own a pair of Gel Flash DS's. That's why I'm so upset. I'm an upset fan. A really upset fan. Very, very upset.

Why did you break things off? Was it greed? A drunken argument with Phil Knight over a Filipino hostess? Does it ever keep you up at night? I mean, <u>you could have been Nike!</u> Instead, you're like the guy that got kicked out of the Beatles. Sure you're doing okay, but Tiger Woods and Michael Jordan never sported your logo. I wouldn't say that's half-assed but kind of like three-quarter-assed.

Why? You could have been Nike!

I can't bear to wear your shoes any more until you <u>tell me what happened.</u> I also want to know why you called your special material at the Seoul Olympics "Russell Crowe." He wasn't even famous at the time. Does he breathe a lot?

Sincerely,

Kirk Dunkirk

ps. Anima Sana In Corpore Sano

pps. This is my SECOND LETTER... won't you please respond?

November 17, 2005

Dear Mr. Kirk Dunkirk,

Thank you very much for your letter dated August 10 and October 24.

It is really regrettable that somehow we have failed to your original inquiry as promptly as we should have. Please accept our sincere apology for it.

As to the matters you have questioned, that is our past relationship with then Blue Ribbon Sports we are providing you our view as follow.

First of all, please be informed that Onitsuka Co. is one of three companies, which merged together to form Asics Corp. in 1977.

The suit brought to us by Blue Ribbon Sports took place in March of 1972 and ended in 1974 by us paying a sum, which cannot be revealed, neither we can reveal the detail of the suit but it had nothing to do us asking for more money. Furthermore, we think that Nike's success has nothing to do with us and we are happy with what we are now.

If you are really interested in finding out what had happen between the two companies please find a book under the title of "SWOOSH". Unfortunately, the copy we once had has been misplaced somewhere in the office and we cannot provide you other than the title.

Anyway, as far as we are concerned there is nothing to be ashamed of the incident except for the fact that we lost the case that we could have won.

It might be difficult for you to be satisfied with the reply we can provide to you but this is all we can do for the matter.

Meanwhile, we will be more than happy to answer you any other questions as long as they are not related with the above-mentioned incident.

Sincerely yours,

ASICS Corporation
1-1, Minatojima-Nakamachi 7-chome
Chuo-ku, Kobe, 650-8555, Japan
S. Matsumura / CS Div.

Kirk Dunkirk
Wan-tastic Conversation School for Dogs
α β α α β α
Kochi City 780-① ① ①
Japan

March 23, 2006

Czech Railways, joint stock company
nábrezí Ludvíka Svobody 1222/12
110 15 Praha 1
Czech Republic

Dear Czech Rail,

Please allow me to introduce myself; I am a man of wealth and taste. I run the "Wan-tastic" chain of English conversation schools for dogs. As you may know, people here in Japan are having fewer children and lavishing attention on their pets instead. We hope to branch out into Taiwan and Hong Kong soon, but our brief experiment in Korea, alas, failed.

We humans and dogs evolved together. To prove my point, I toured Europe by rail accompanied by a dog disguised as a baby. An ugly baby to be sure but still beautiful to her mother's eyes. This is something you might want to consider next time you are thinking of ways to boost passenger numbers. It was all filmed and the documentary should be out just as soon as I get my mojo back.

Which brings me to the main reason for writing this letter: While riding your lovely "Vlak" trains during the week of Feb. 12th I seem to have lost it. My mojo. Were there any turned in to lost and found? It was a gift from my grandfather. Since the loss, my personal and professional life has become a disaster.

During much of the trip I sat next to a funny young british man named Scott Linyard. He may have been a Homo Sapien, if you get my drift, but it's hard to tell with you Europeans sometimes. It's not much to go on, but the cops I met during my tour seemed competent, not at all the fascists I expected them to be.

By the way I'm willing to pay a reward for the safe return of my treasure.

Sincerely

Kirk Dunkirk
President and Top Dog

 Czech Railways, joint-stock company - General Management

PASSENGER TRANSPORT AND SERVICE DEPARTMENT

Reference No.: 344 /2006 – O 16/7
Date: 12.04.2006
Referent: Hladíková Kateřina
Tel.: +420 972 32 253
E-mail: Hladikova@gr.cd.cz

Mr. Kirk Dunkirk
Wan-tastic Conversation School for Dogs
███████████
Kochi City 780 – ███
Japan

Dear Mr. Dunkirk,

Having received your letter of March 23rd, we tried to probe the case you described .

To our regret we can´t give you a positive reply without a specification of trains you used also with the exact time when your loss seemed to happen.

So far we haven´t got any news from our lost and found office either.

We apologize for any inconvenience made by your loss.

We remain,

Yours faithfully,

Luďka Hnulíková, Dipl. Ing.
Director
Passenger Transport and Service Department

 České dráhy, a. s. – registration in nomenclature court of municipal Prague, head B, contents 8039
Nábřeží L. Svobody 1222, 110 15 Praha 1, tel. +420 972 232 218, fax +420 972 233 306, IČ: 70994226 DIČ:CZ 70994226
e-mail: info@cd.cz, www.cd.cz

PKP INTERCITY
spółka z o.o.

Biuro Sprzedaży
02-021 Warszawa ul. Grójecka 17
tel.: (022) 474 26 53
fax: (022) 474 26 53
e-mail bws3@intercity.pl

Warsaw, 8th of Mai 2006

Letter: BWC3c - 772-641/06

Kirk Dunkirk
Wan - tastic Conversation School for Dogs

Kochi City 780-
Japonia

Dear Mr. Dunkirk,

we are very sorry about your troubles during your journey on 12th of February in the train "Polonez". We wish, such accidents did not happen in the future.

Certainly, we will take care of your case but in order to consider your claim we need the original tickets which are to be sent to our company. Furthermore, please indicate the number of the letter as mentioned above. Having your tickets, we will be able to find out which relation you were going and which car you were in.

Simultaneously, we would like to have a more detailed description of your lost precious thing.

We would like to apologize for your troubles.

Best regards
Eva Markiewicz
Chairman
Customer service
PKP Intercity Ltd. Co.

Kirk Dunkirk
x x x x x
Kochi City 780- ☠ ☠ ☠

Paloma Co., Ltd.
6-23 Momozono-cho, Mizuho-ku
Nagoya, 467-8585, Japan

Aug. 15, 2006

Dear Paloma,

I have been reading with great interest the scandal surrounding your company; about how for years you covered up faults with your products that resulted in several (29?) deaths. I have experience with Japanese commercial justice, so take heart: you'll probably get off with an apology, a small fine (about the cost of an economy car) and 6 mos. to 3 years jail time, suspended.

I own a PH-E50B gas water heater, purchased new about 6 months ago. Should I worry about carbon monoxide poisoning and / or fire?

My wife Miki and I have a bet. Her former co-worker in Matsuyama died of carbon monoxide poisoning at home 5 years ago. She thinks it was suicide due to his debts, I think it was accidental due to his dumbness. Have there been any deaths in Matsuyama at the time attributed to your products? Please inform.

Don't worry. In spite of all the sensational headlines about deaths due to coverups by Mitsubishi, Toyota, Snow Brands, every other hospital, et al., not to mention shady financial dealings by the likes of Kanebo, Seibu, NHK, Sogo, most major banks and so on, I still have great faith in business leaders such as your president Toshihiro Kobayashi and the rest of his wealthy family who own you. Japan must never allow its corporate culture to succumb to international standards of transparency and accountability.

As a matter of fact, I think the "Company perspective" section of your website is worth a re-read. (See next page.) Don't worry, I believe you, I believe you!

Good luck! Gambatte! がんばって！ファイト！ファイト！Faito, faito!

Sincerely,

Kirk Dunkirk, Esq.

From the Paloma Website:

Ever since our founding in 1911, Paloma has consistently continued to maintain an unflinching stance about one thing: providing our clientele with products that put priority on safety above all else. No matter how sophisticated or easy to use it may be, we believe that only true technology is also furnished with safety.

People make mistakes. That's precisely why it's Paloma's unchanging corporate mission to adopt this stance in our quest for responsible technology. As a manufacturer, we must engage in product development that is grounded in good conscience as we actively strive to ensure safety.

For this reason, we have always placed safety before cost and productivity. We have established our own stringent standards for safety and tackled safety measures before all else. We have brought into the world such innovations as flame-failure safety devices for portable gas cooking stoves and oxygen depletion safety shut-off devices for gas water heaters. In this way and others, we're seizing the initiative to enlighten the entire industry about safety.

In bringing reliance and comfort into people's daily lives, Paloma's reliable and safe technology makes no compromise. The form and specs of our products are an eloquent testimonial to this.

Kirk Dunkirk
☠ ☠ ☠ ☠
Kochi City 780-☢ ☢ ☢

Paloma Co., Ltd.
6-23 Momozono-cho, Mizuho-ku
Nagoya, 467-8585 Japan

Oct. 20, 2006

Dear Paloma,

I wrote you a letter dated Aug. 15, 2006 regarding the safety of my PH-E50B gas water heater but have yet to get a reply.

Considering that your product has the potential to kill me and my followers, the least you can do is acknowledge that and write back.

Won't you please find the time to assuage my fears?

Sincerely,

Kirk Dunkirk

Paloma

6-23, Momozono-cho, Mizuho-ku,
Nagoya, Aichi, 467-8585, Japan
Phone: 052-824-5111, Fax: 052-824-5414

November 6, 2006

Mr. Kirk Dunkirk

Kochi City 780-

Dear Mr. Dunkirk,

We received your letters dated Aug 15th and Oct 20th.
Please accept our most sincere apology for late response.

As to PH-E50B which in current use, you can use it without problem for it has safety device (oxygen depletion safety shut-off device).
Just to make it more certain, please keep your room well-ventilated while in operation of gas appliance.

We apologize for any inconvenience caused to you this time.

Sincerely,

Toshimasa Ura

Toshimasa Ura
Deputy general manager
General Affairs Department

TIMES

and the world, Pages 11-17

YOMIURI

RY 11, 2007

PRICE ¥120 (¥2,650 per calendar month)—tax included   EDITION A

es agreed

Rinnai water heaters tied to 3 CO deaths

Lack of safety devices also led to 12 injuries

The Yomiuri Shimbun

Three people have died and a dozen have been injured in five instances since 2000 due to carbon monoxide poisoning by Rinnai Corp. water heaters, according to the Economy, Trade and Industry Ministry.

The three fatalities were each caused by the same model of water heater, while a similar model caused injury in one of the remaining two cases. The ministry on Friday ordered the Nagoya-based major manufacturer of gas appliances to determine the cause of the accidents.

Rinnai on Saturday held an emergency meeting, where the company decided to open up a 24-hour telephone help line, to

safely devices to prevent incomplete combustion extinguished the flame, disabling the device.

Rinnai said the ministry informed it Thursday of Wednesday's accident.

Rinnai President Hiroyasu Naito, 51, apologized saying: "We offer our deepest condolences to those who lost their lives. We'll work to confirm if there was a common cause behind the accidents."

In August, the ministry confirmed that Rinnai products were behind four of the five incidents, following an investigation into water heaters spurred by similar accidents linked to Nagoya-based Paloma Industries Ltd.

But the ministry did not make the four accidents public at the time, only releasing the information after Wednesday's fatality in Yokohama. As for why the ministry did not disclose the information about questionable Rinnai products in August, one official said, "We concluded the accidents were likely the result of incorrect usage."

Later on Saturday, industry sources said the five water heaters in question had not been equipped with devices to prevent reignition during incomplete combustion.

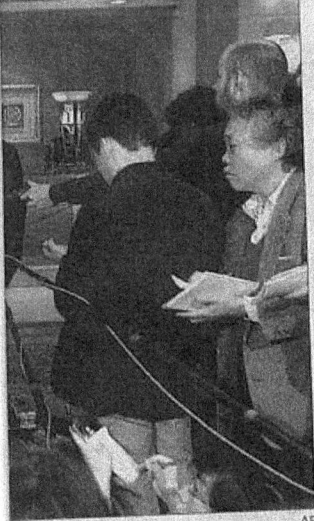

l, center, speaks to reporters be-
ea's nuclear program in Beijing on

osal after further discussions.
Friday, Hill said without giving
fics that North Korea disagreed with
vording in one paragraph of the new
osal.
l said two other key issues that have
iously stalled the negotiations were
roblematic this time. They include U.S.
ictions on a bank where North Korea
accounts for its complicity in alleged
cial crimes, and demands that North

Kirk Dunkirk
☣ ☣ ☣ ☣
Kochi City 780-☢ ☢ ☢

Kao Corporation
14-10 Nihonbashi Kayabacho, 1-chome,, Chuo-ku
Tokyo, 103-8210

Aug. 15, 2006

Dear Kao,

I love your products, everything from your Attack™ laundry detergent to Merries™ diapers to, heck, even your copier toner. You do it all and you do it all so well. I can tell that you are a COMPANY THAT CARES.

That's why I'm writing. I need your advice. There is a problem in my office and I don't know what to do!

There is a woman I work with whose large shapeless garments seem moldy. Her hair smells like a wet dog and her teeth are mossy. She's only 35 years old or so but because of this looks at least 46. Then there's the older guy who is fond of vinegar and riding his bike one hour to work w/o a change of clothes. Together they form an Axis of Odor that threatens our way of life.

I'd like to make suggestions to them about how to improve their hygiene, perhaps by using your products but I face a cultural conundrum. How can I do so without seeming rude? (I'm Irish, Axis of Odor is Japanese.) I just want to help them and make the office a pleasant place to work.

Can you help me? Please advise regarding the best products to use and how to tactfully recommend them.

Thank you.
Sincerely

Kirk Dunkirk

Mr. Kirk Dunkirk

Kochi City 780-

                                                        Ms Naoko Tomie
                                       Consumer Information Center
                                                Kao Corporation
                                        2-1-3 Bunka Sumida-ku
                                                Tokyo 131-8501
                                                   2006/08/31

Dear Mr. Dunkirk

Thank you for your letter of 15 Aug. enquiring about our products. we are very pleased to know you favor Kao products.

I understand it is very difficult to advise to your colleagues about their hygiene, as it is a personal and delicate matter.

I enclose a Kao products catalogue and a booklet which suggest some ideas to keep our body healthy and beautiful.

Would you please recommend them to your colleagues with your humorous talks and I hope your working conditions will be improved.

Yours sincerely

Naoko Tomie

Naoko Tomie

月のマークのうつりかわり

1890　　1897　　1912　　1925　　1943　　1948　　1953
(明治23年)(明治30年)(大正元年)(大正14年)(昭和18年)(昭和23年)(昭和28年)

本冊子の姉妹編として「くらしの清潔ノート 生活編」があります。

[内容]　●洗濯機洗い、手洗い
　　　　●漂白する
　　　　●仕上げ、乾かす、アイロンをかける
　　　　●台所の清潔
　　　　●住まいのお手入れ、台所のお手入れ
　　　　●トイレ、浴室のおそうじ
　　　　●洗剤、洗浄剤と住まいのお手入れ

花王製品に関するお問い合せは、
　　　消費者相談センター　　TEL.03-5630-9911

発行　花王生活文化研究所
〒131-8501　東京都墨田区文花2-1-3　TEL.03-5630-9963

★本冊子掲載の記事・写真の無断転載・複写を禁じます。
★再生紙を使用しています。

2004.3 改訂版　　10,000 ①

KIRK DUNKIRK
✪ ✪ ✪ ✪
KOCHI CITY 780-✯ ✯ ✯

CORONA CORPORATION, HEAD OFFICE
7-7 HIGASHI-SHINBO, SANJO
NIIGATA 955-8510,
JAPAN

OCT. 20, 2006

DEAR CORONA,

WHAT'S GOING ON?

BACK IN JULY I BOUGHT ONE OF YOUR VACUUM CLEANERS BUT I'M STILL WAITING FOR MY CASE OF BEER TO SHOW UP.

WHEN I BOUGHT THE APPLIANCE, THE SALESGUY TOLD ME THERE WAS A PROMOTION AND THAT IF I BOUGHT THE CLEANER I'D GET A CASE OF YOUR BEER TOO. WELL, IT'S BEEN LIKE 3 MONTHS, I VACUUMED THE HOUSE A BUNCH A TIMES AND THERE'S STILL NO BEER. IT'S LIKE A FAIRY GODMOTHER OR SOMETHING. I'M STILL WAITING.

I WENT TO THE SHOP THAT SOLD ME THE MACHINE BUT THEY SAID THE GUY NO LONGER WORKS THERE SO THERE'S NOTHING THEY CAN DO. THEY SAID I SHOULD WRITE A LETTER TO YOU DIRECTLY.

WHAT DO I HAVE TO DO TO GET MY CORONA BEER? I MEAN I CAN JUST GO OUT AND BUY A CASE OF BEER, I'M NOT STUPID. BUT I FEEL LIKE I GOT LIED TO AND I DON'T THINK THAT'S A GOOD WAY TO DO BUSINESS. SOMEBODY OWES ME A CASE OF BEER. I DESERVE IT.

I'M STARTING TO THINK YOUR VACUUM CLEANER <u>SUCKS</u>.

HURT AND DISAPPOINTED,

KIRK DUNKIRK

CORONA CORPORATION

7-7 HIGASHI-SHINBO, SANJO, NIIGATA 955-8510, JAPAN
TEL: 81-256-32-2111   FAX: 81-256-35-6892   http://www.corona.co.jp/

CORONA

November 1, 2006

Mr. Kirk Dunkirk

Kochi city 780-

Dear Mr. Dunkirk,

We duly received a letter from you.

Thank you very much for your purchase of our vacuum cleaner.

But unfortunately, Corona Corporation already stopped to produce vacuum cleaners about 10 years ago, and we have no relation to the promotion campaign at which you bought a vacuum cleaner.

It is the shop that conducted the promotion campaign and sold you the vacuum cleaner. We, therefore, cannot help you regarding this matter.

Could you please negotiate again with the shop for a case of beer.

Please kindly understand this situation.   Thank you.

Sincerely yours,

CORONA CORPORATION

Takao Yoneyama
Assistant Manager
Export Section, Sales Dept.

Kirk Dunkirk
ΔΣΦ
Kochi City 780-AΔ

Hato Bus Tours
World Trade Center Bldg. 1F
2-4-1 Hamamatsu-cho, Minato-ku, Tokyo

Oct. 30, 2006

Dear Hato,

I am Field Researcher for the Diepne Benz Dance Troupe, named after our founder and dedicated to spreading crappy revolutionary art to the masses. We are currently putting together an operetta version of "Godzilla vs. The Smog Monster" hopefully leading to a movie one day as well.

In order to get the feel of the original film, 3 members of my troupe are here in the Japanese archipelago to tour Godzilla locations and need a guide for the Kanto area sometime during early December. Also, since English and Japanese are languages of Imperialism, in accordance with our Troupe's manifesto the tour must be given in Esperanto. I'm sure you are *trolaborigata kaj maltropagata* so I appreciate your time. *Kion vi opinias*? Can you accommodate our needs?

Sincerely,

Kirk Dunkirk
Tour Commander

ps: I saw your ad in online Townpage

HATO BUS CO., LTD
INBOUND TOUR SECTION
〒105-6101 WORLD TRADE CENTER BLDG 2-4-1
HAMAMATSU-CHO, MINATO-KU TOKYO JAPAN
TEL 03-3435-6081   FAX 03-3433-1972

December 8, 2006

Dear Kirk Dunkirk-san

Thank you very much for your inquiries. It is regrettable that we weren't able to reply sooner. We are not quite sure what was written in the previous letter, but we would do our best to answer your question.

Regarding Godzilla tours you are interested in, we have no such tours operated in the past nor do not have any plan to do tours related with Godzilla right at the moment.

If you mean Godzilla is Yankees' baseball star, Hideki Matsui, we have operated a tour of children sponsored by him in summer this year, for your information. We are afraid that we do not have any information on this tour, such as how the trip was organized.

This is as far as we can inform you. If you have any further questions, please feel free to ask again, by letter or phone written above.

Thank you very much for your understanding.

Sincerely yours,

Yukiko Oka(MS)
National Certified English Tour Guide & Tour Operator

HATO BUS CO., LTD
INBOUND TOUR DEVISION

Kirk Dunkirk
½ ⅓ ⅔ ¼ ¾
Kochi City 780- ¾ ⅔ ½

HARA SHOBO
2-3 Kanda Jimbocho
Chiyoda-ku, Tokyo 101-0051

Oct. 11, 2006

To Whom it May Concern,

Thank you for offering your services in English. They are a great help to those of us who appreciate Japanese art but have not yet mastered your beautiful language. You are doing a wonderful service by helping to spread Japanese culture across the globe.

My interest in collecting Ukiyo-e began when I bought a few works by Kuniyoshi near the military base I was stationed at in the 1980's. Since then my collection has grown, step by step, a Hiroshige here and a Gessan there, but there is one set of works that escapes me.

I seek a print from the fabled Sailor Moon "patriotic series" during the Second World War. Any print will do, as they are so rare, having been hunted down and burned during the occupation, but I hope to find the one where she and Sailor Mercury catch Bugs Bunny poisoning the water supply and roast him on a spit.

If you carry this print or could provide some advice as to where I might look for it, I would be most grateful.

Sincerely,

Kirk Dunkirk

原書房
HARA SHOBŌ

Mr. Kirk Dankirk

Kochi-City 780-

Dear Mr. Dankirk

I am sorry for the delay of my reply.

Maybe my English not as good as I thought. I have been at a loss as I could not understand what your first letter says.

I am not sure what is "Sailor Moon Partiotic Series". You also mentioned that the series was during WW2. There is not longer woodblock prints at that time, but lithographs, which we do not handle. We primarily handle woodblock prints. We have some of Japan-China or Japan-Russo Wars, but not of WW2.

Unfortunately I think that we could not be of your help. I am sorry for the disappointment.
Sincerely yours,

Toshiyuki Hara
Hara Shobo

Kirk Dunkirk
x x x x
Kochi City 780- x x x

HARA SHOBO
2-3 Kanda Jimbocho
Chiyoda-ku, Tokyo 101-0051

Nov. 29, 2006

Dear Mr. Hara,

Thank you so much for your kind and quick reply.

Your English is excellent. It is I who must apologize for my lack of knowledge and for wasting your time.

Thanks to you I learned something very important.

Sincerely,

Kirk Dunkirk

Kirk Dunkirk
☠ ☠ ☠ ☠
Kochi City 780-✂ ✂ ✂

〒651-0087
Hyogo-ken, Kobe-shi, Chuo-ku
Gokoh-dori, 7-1-15, Nestle House
Nestle Customer Service

Dear nestle,

I've been a huge fan of your Powerbars. Whether I'm haulin a** on a mountain bike trail or catchin air on a windsurfer, they are totally bitchin.

But anyway I was on this awesome rockclimbing trip in western Kochi when something totally weird happened. I was like 50 feet up, just hanging there by my toenails basically and I needed a power boost. So I ripped out one of my powerbars and this big bird, like a hawk or falcon, not like just a crow, comes out of nowhere and just freaking <u>rips</u> the bar out of my hands.

I was like "Whoah, Topher did you see that? " and he goes "No way dude! -- You're totally lucky that eagle didn't like cut your hand off!" And he was right. He was always my lab partner in AP Bio and I just copied everything off him cause he knew all the answers.

So we figured the bird was gonna come back and attack us because of the power bars so Topher gave the box of them to some loser who was nearby and cut us off in the parking lot earlier. <u>Your bars are totally dangerous.</u>

Then I got to the top and I noticed I had one apple cinnamon bar left so I ate it fast as I could in case that attack bird came back! It got all over my fingers. <u>Can't you guys include disposable plastic gloves or something with the bars?</u> I don't mind sticking food in my mouth but I hate it when it gets on my hands. It could be a good selling point. Topher thinks so too.

Anyway, I think you ought to change your formula or at least warn people. I could of gotten hurt. And I think you owe me 6 powerbars too. I don't care what flavor, as long as eagles don't like them. Please send my bars or coupons to the address above. It's my house.

Thanks

Kirk Dunkirk, Nov. 20, 2006

November 28, 2006

Dear Mr. Dunkirk,

We hope this letter finds you well.
Thank you for choosing our products.

We are sorry to hear of the misfortune that happened to you. However, we are afraid we are unable to satisfy your request as the incident was not responsibility.

Nestlé Japan Ltd. is dedicated to the constant improvement of our quality control system so as to offer products whose safety is unquestioned by consumers. We hope that you will continue to extend your kind patronage to our products in the future.
In closing, I send my best wishes for your health.

Sincerely yours,

Consumer Hot Line Section
Nestlé Japan

Kirk Dunkirk
x x x x
Kochi City 780-x x x

Taiyo Kogyo Corporation, Camping Equipment
2-33-16 Ikejiri
Setagaya-ku, Tokyo

Nov. 6, 2006

To Whom it May Concern,

I recently purchased one of your filibuster machines to take on my Shikoku 88 Temple Tour but it doesn't work anymore. I feel banquished. Don't worry, I admit that I broke it myself; I'd just like some information on how to fix things.

Due to the extreme wilderness conditions experienced by pilgrims on this tour, I needed to make sure all my equipment was in top-notch condition. So I opened the machine up to clean the zardoz element but I think I may have inadvertently gerrymandered the caucus. Either that or the primary runoff lobbyist got knocked out of whack. It certainly is bent, that's for sure.

I'm sorry my explanation isn't very clear. I checked the online forums but couldn't find any information there either. If you don't have any suggestions, could you at least refer me to a place where I can order mutonic brokstoff clips and titanium salamander springs?

I want to reiterate that I am a very satisfied customer... I just made a mistake.

Thank you for your time.
Sincerely,

Kirk Dunkirk

TAIYO KOGYO CORPORATION

2-33-16 Ikejiri Setagaya-ku
Tokyo 154-0001 Japan
Tel : 03-3714-3368
Fax : 03-3714-3381
http://www.taiyokogyo.co.jp/

Reiko Harada / Overseas Operations
E-mail :hr900242@taiyokogyo.co.jp

Jan. 26, 2007

Mr.Kirk Dunkirk

Kochi City 780-

Subject: Your letter dated Jan.12

Dear Mr. Kirk Dunkirk,

First of all, our sincere apologies for not replying sooner to your letter dated Jan.12.
However, somehow we still cannot find anyone who received your original letter dated Nov.6, 2006, and the latest letter had been circulated in office for long time.
Eventually, overseas operations department where I belong to received your letter today only because it was written in English.
Now, we would appreciate it if you would contact us again and let us know your inquiry in detail so that we can forward your request to appropriate department and provide you our product exactly you need.   You can also check our products on our web page shown above.

We wanted to contact you by phone or E-mail but we could not since there was no information other than your address in your letter.   We ask for your kind understanding for this.

We will be waiting for either your phone call or E-mail soon.
Of course replying by letter also would be fine, but it would take some more time.

Best regards,

R. Harada

Reiko Harada
Overseas Operations,
Taiyo Kogyo Corporation

Kirk Dunkirk
x x x x
Kochi City 780-x x x

MakMax
Taiyo Kogyo Corporation
2-33-16 Ikejiri Setagaya-ku
Tokyo 154-0001 Japan

Feb. 7, 2007

Dear Miss Harada,

Thank you very much for your letter. You sound like a nice young lady.

I don't know what happened to my first letter. I'm not the sharpest knife in the drawer so I probably sent it to the wrong people or forgot to put a darn stamp on the thing.

I also don't have email. A shame, seeing how you young folk like it so much. Thing is, I'm a backwards old coot and I don't like all this new technology. I'm only using my wife's word processor because my old typewriter's done gone and died. If you ask me, we never shoulda came down from the trees in Africa a million something years ago. Eating bananas and picking fleas off each other is about as good as it gets, I reckon.

So for me camping is the next best thing. And from what I hear, your Buddha fellow had some similar ideas too, so I've been planning a walk around the 88 temple tour here on lush, gorgeous Shikoku.

I bought one of your filibuster machines for the trip but it doesn't work now. I admit it was me that broke it while tinkering around. I'm not sure about the model number as everything's in Chinese, but looks like it's either a "Y-68" or a "Portable Convenience Apparatus."

All I'd like from you is to information on how I can repair it. I don't know all the newfangled terminology - heck I still have trouble with "350ml" vs. "350cc," but here's what I suspect happened: while I was cleaning the zardoz element, I must've gerrymandered the caucus. So to repair it I think I need mutonic brokstoff clips and some salamander springs. Clockwise ones.

If you could either send me a repair guide or tell me where I can buy the parts I think I can take care of the rest by myself. I'm not angry. It was my own dang fault. I was born an old fool.

Thank you for your time. Much obliged.

Kirk Dunkirk

TAIYO KOGYO CORPORATION

2-33-16 Ikejiri Setagaya-ku
Tokyo 154-0001 Japan
Tel : +81 (0)3-3714-3368
Fax : +81(0)3-3714-3381
Http://www.taiyokogyo.co.jp/

Feb. 15, 2006

Mr. Kirk Dunkirk
███████████████
Kochi City 780-█

Subject: Reply to your letter dated Feb.7.

Dear Mr. Dunkirk,

Thank you for your reply letter, and I am sorry that I could not send you a reply letter earlier.
Reviewing your letter, actually we could not tell which product of ours you meant by
"filibuster machine" with model number like "Y-68" or "Portable Convenience Apparatus."
According to your letter, I guess it might be a camping goods or something.

Our company is now handling with Architectural Structure (membrane structure such
as Tokyo Dome or Soccer Stadium), building materials, distribution facilities,
civil engineering and others.

I am sorry, but only from the information you gave us, we cannot tell which product you mean,
and we don't have any idea how to support you.
So, could you ask one of your friends or neighbors and check what it says in Chinese Characters.
Or, if possible, it might be helpful for us if you would send us a photo of the product.
And also you could call me any time at 03-3714-3368 (Harada).
However, it might be difficult to repair depending on the product.
I would appreciate it if you would understand in that case.
I look forward to having your reply first.

Sincerely Yours,

R. Harada

Reiko Harada
Overseas Operation
Taiyo Kogyo Corporation

Kirk Dunkirk
Passing Wind Pub
x x x x
Kochi City 780-x x x
Japan

Unicharm/Kobayashi Pharmaceutical
4-3-6 Doshomachi, Chuo-ku
Osaka 541-0045 Japan

Jan 10, 2007

Dear Unicharm,

Happy New Year of the Wild Boar!

I own a bar in Kochi and often use your products. Please don't confuse me with Norm in Tokushima –he's the <u>other</u> gaijin on Shikoku who runs a bar. I used to be in the English conversation business but one day I finally realized that I wasn't cut out for talking all day long to rich post-menopausal housewives who think everything is dangerous.

But I digress.

On the whole, I find your cleaning products both useful and fun. But I have some questions and suggestions about how to make them even better. In particular I'd like to focus on "Toire no shō nioi moto" or "Going Out of Restroom Ill-Smelling Cause" brand air freshener.

I serve traditional Japanese pub fare at my shop, things like fried pork cutlets, fried chicken, fried octopus and fried eggplant with bacon and mayonnaise. But when my customers go into the rest room to take care of business they are shocked by the sudden rush of "Passion Orange" or "Blue Jasmine." Instead of fighting the nature of pub odors you should <u>work with them</u>. So please make scents like "Recycled Lard" or "Dank Hairy Floor."

By the way, I'm baffled by how your products actually find the bad odors and get rid of them. I mean, how do they know?

Thank you for hearing my request. I look forward to your reply.
Sincerely,

Kirk Dunkirk

30-Jan-07

Dear Mr. Kirk Dunkirk

Thank you for always using KOBAYASHI's product, especially
'Sho-shu-gen' for toilet use.

We're very sorry to reply to you after receiving your letter.
Please let us explain about the function of 'Sho-Shu-gen' for toilet use.
Our product is absorbing bad smell to the filiter
and prevent bad odor from going again by detergent.
And in the same time, our product is releasing nice smell to the air.

We'd like to highly appreciate your advice of new Scent,
'Recycled Lard' or 'Dank Hairy Floor'. It's nice and interesting
for us to hear such kind of scents. Please let us take into accounts
your idea to develop new product in near future.

We hope you to continue using our KOBAYASHI's product and thanks
for your attention this time.

Sincerely yours,

K. Yamashita
Customer Services department
KOBAYASHI Pharmaceutical Co., Ltd.
TEL: 06-6203-3625
     06-6203-3673

Kirk Dunkirk c/o
Japan-Belarus Go Friendship Association
✪ ✪ ✪ ✪
Kochi City 780- ❀ ❀ ❀

Japan Go Association
7-2 Gobancho
Chiyoda-ku, Tokyo 102-0076

Nov 13, 2006

Dear Go Association,

I am here Kochi, Japan on 6-month Katarina Ingeborg Von Schtanck Foundation* grant to study go (also called *igo.*) I am much grateful for one opportunity to improve my game in the Land of Go. Sure, China is place to invent and can be popular of wideness in Korea, but Japan is remains The Land of Go.**

Since I come to The Land of Go, aka Japan, my weeks of intensity study have to increase of my appreciate on the depth and beauty of the game so large. Thank you so very. However the few revelations cause me great concern this go future. These are the topics of heat on the internet blogs.

I think the adoption start in 2009 of so-called "bin-go" rules is tragedy indeed. Players to win packets of instant coffee or grease of cooking if an announce man calls out a random of number line where they have a piece?!? This goes against the spirit of the game what players compete just for sheer pleasure, and occasional money, and maybe even love. There must be an better other ways to enticement to new players. Go figure.

Also, it true? that when Chairman of one Australian Chess Association recently threatened to "Kick go's arse" and for us to "Go [blank] ourselves", the Chairman of Japan Go Association (Nihon Ki-in) has run and hide behind tall corn plant? Why? I am so sick of bully chess hotshots push us around! We need fighting them back!

One way push back is change the name so is harder make joke. May I humbly suggest following names change: Goo, Gno, Og, Ogi, Gomega, Gomopoly, Gort, Gobancho, I. G.O., and Gothello.

Thank you for your time. Please soon write back me about these terrible developings.
Sincerely,

Kirk Dunkirk
Belarus Go Association, 3-kyu

* Patron Saint of Igo in Belarus. Learned go under in arrest by Japanese forces in Manchuria in WWII

** Korea is of course The Land of Baduk and China The Land of Weiqui.

THE NIHON KI-IN

7-2, Gobancho, Chiyoda-ku, Tokyo 102-0076, Japan

Dear Mr. Kirk Dunkirk,

Thank you for your letters and we are sorry for my slow reply.

We are glad to hear that you got this opportunity to learn more Go in Japan and we have searched Katarina inggeborg Von Schtanck Foundation, but we could not find a good one. If you have any information, please let us know.

Well, we do not understand your meaning of "bin-go" rules very well. We've never heard of that and other things. Could you send us the page of the internet blogs? And there are some people who talk nonsense which we can not stop.

Faithfully,

Hideko Okada
Overseas dep.
Nihon Kiin

Time out for some more…

Haiku by Stymie

Autumn wind blowing
The scent of leaves turning brown
Or is it just farts.

Take fish parts and bake
Now mash them up and reshape
Some folks call this food.

Kirk Dunkirk
© © © ©
Kochi City 780- ® ® ®

Sanyo Electric Co.
5-5, Keihan-Hondori 2-Chome,
Moriguchi City, Osaka 570-8677
Japan

Feb. 26, 2007

Dear Sanyo,

Years ago you had a TV ad campaign in the US. It was great and I really miss it.

In the spots, there would be some of your products, usually a TV or radio. Then suddenly, this glamorous woman in sexy evening wear would strut out from the product and burst into a big band rendition of Frank Sinatra's "That's Life." But she was really tiny so she could fit inside the TV set, like the Mothra chicks.

It gets better – She'd sing the Sinatra song but the words were a little different! So at the climax of the song, when everyone's expecting the usual song words, she'd sing "Saaaaaaaannn....yyoohhhhh!" In fact, when I was a kid I thought your version was the real one and that Sinatra copied it. "Why is Frank Sinatra singing the Sanyo song?" He was still alive then, and had hair.

Me and my friends used to sing it at school all the time, mostly just the "Sanyo!" part. We'd stand on desks, arms spread wide, using the green lefty scissors as a mic, shouting the name of your brand. The teachers complained but I think secretly they liked the ads too. I caught them doing it once while smoking in the teacher's lounge. There was an Indian kid in my class named Sanjoy and we'd sometimes shout his name instead. Just for fun, not to tease him, he was our friend. I think he liked the ads too.

What a great ad campaign. Obviously I never forgot it. You should bring them back. I mean, you stopped the ads and now you're having all sorts of problems. And whatever happened to the "That's Life, Sanyo" babe? Please write back and let me know. Thanks a lot. And I'm glad you keep jobs in Osaka.

Kirk Dunkirk

 SANYO Electric Co., Ltd.

Corporate Communications Headquarters
3-23-1, Celestine Bldg 13F, Shiba, Minato-ku
Tokyo 105-0014, Japan

March 5, 2006

Dear Mr. Dunkirk,

Thank you for your letter dated February 26, 2007. We appreciate your feedback on the appeal of the "That's life" commercial at the end of the 70s.

This commercial, featuring Susan Anton, was very popular at the time even winning an award at the 1985 Gong Gold Awards in Singapore, but was targeted just for the USA market.

At this juncture we do not have any plans to repeat any such commercial; however we appreciate your feedback.

Once again thank you for your letter. We appreciate your continued support for SANYO.

Best regards,

Global PR Team, Public Affairs Unit
Corporate Communications Headquarters
SANYO Electric Co., Ltd.

Corporate Communications Unit is ISO14001 Certified.
Promoting Environmental Management aiming for co-existence between the Environment & Economy.

Kirk Dunkirk
x x x x   x x x x
Kochi City   780- x x x

Yamato Protec Corporation, Head office
5-17-2 Shirokanedai
Minato-ku, Tokyo 108-0071

March 9, 2007

Dear Yamato Protec,

Your smoke alarms help me sleep at night. I can wake up fresh and be on time for work and know that my home will still be there when I return, ready for another night of good sleep. If your smoke alarms had hands, the fate of my family would rest in them. Except for my mom, who lives in a "home."

At first I found the Jackson 5 ringtones intriguing, but now I want to change them to something more urgent such as Daft Punk. I have uploaded the mp3 files into the detector but the new songs aren't showing up in the menu. Since it's set to random, whenever my wife Miki burns the toast we tend to get "ABC 123" or "I'll Be There." Salmon on Monday night often results in "Don't Stop 'til You Get Enough" perhaps due to the concentration of omega-3 oils.

The staff at the big DIK home center where I purchased the product were befuddled and suggested I write you.

By the way, there are some mistakes on your English homepage. You misspelled "corporation" as "corpration" and "profile" as "profil", "outline" as "outlin" ...all on the same "branch offices" page! Sorry to point this out, I just want to make the world a better place.

Otherwise the smoke alarms work great. If only I could get Miki to stop burning the damn toast!

Please write back soon with any suggestions. Thank you.
Sincerely,

Kirk Dunkirk

ps: I noticed you like the Futura font. Me too!

Dear Mr. Kirk Dunkirk

Thank you for your inquiry.

I'm afraid that the fire alarm which you stated in your mail is not our product.

Please confirm the manufacturer and ask the customer service.

Sincerely,

Yamato Protec Corporation

Matsuyama Sales Office

March 14th, 2007

Marukome Co ,Ltd
883, Amori
Nagano, Nagano Japan

March 5, 2007

Dear Marukome,

I'm a big fan of your instant miso soup with fried spiderbeans. It's simply the best instant fermented soybean soup type product on the market.

After a long day of clowning for 8 year-olds (part-time teaching) followed by the million-and-sixth rendition of "Country Road" for drunk and rhythmically -challenged salarymen (part-time street busker) in turn followed by paying off gangster operatives for my busking spot on the street – after all that, there's nothing like coming home to rice gruel flavored with your instant products and washed down with hot potato liquor.

One problem though. I've been feeling bloated lately and I wonder if it's your product. I'm bloated like a lactose intolerant cow. Bloated like the Duchess of York. Same thing? I don't know, I'm too bloated to care.

Don't get me wrong, the fried spiderbeans taste great. Even my pet pug Gingrich demands a bowl before performances on Wednesday, his "80's Rock Chicks Dance Medley" night. He's usually ok with the Debbie Harry stuff but can no longer hit the high notes of "Shadows of the Night" (Pat Benatar.) Fuhgeddabout any Sheena Easton, I've had to drop her from the show.

Like I said, we are BLOATED. Like dead goldfishes. Bloated like a Bush budget.

Why do you think we are so bloated? Too much MSG? I've lived in Japan for only 6 months but everyone tells me it's because Japanese intestines are longer than those of other people. (I'm not Japanese.) Do you think this is why? What about Japanese dogs? Are their intestines longer than those of other people?

Every day I look forward to ingesting your products, so <u>please write me back</u> with advice. As Pat would say, hit me with your best shot!

Kirk Dunkirk
Kochi City

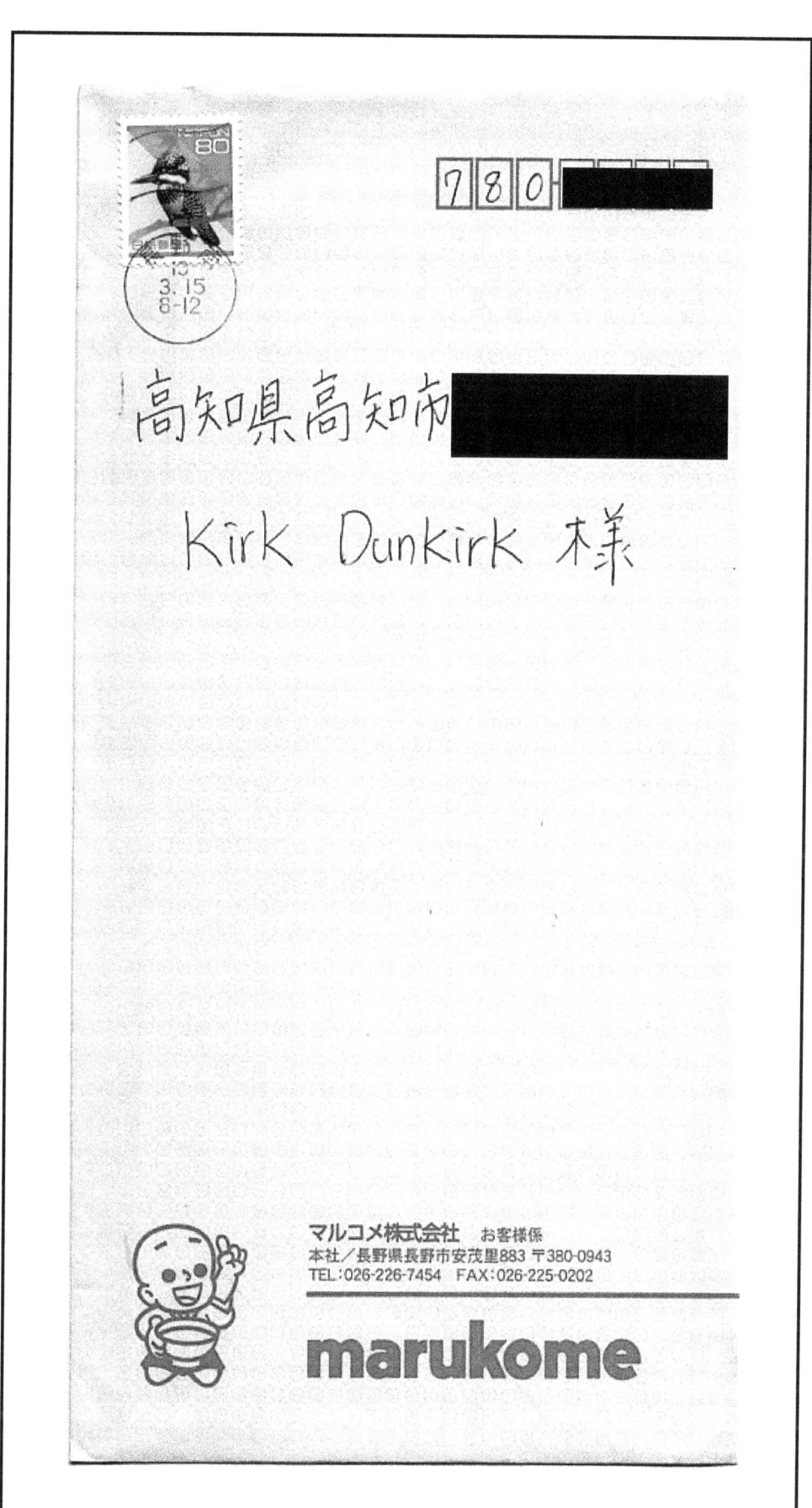

marukome Co., Ltd.

March 14th, 2007

Dear Mr. Kirk Dunkirk,

Thank you very much for purchasing our products.
We have received your letter on March 9th, in which you informed us that you gained weight by eating our instant miso soup with fried spiderbeans.

We are not conducting a study on whether consumption of our instant miso soup would cause gaining weight; therefore, we are afraid we will not be able to respond to your inquiry regarding the linkage between the product and fatness.
For your information, we have not received the similar inquiry so far.

We strive for improvement and constantly provide high quality products.

Sincerely yours,

Masahiro Wakasa
Masahiro Wakasa

General Manager
Customer Service
Marukome Co., Ltd.

883 AMORI, NAGANO-CITY • NAGANO PREFECTURE 380-0943, JAPAN
PHONE: (026)226-0255 • FAX: (026)225-0202

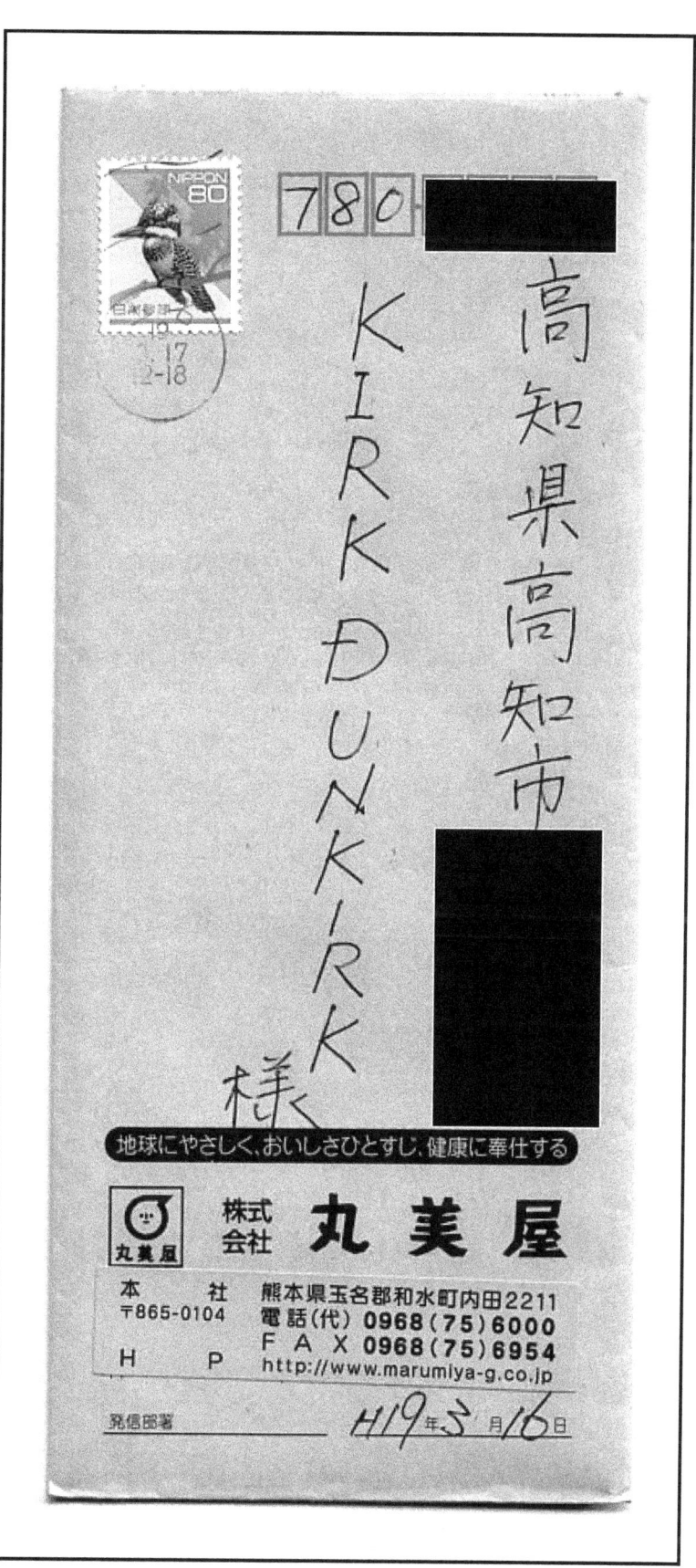

Marumiya,KK
2211,Uchida,Nagomi-Machi
Tamana-Gun,Kumamoto Japan

Kochi City ,Kochi Japan

March 16,2007

Dera Mr. Kirk Dunkirk,

Thank you for sending a letter.
Unfortunately, we do not understand what you wish to say.
Probably, you sent your letter to us by mistake. Our company has been making " Natto "and " Tofu " for more than 50years. We do not produce burdock root flavor rice additive products. We sympathize with your condition. However, we are not able to provide you with any information about another company's product.

Sincerely,

Kirk Dunkirk
☹ ☹ ☹ ☹
Kochi City 780-☹ ☹ ☹

Skylark Co. Ltd.
1-25-8, Nishikubo
Musashino, Tokyo 180-8580

March 12, 2007

Dear Skylark,

First of all, the public service your cheap restaurants provide is just right for people like me: on a budget and not too choosy. I really appreciate it. You must be doing something right to sell $3 billion of fast food a year!

I haven't been in Japan long, but I already feel nostalgic about the happy times I spent every day at your restaurant Jonathan's, nicknamed "Jonathongs" by the other members in my Tokyo Orientation Study Group. Still, I can't for the life of me figure out how to pronounce "Restaurant BLDY." Is it bloody, or boldy, or bildai, or buldee, or what? And what the heck does it mean?

Though I like your casual eateries, sadly, The Real Reason I Am Writing is to express my strong disapproval for your new chain of theme restaurants called "Stalkers." Staff that follow you to the restroom and hide behind potted ferns? No way. Hysterical waitresses? Yuck. A host that demands to know who your date is? Kind of sick.

Here's a section from the news article where I first read about it:
    ...And whatever you do, don't give your real telephone number when making reservations. You'll soon regret it after the 50th phone call 'just to check up on you.'

It might seem like just a game, and I'm sure people will say that I don't have to eat there if I don't want to. But stalking is a real problem and I don't think you should make fun of it, especially not for profit.

As a recovering stalker, I feel quite strongly about this. I know I'm just one person, but I am determined to keep at it until I can change your mind. Please write me back. I need to hear from you! Soon… I can't stop thinking about you.

Sincerely,

Kirk Dunkirk様へ

拝復　日頃のご愛顧、ご厚情を心より感謝申し上げます。
この度はお客様に弊社店舗においてご不快な思いをお掛けし深く
お詫びもうしあげます。
該当店舗および従業員に確実に指導・教育をする必要を感じて
おりますゆえ　店舗名・ご利用日時をお教え頂きたく何卒よろしく
お願い申し上げます。

また、「BLDY」はビルディという名称で営業しております。

この度の私どもの不手際にお懲りになることなく、変わらぬご愛顧を賜わりますよう
お願い申し上げます。

　　　　　　　　　　　　　　　　　　　　　　　　　敬具
平成19年3月16日

　　　　　　　　　　　　　　　　　　　株式会社すかいらーく
　　　　　　　　　　　　　　　　　　　お客様相談室室長
　　　　　　　　　　　　　　　　　　　　宇都木　敏也
　　　　　　　　　　　　　　　　　　　TEL:0120-12-5807

Mr Kirk Dunkirk,

Greetings. We thank you from our hearts for your kindness and patronage.
We would like to apologize deeply for the unpleasantness you experienced in one of our establishments.
Would you be kind enough to inform us of the location name as well as the time and date you went there as to ensure the necessary education and guidance is given to the applicable staff and premises.

Also, the name "BLDY" is pronounced "birudy".

We wish for your continuing patronage despite our ineptitude.

March 16, 2007

Regards

SkyLark Co.
Chief of Customer Relations
Toshiya Utsugi

```
(Skylark Co. "Stalkers" Restaurant reply, translation: Evan Coombes)
```

x x x x
Kochi City 780-x x x
Japan

Format Entertainment Development Team
Room 4010, BBC Television Centre
Wood Lane
London, W12 7RJ
England

5 March, 2007

Dear BBC,

Love your BBC World satellite broadcast, I think it's ace, it's the bees knees. A nice taste of home here on the other side of the world. It's also much less "cheesy" than CNN, though not without fault -let's not get carried away. For example, the Fast Track travel duo curdles my innards, and I wish Martine Dennis wouldn't act so bored all the time. Plus you have a lot of audio trouble, and the volume levels jump between the programmes and the commercials.

Anyway, I've got a great idea. Why not let amateurs present the weather? It's not really necessary for the "weatherman" to be an actual meteorologist, is it? After all, lots of newsreaders are just that: they simply read the news off a teleprompter, news that was gathered by someone else. If it's good enough for serious news, why not for something less important, like the weather?

I'm not suggesting dedicated "weatherman actors." Like I said, amateurs. People could audition, be screened, perhaps even via the Internet or YouTube &c. Then they get one shot at a real weather report. I have an American friend in Louisiana who would be great at it! You'd invite him back for sure.

More people would tune in, meteorologists would have more time to focus on accuracy and forest fires and so on. What do you say? Please write me back and let me know. Mr. Fantastico, the man who lives in my finger, thinks it's a great idea.

sincerely,

Kirk Dunkirk

ps. has anyone checked Rob Bonnet's pulse lately?

British Broadcasting Corporation Television Centre Wood Lane London W12 7RJ
Telephone 020 8743 8000

Entertainment Development

Kirk Dunkirk
Kochi City
780-
Japan

Monday, 19 March 2007

Dear Mr Dunkirk,

Re: Weatherman Actors

Thank you very much for contacting the Format Entertainment team about your idea about getting people to audition for the role of weatherman. Please accept our apologies for any delay there might have been in getting back to you.

Unfortunately, we have decided to decline your format. Though your idea has an interesting format point, we feel it is not enough to create a full television programme around.

We would like to thank you for your interest in Format Development and wish you much luck in the future.

Yours sincerely,

Karen Murphy,
Format Entertainment Development Team

INVESTOR IN PEOPLE

Kirk Dunkirk
x x x x
Kochi City 780-x x x

Mitsukoshi, Ltd.
1-4-1 Nihonbashi Muromachi, Chuo-ku
Tokyo, 103-8001, Japan

March 19, 2007

Dear Mitsukoshi,

I don't like change. Who does? Nobody I know. Some folks say "Change is inevitable," or even "Change is good," but they're just trying to buck themselves up.

One of my friends dislikes change so much he tosses it over his shoulder and spits, if he's in a bad mood that is, which is most of the time because dealing with change puts him there. So I said to him "Jake, (not real name) you need some change in your life." Woo hoo, you should have seen the look on his face before he punched me!

Anyway, I have a suggestion for your shop that would make a lot of people happy.

When customers make a purchase, instead of handing them their change, which they DON'T want, how about giving them something they DO want? Since they are at your store they obviously want to buy goods you have for sale.

So instead of giving someone change, you should let them acquire an item or items equal in value to the leftover money. Tell them how much the change is, maybe give them a receipt or some round metal tokens with numbers to represent the value, and they can go back into to the store and exchange it for goods of their choice. If they're in a hurry they might even be able to keep the tokens for later use. A kind of abstract barter system.

I'm not complaining. I like your stores a lot. I often buy hats there. I just think that my humble suggestion would make shopping an even better experience. Don't you agree? Please write me back and let me know. Mr. Fantastico, the man who lives in my finger, thinks it's a great idea.

Sincerely,

MITSUKOSHI

MITSUKOSHI LTD.
4-1, NIHOMBASHI MUROMACHI 1 CHOME,
CHUO-KU, TOKYO-103-8001, JAPAN

September 4, 2007

Mr. Kirk Dunkirk

Thank you for the letter you sent us on the 27th of August.
After we received your letter on the 4th of September, our customer service looked over all the letters we have received in March, and in the months around the time.
Unfortunately, we could not find records of receiving your letter.

We are very sorry for the trouble, but could you kindly send again the first message you gave us in March?

We thank you again for your continuous support.

Sincerely,

Mariko Iwamoto.

Mariko IWAMOTO
Overseas Business Department
Planning and Organization
Departmentstore Business Headquarters
Mitsukoshi, Ltd.
1-4-1 Nihombashi Muromachi, Chuo-ku
Tokyo, 103-0081 JAPAN
Email: info@mitsukoshi.co.jp

from: Kirk Dunkirk <kirk@silicon_carne.com>
to: info@mitsukoshi.co.jp
date: Tue, Apr 3, 2012 at 11:49 AM
subject: Change is bad, attn. Iwamoto Mariko

Dear Ms. Iwamoto / Mitsukoshi,

This is a follow up to a letter I wrote in the Fall of 2007. I'm sorry for the delay but I was participating in a sleep study.
Let me just say that I never want to listen to REM again.

A dream I had and still have is a plan for Mitsukoshi that would radically cha-, um, alter the way we do business.

Everyone hates change. C'mon admit it, you do. So why not get rid of change?

When people buy something at your stores, instead of returning their change, you could give them small tokens that represent the value of their change.

Round chips made of metal could be used for the smaller amounts and ornate paper ones could represent larger amounts. These can then be used for future purchases at Mitsukoshi or other shops who participate. Pictures of past Mitsukoshi presidents or local heros and products could be printed on the tokens, with new ones coming out every year or so. Customers can be assured that the abstract chips actually represent true wealth such as gold or yams or chickens that can be redeemed if necessary. You could pay your suppliers and staff this way, maybe eventually get the whole nation, even the government on board using your system.

But people do hate change, so a clever campaign would help. How about "Change will never be the same again!" Write it in stone and have performers in Edo Period style or Tokyo Olympics Era costumes stand frozen in various parts of the store.

By the way, I bought a sweatshirt at Mitsukoshi but when I got home and opened the package, I noticed the sleeves and zipper and pockets - everything but the part that covers your head and collar bone - was missing. It is like a mock turtleneck but called a "false hood." Can I return it for cash or store credit? No coins. I don't want coins.

Now is the season when Japanese have to pack up their lives on 3 days notice and move to new jobs, often far away from home, so it's a good time to institute the program. Time's a wastin'! Let's get a move on Mitsukoshi. Giddyap. Yah!

Thank you very much.
Sincerely,

Kirk Dunkirk
Kochi City

* * * * *

from: Kirk Dunkirk <kirk@silicon_carne.com>
to: iclub@isetanmitsukoshi.co.jp
date: Fri, Apr 6, 2012 at 10:46 AM
subject: Waiting for reply

Hi,

I sent a mail three days ago offering some suggestions and asking about refunds but haven't heard back yet.
Is a reply forthcoming?

Thank you.
Kirk Dunkirk
Kochi City

* * * * *

from: iclub@isetanmitsukoshi.co.jp
to: Kirk Dunkirk <kirk@silicon_carne.com>
date: Fri, Apr 6, 2012 at 12:08 PM
subject: Re: Waiting for reply

Dear Mr. Kirk Dunkirk,

Thank you for your email.

As for your email, it has been transferred to Ms. Iwamoto Mariko.
We kindly ask for your patience for her response.

Thank you for your understanding.

Foreign Customer Service
****
I CLUB
Foreign Customer Service
Isetan Shinjuku
3-14-1 Shinjuku, Shinjuku-ku, Tokyo 160-0022
Tel: 03-3225-2514 Fax: 03-3225-2513
http://www.isetan.co.jp/iclub

* * * * *

from: Kirk Dunkirk <kirk@silicon_carne.com>
to: iclub@isetanmitsukoshi.co.jp
date: Fri, Apr 6, 2012 at 3:50 PM

subject: Re: Waiting for reply

Thank you very much. I addressed it to Ms. Iwamoto but really anyone is ok. It is of general interest.

Thank you again.

K. Dunkirk

* * * * *

from: Kirk Dunkirk <kirk@silicon_carne.com>
to: iclub@isetanmitsukoshi.co.jp
date: Fri, Apr 13, 2012 at 3:16 PM
subject: Re: Waiting for reply

It has been over ten days since I sent my original inquiry, and a week since I sent my follow-up inquiry. But still no reply from you. When can I get a reply? My knees hurt.

* * * * *

from: iclub@isetanmitsukoshi.co.jp
to: Kirk Dunkirk <kirk@silicon_carne.com>
date: Sun, Apr 15, 2012 at 4:23 PM
subject: Re: Waiting for reply

Dear Mr. Kirk,

We are sorry that Ms. Iwamoto Mariko did not reply to you.
We are not sure what kind of reply you are waiting.
If you are asking our suggestion regarding your sweatshirt,
you would need to contact the shop you purhased at, in this case,
Mitsukoshi Department Store, and show the receipt and the item.

Again, we are sorry that we cannot be of your help this time.

Best regards.
Foreign Customer Service
****
I CLUB
Foreign Customer Service
Isetan Shinjuku
3-14-1 Shinjuku, Shinjuku-ku, Tokyo 160-0022
Tel: 03-3225-2514 Fax: 03-3225-2513
http://www.isetan.co.jp/iclub
****

* * * * *

```
from: Kirk Dunkirk <kirk@silicon_carne.com>
to: iclub@isetanmitsukoshi.co.jp
date: Mon, Apr 16, 2012 at 12:40 AM
subject: Re: Waiting for reply
```

I see. Thank you very much. I appreciate your reply but do wish you had told me this sooner.

I will try to clear up the issue of the false hood directly myself.

Furthermore, have your bosses been informed of my suggestions regarding changing the change?

thank you.
Kirk

* * * *

```
from: iclub@isetanmitsukoshi.co.jp
to: Kirk Dunkirk <kirk@silicon_carne.com>
date: Mon, Apr 16, 2012 at 11:56 AM
subject: Re: Waiting for reply
```

Dear Kirk,

Thank you for your reply and sorry for our late response. Regarding your suggestion of changing the change, we have passed it onto another section as we are not in charge.

Thank you for your attention.

```
Regards
Foreign Customer Service
*************************************
I CLUB
Foreign Customer Service
Isetan Shinjuku
3-14-1 Shinjuku, Shinjuku-ku, Tokyo 160-0022
Tel: 03-3225-2514  Fax: 03-3225-2513
http://www.isetan.co.jp/iclub
*************************************
```

Left on virtual hold for two weeks, only to have the buck passed.
Who's the joke on now?
I got digital chump change. -KDK

Kirk Dunkirk
x x x x x x x
Kochi City 780-x x x

Aixia Corporation
Shibanichomedaimon Bldg 4f
Minato-Ku, Tokyo Japan

August 27, 2007

Dear Aixia,

I have a question regarding your Tsumemigaki cat scratch.

Overall, I'm satisfied with the construction of the product. The cardboard and matatabi-type catnip appear to be of the highest caliber.

My cat, Kilgore Trout, however, seems to think otherwise. In fact, he plum refuses to scratch, even though I never had him declawed like those hippie commie pinko asswipes down the road who'd prefer we all celebrated Kim Il-sung's birthday with lavish mass gymnastics want to do to this country and did to their poor animal.

I opened said cat scratch box according to the instructions on back. And I gave me cat the catnip and waited a minute for it to take effect. Then I pinned him down to the carpet with my knees, gently, and rubbed his front paws all up and down the box, like a cheese grater: back and forth in a firm shaking motion, just like I'd do to my own nails with an emory board. "How do you like that, Kilgore?" I yelled while a helicopter circled overhead.

But he didn't like it at all! He struggled and resisted, cried and twisted. I increased the dosage and sprinkled more catnip in his eyes and kept filing away but he flat out refused to cooperate. Even taping a sepia tone photo of Justin Timberlake to the top of the box just made poor Kilgore howl for his momma.

Am I doing something wrong? Please write back and let me know ASAP. His creepy long nails are giving me nightmares. Thanks.

Sincerely,

Kirk Dunkirk

平成19年9月7日

Dear　Kirk Dunkirk

アイシア株式会社

お客様センター
〒105-0014 東京都港区芝2-3-3
フリーダイヤル　0120-712-122

拝啓　時下益々ご清祥のこととお慶び申し上げます。
「つめみがき」についての、お手紙を拝読致しました。
弊社では、「つめみがき」を作っておりません。猫用・犬用のペットフードを製造販売しています。別の会社へお問い合わせをされてはいかがでしょうか。

敬具

Our company doesn't manufacture the "Tsumemigaki". Our company is making only the Cat food and Dog Food. You have sent a letter to making a mistake as another company.

Kirk Dunkirk
☠ ☠ ☠ ☠
Kochi City 780- x x x

Isuzu Motors
6-26-1 Minami-oi, Shinagawa-ku
Tokyo 140-8722   Jan. 23, 2008

Dear Isuzu,

It is a well established scientific fact that the Japanese appreciate nature more than other people do. Everybody knows this to be true, since Japanese have gardens, arrange flowers to look nice, and write poems about mountains and such, unlike most societies on Earth.

How I envy you. Every time I leave my tiny tin shack of a home I am bombarded by noise! Birds singing, frogs croaking, even water in a nearby stream gurgling over rocks drives me crazy. The only relief I can find is to put a on big pair of headphones and play loud pop music on my Sony Walkman as I move about.

The time I envy the Japanese most is in the summer. The humid, sweltering summer. All around me, even with the windows closed and the Toshiba A/C and Sharp Aquos TV on, I can still hear them: THE CICADAS *("semi" in Japanese.)* Aagh!

As a non-Japanese, the buzz of cicada and grasshoppers etc. is just plain irritating, but it's well documented that to Japanese ears, especially those that didn't study a foreign language as a child, it sounds like music.

But when I stop next to one of your large diesel trucks with its blinker on and an artificial female voice announces repeatedly *migi he magarimasu* ("I am turning right,") it sounds wonderful! It reminds me of the crowded, bustling streets of Memphis where I grew up.

Okay, that's the background. **My question for you, Isuzu Trucks, is this:** Do your truck announcements sound good to Japanese ears too, or are they processed in the same part of the brain that tunes out police sirens and right-wing bus parades?

<u>Please write back</u> and let me know. I'm an exchange student and hope to include this in my social studies senior thesis when I go back my country soon.

Sincerely,

ISUZU MOTORS LIMITED
Atsushi Sato
Customer Relations Dept.
6-26-1Minami-oi,Shinagawa-ku
Tokyo,140-8722

Mr. Kirk Dunkirk

Kochi City 780

Feb.16, 2008

Dear Sir,

The letter was read.
The answer of the received question.
At present, the device that raises an alarm when turning to the left and retreating by the sound installed in the manufactured vehicle has both of the vehicle with the device that originates the electronic sound caused by the vehicle with the device and the buzzer that informs of the direction in which the driver tries to go by a Japanese voice that exists in the letter and informs in our company.

Sincerely,

Atsuki Sato

Miki Dunkirk
x x x x x x
Kochi City 780- x x x
Japan

2008 22 January

H.W Naylor Co.
POBOX 190
Morris, NY 13808
USA

Dear Doctor Naylor

I recently buy your Doctor Hess udder Ointment at local boutique.

I am very happy because my skin become good. Softness and pliability is foregone conclusion.

But after the 5 weeks period of usage, enlargement of my breast area recognize ability is nothing.. The application of product is twice each daily. Morning and before asleep is.

Nipple (teat ok?) maybe become bit bigger. Recognize is uncertainty. But breast no. still small.

Sorry my poor English but please explain towards myself defective application procedure.

In your debt.

H. W. NAYLOR COMPANY, INC.

P.O. BOX 190 • MORRIS, NEW YORK 13808

MANUFACTURING CHEMISTS

Area Code 607
Telephone 263-5145
FAX 263-2416

February 12, 2008

Miki Dunkirk

Kochi City 780-
Japan

Dear Ms. Dunkirk,

Thank you for your recent letter. We were not aware that our product was being sold in Japan. Concerning your general comments, our product and label claims are for usage on animals. We are aware that people do use the product and that it does soften the skin, however we have no knowledge and cannot suggest that the product has any other properties.

Once again, thank you for using our product and should you have any other questions please feel free to contact us.

Sincerely,

David Lucas
President
lucas@drnaylor.com

DEPENDABLE VETERINARY PRODUCTS

Kirk Dunkirk
x x x x x
Kochi City 780- x x x

Ryohin Keikaku Co., Ltd.
4-26-3 Higashi-Ikebukuro
Toshima-ku, Tokyo 170-8424

Dec. 19, 2007

Dear Ryohin Keikaku aka "Muji",

I love your store and buy all my dog clothes there but I have to take issue with the boiled instant frogs' legs. Wouldn't it be more humane to keep them in a large clear acrylic tank in the front of the store instead? That way they wouldn't be so bored and could greet (s)hoppers as they entered.

BUT the REAL REASON I am writing this LETTER is because your CEO, Matsui Tadamitsu, aka "Mr. Muji", has stopped sending me either Xmas or New Year's cards (*nengajou* in Japanese). I met him once at a yattai a couple years back, had a few beers and gyoza together, and ever since then he's been sending me cards.

But last year I didn't get one, so I just wanted to remind him and the rest of the team not to forget me. He's not mad is he?

I really need that card! I look forward to it all year.

Thank you and happy holidays.

ps. At the annual Muji employee softball game does Mr. Matsui wear No. 55, 2 or 7? He won't tell me.

Kirk Dunkirk
x x x x
Kochi City
780- x x x

Nescafe Japan
NESTLE HOUSE
7-1-15, Gokodori,Chuo-ku
Kobe, Japan
651-0087

March 13, 2008

Dear Nescafe Japan,

You make many fine, coffee-flavor inspired products.

About your "Single Bean" can coffee though: how do you get so much coffee from a single bean?

Thank you.
Sincerely,

Kirk Dunkirk

Dear, Mr. / Ms Kirk Dunkirk

We thank you for contacting us concerning NESCAFE SINGLE BEAN.

We selected a single bean with enough amount to our production.

We would like to express our sincere gratitude for your using Nestle products, at the same time we hope that you will continue to extend your kind patronage to our products in the future.

Sincerely yours,

Consumer Hot Lines Section

Nestle Japan Group

〒651-0087

Toll-Free-Dial 0120-00-5916

(Open weekdays from 10:00 - 17:00)

http://www.nestle.co.jp/

mail: Consumer.Services@jp.nestle.com

Kirk Dunkirk
x x x x x
Kochi City 780- x x x

Ryohin Keikaku Co., Ltd.
4-26-3 Higashi-Ikebukuro
Toshima-ku, Tokyo 170-8424

March 5, 2008

Dear Ryohin Keikaku aka "Mujirushi",

I sent a letter regarding product placement and New Year's cards dated December 19, 2007 but have not yet received a reply. That was almost three months ago. It was last year, even.

Won't you be so kind as to address my concerns as a customer?

Thank you and be spring.

Dear Kirk,

Thank you for your letter.
Please accept our apologies for delay in replying to you.

First of all, we inform you that we did not receive your letter last year.
Therefore, this is the first time that we received a letter from you.
Could you send us your plan of the product placement again?
If you could send an email, you could email us to the following address:
call3@muji.co.jp

Thank you again for your interest in MUJI.

Best regards,

Customer Relations Office
Ryohin Keikaku Co., Ltd.

Mar./21/2008

4-26-3, Higashi-Ikebukuro,
Toshima-ku, Tokyo, 170-8424

Kirk Dunkirk
x x x x x
Kochi City 780- x x x

Ryohin Keikaku Co., Ltd.
4-26-3 Higashi-Ikebukuro
Toshima-ku, Tokyo 170-8424

March 31, 2008

Dear Ryohin Keikaku, aka "MUJI", Customer Relations Office,

This is my reply to your reply to my letter asking why you Hadn't replied to my original letter from December of last year. I'm sorry I didn't make myself clear before. I always strive for clarity TKLF.

My product placement idea was in Regard to where you keep the frogs. I suggest putting them In a large tank at the entrance, much like in a seafood Restaurant, where customers can pick out the cute ones they want to eat.

In addition, this is the first year I didn't Receive a New Year's Card from CEO Matsui. Is he ok?

Thank you for your time.
Sincerely,

Kirk Dunkirk

Dear Kirk,

Thank you for your letter again.
Please accept for our apologies for the delay in replying to you.

Thank you very much for sending us your idea of product placement.
We regard it as a precious opinion and think it may be an opportunity
to have a better operation for MUJI in the future.
Thank you very much for your kind attention to us.

On final note, we inform you that Mr matsui is fine
but he is very busy in his tight schedule nowadays.

Again, we apology for the delayed reply to you.

Thank you very much and best regards,

Customer Relations Office
Ryohin Keikaku Co., Ltd.

Apr./23/2008

4-26-3, Higashi-Ikebukuro,
Toshima-ku, Tokyo, 170-8424

Kirk Dunkirk
X X X X X
Kochi City 780- X X X
Japan

Hoshino Gakki aka Ibanez Guitars
3-22 Shumoku-cho, Higashi-ku
Nagoya, 461-8717   Jan 15, 2008

Dear Hoshino Gakki,

First of all, I was pretty surprised to hear that Ibanez guitars are a Japanese company. Seems kind of sneaky to me, like the way you guys made Toyotas seem German when you introduced Lexus in the late 80's. But, just as Lexi are great cars, Ibani are equally great guitars.

One of my (Japanese) friends, named Isabel (just kidding) recently visited Paris. She was shocked that the taxi driver tried to overcharge her a few euros because she is Japanese and we all know how cultured and refined every single French person on the planet is. She went on to explain how such a thing is unheard of in Japan. This is from someone who had willingly paid the several thousand yen fee for the Japanese tour operator to "process" her passport.

So I told her about my Ibanez guitar. It has a spanish name and was made in China by a Japanese company. Fair enough. I found a great deal on it from a shop in the US but you guys won't permit them to ship to Japan because the US price is that much lower. So I had them ship to my friend in the States who then sent it to me in Japan. So there you have it: a Japanese guitar along with case and heavy amp is cheaper to have shipped from China to the US then to another private residence then back here secretly in order to keep prices high in Japan.

What I'm getting at is this: Japanese don't need to go abroad in order to get reamed. I mean, what did the tour to France cost?

You might not agree with me but the least you could do is ask the following question to your president Toshitsugu Tanaka: *Hey Toshi, where the heck is my New Year's card? You've been sending me them for several year's now but why did you stop? Am I off the list? Are you still angry about the girl in the park? C'mon buddy, don't be sore.*

Thank you and <u>please write back soon</u>. I want to put this year's New Year's card collection away ASAP and get ready for Valentine's.

Kirk Dunkirk

HOSHINO GAKKI CO., LTD.
NO.22, 3-CHOME, SHUMOKU-CHO, HIGASHI-KU, NAGOYA, 461-91, JAPAN
TELEPHONE: 052-931-0381   FACSIMILE: 052-932-2684

April 4, 2008.

Mr. Kirk Dunkirk
▓▓▓▓▓▓▓▓▓▓▓▓▓▓▓▓
Kochi City 780-▓▓▓▓▓▓▓▓

Dear Mr. Dunkirk,

We thank you very much for your letter dated March 31, 2008.

My name is Kuniko Mori and I'm a staff of overseas sales department of Hoshino Gakki Co., Ltd.

Unfortunately we haven't received your letter dated January 15, 2008, and we don't know the contents of that letter. So we are very sorry to bother you, but if you don't mind, could you kindly let us know the contents of that letter by e-mail to my following address in order to reply to you?

   kmori@hoshinogakki.co.jp

Your kind cooperation is highly appreciated.

Thanks in advance for your kind attention.

Very truly yours,

HOSHINO GAKKI CO., LTD.

[signature]

Kuniko Mori

Kirk Dunkirk
x x x x x
Kochi City 780- xxx
Japan

Kuniko Mori
Overseas Sales Dep't
Hoshino Gakki aka Ibanez Guitars
3-22 Shumoku-cho, Higashi-ku
Nagoya, 461-8717

April 7, 2008

Dear Ms. Mori,

I'm sorry this reply is not sent by e-mail as you requested but I always follow my grandfather's advice who warned me of all the trouble it caused back in the Old Country. Rest his Luddite soul.

Regarding my January 15 letter, I had three points.

1. Why the name Ibanez? It's not very Japanese. It seems sneaky to me. I felt tricked after I bought my new guitar. Imagine buying a German Shepherd only to learn later that it's a French Poodle.

2. Shipping. It was cheaper for me to buy an Ibanez guitar from a shop in the United States and have it shipped to Japan. The shop couldn't ship to Japan though, because of Ibanez rules, so I had it shipped to a friend in America who then shipped it to Japan.

Thus it was cheaper for me to buy a guitar (and amp!) that had been made in China, shipped to the USA, shipped to my friend's house, then shipped back to Japan -- cheaper than if I bought an Ibanez guitar here in Japan. Why? Please don't say it's because you have an agreement with Ibanez USA or something. My question would then be why do you have such a rule?

Regardless of the explanation, please keep this example in mind next time you travel abroad and think "How unfair of these foreign taxi drivers to try and overcharge me! This would never happen back home."

3. I'm still waiting for CEO Toshitsugu Tanaka's Christmas or New Year's card. He's not still upset about the girl in the park, is he?

That's about it. If you would like, I can send a copy of the Jan. 15 letter next time, or a picture of my guitar or something. You sound kind of cute, maybe we could become pen pals, if that's ok with your boss.

Sincerely,
Kirk Dunkirk

```
from: kirk dunkirk <kirk@shaman-you.com>
to: Kuniko Mori <kmori@hoshinogakki.co.jp>
date: Tue, Apr 3, 2012 at 10:35 AM
subject: Re: Old Letter
```

Dear Ms. Mori,

Thank you very much for your quick reply, cutie.

An acquaintance of mine was complaining about how a taxi driver in Paris tried to rip her off and how such a thing would never occur in Japan because it is an island nation.

So I related an anecdote about my purchase of an Ibanez guitar. It was cheaper for me to buy the Japanese electric guitar and heavy amp with a spanish name that was made in China and shipped to a music shop in the USA then to a friend in the US then back across the ocean to Japan than to buy from a shop, online even, in Japan.

It would have been cheaper still to buy the guitar from the American shop and have it shipped directly back to Japan, but the shop had an agreement with Ibanez not to do that in order to prop up prices in Japan. I'm ok with the practice, lots of companies and not just Japanese ones do it, from National Geographic to snowboard maker Burton. In fact I wholeheartedly encourage the process as it keeps our streets clean and a small part of the tax revenue it generates is diverted to fund my Nasal Academy.

My acquaintance however refused to believe that such policies even exist and that I must have misunderstood my exchange with the US guitar shop due to language differences (?!) and my lack of familiarity with Japanese culture. Then she finished her chocolate covered potato chips and went to play Hello Kitty pachinko across the street.

I was wondering if Ibanez could clear this up. Is it necessary to leave the country to get price gouged? And why the sneaky Spanish names?

Sincerely
Kirk Dunkirk
Kochi City

```
From: Kuniko Mori <kmori@hoshinogakki.co.jp>
Date: Wed, Apr 4, 2012 at 7:28 PM
Subject: Re: Old Letter
To: kirk dunkirk <kirk@shaman-you.com>
Cc: Jun Hosokawa <hosokawa@hoshinogakki.co.jp>
```

Dear Mr. Dunkirk,

Thank you for your e-mail.

We have the distributors in each area/country, and each distributors have their own territory that only they can distribute. Under this system, it is not allowed to sell the products beyond their own territory. So the products distributed by the distributor in USA is available only in USA...

This way of distribution is common in the business of musical instruments.

Your kind understanding would be highly appreciated.

Thank you very much for your inquiry.

Best regards

Hoshino Gakki Co., Ltd.
Kuniko Mori

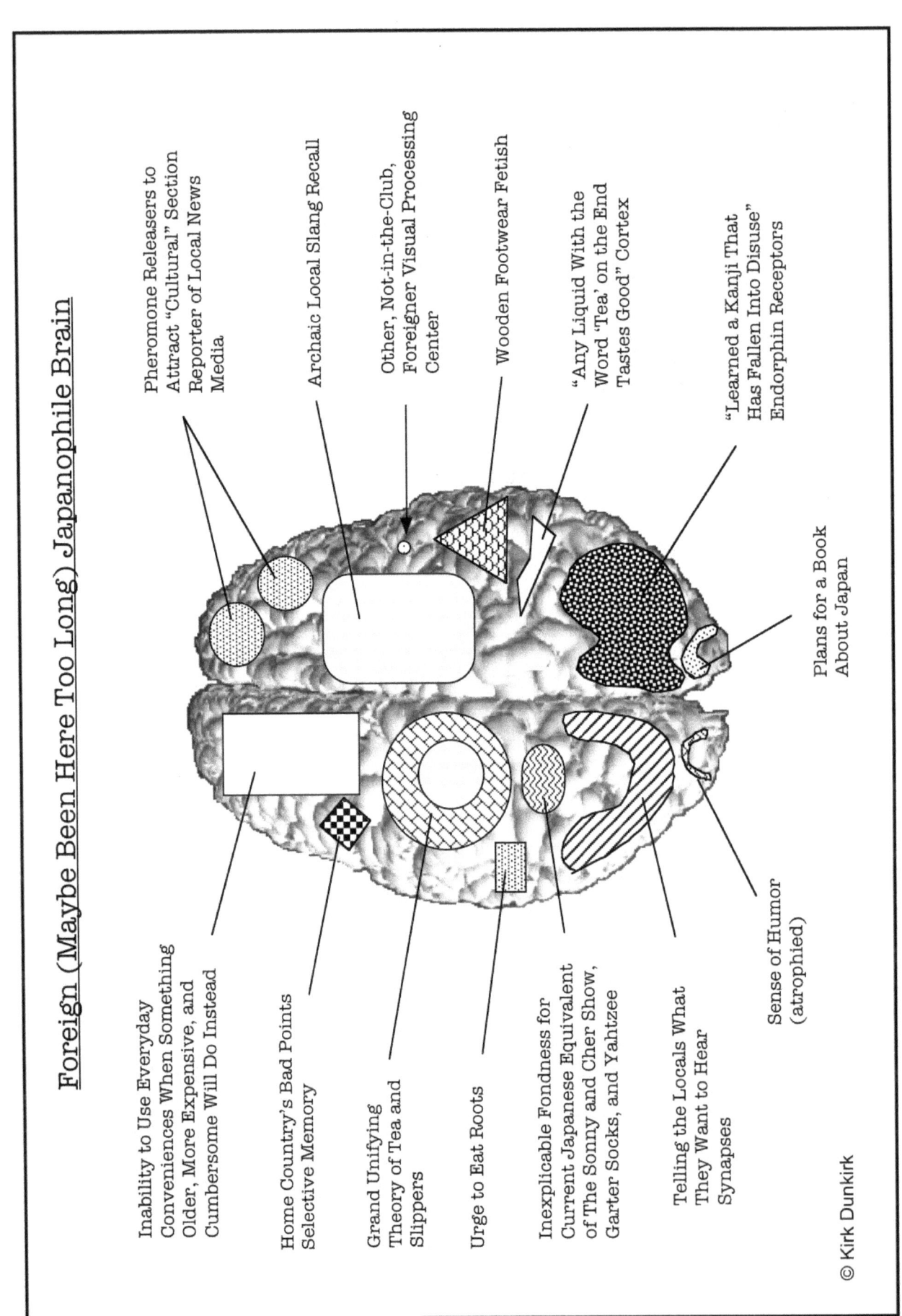

Kirk Dunkirk
x x x x x
Kochi City 780- x x x
Japan

Asahi Keisei Co., Ltd.
1-1-2, Yuraku-cho
Chiyoda-ku, Tokyo 100-8440

Jan 23, 2008

Dear Asahi Keisei,

I tip my hat to you for the amazing variety of products you make: flat panel LCD screens, beer, newspapers, even apartment hotels.

I myself am a simple pomegranate farmer, but I use your products all the time. My life is better thanks to you. Kudos maximundos as we PF's like to say.

This letter, however, is about business. I would like to buy between 317 and 441 kilograms (699 - 972 lbs.) of your soda ash to put in my pomegranate orchard, specifically Mitsuya Cider ash as I believe its melony aftertaste would best suit the type of fruit I cultivate. Other Asahi soft drink soda ash might work too. I am eager to grow and sell my own soda, as the profit margins are much higher than for plain old fruit.

This could be win-win for both of us since I imagine you normally just throw away the leftover soda ash. Dumping it into rivers or shipping it to China must cost money. I can even come pick it up myself with my Bongo van if you have factories in the Kansai area, or shipping it by boat to the New Port of Kochi is another option. My close friends consider me proactive in these matters.

Please write me back at your convenience.

Thank you for your time. I eagerly await your reply.

AGC

May 23, 2008
1-12-1, Yuraku-cho
Chiyoda-ku, Tokyo 100-8405

Mr. Kirk Dunkirk
████████
Kochi City, Kochi Pref 780-████

Dear Mr. Kirk Dunkirk,

Thank you for sending your mail, and I'm so sorry that our replying so late. My name is Akira Muraisi. I was in charge of Soda Ash in ACG chemicals company. Because we haven't been able to find the letter that you sent in January, we haven't replied it. Please forgive our late response.

About your inquiring of purchasing Soda Ash from our company, unfortunately we have to say we cannot supply it. We already have terminated our sales business of Soda Ash in Japan from May in 2005. Our company transferred it to another company, "SODA ASH JAPAN Co., Ltd." in Tokyo.

I'm sorry but if you can, please inquire again to her.

"SODA ASH JAPAN Co., Ltd."
Harumi-Islanmd-Triton Square Office Tower "Z"
1-8-12, Harumi, Chuo-ku, Tokyo 104-6221
tel; +81-3-6219-7531 facsimile;+81-3-6219-7520
URL; http://www.s-a-j.com/

Best Regars,

akira muraishi

Akira Muraisi
Supply Chain Management Group
Operation Controlling Office
Chemicals Company
Asahi Glass co.,ltd.
Phone) +81-3-3218-5537
Facsimile) +81-3-3218-7845

mailto:akira-muraisi@agc.co.jp

ASAHI GLASS CO., LTD.   Shinyurakucho Bldg., 1-12-1 Yurakucho Chiyoda-ku, Tokyo 100-8405 JAPAN   http://www.agc.co.jp/

Kirk Dunkirk
X X X ✏ X ✏ X
Kochi City 780 ✏X ✏ X ✏
Japan

北星鉛筆株式会社　　　　　Kita-Boshi Pencil Co.
〒 124 - 0011　　　　　　　1-23-11 Yotsugi Katsushika-ku
東京都葛飾区四つ木 1-23-11　　Tokyo　124-0011, Japan

March 25, 2008

Dear Kita-Boshi,

Your sales reps have a reputation for bragging after a few drinks about how you make the best damn wooden pencils in the world. As an American I admire their swagger and overconfidence, which in turn has led me to consider making Kita-Boshi my official wooden pencil.

I don't take such decisions lightly, especially about a company that would name itself "North Hat" and then go on to make wooden pencils, no matter how damn good they are. You should have seen the grilling I put TAG Heuer through.

So what exactly about your wooden pencils makes them so special? They are just dead trees with dyed cat guts squeezed into the middle, after all.

I appreciate your cooperation in this endeavor and eagerly await your reply.
Sincerely,

Kirk Dunkirk

KITABOSHI PENCIL CO., LTD.
NO.23-11, 1-CHOME, YOTSUGI, KATSUSHIKA-KU,
TOKYO 124-0011 JAPAN
TEL: 03-3693-0778   FAX: 03-3693-0817
E-mail: purchasing@kitaboshi.co.jp   URL: http://www.kitaboshi.co.jp

To:
Mr. Kirk Dunkirk
█████████
█████████ Japan

June 16, 2008

Dear Mr. Dunkirk,

Thank you very much for your letter dated June 11, 2008.

I am very sorry that I had not received your letter dated March 25, 2008, due to some mistake in our company. In order to avoid same mistake, please kindly contact me directly because nobody can understand English in our company, except me. And if possible, I would like you to contact me with E-mail or Facsimile, mailto: purchasing@kitaboshi.co.jp Fax: 03-3693-0817, because I can also speak English only a little.

Your cooperation and understanding would be very much appreciated.

Best regards,

[signature]

Hide Sugitani, Purchasing Manager
Kitaboshi Pencil Co., Ltd.

Kirk Dunkirk
x x x x x x x x
Kochi City 780- x x x
Japan

Mizuho Bank, Ltd.
1-1-5, Uchisaiwaicho
Chiyoda-ku, Tokyo 100-0011, Japan

June 11, 2008

To Whom it May Concern,

I read with great trepidation your foray into the vaunted depths of ersatz ego gratification.

Such histrionics notwithstanding, collective wisdom as such would preclude haughty ecumenicism ipso facto: hence, the departed. Kudos abound, such as we must, with nary the acclaimed pedantic underscoring this lapse.

To wit: fourteen yet or confidence beyond? Either way musters the zero sum game. The essence of nil, a virtual financial moebius strip. But what of the Rick?

Indeed, what of the Rick? Inaction eschews such joy as it were, the paradigm sadly calculated to rattle and harrow. Cruel is the morn of base instinct, for were it not from whence all lustre passes, the marveled gate of epiphany.

Furthermore, best of luck! This is great news. If I may be of any assistance let me know. And <u>please write back ASAP</u> about the new shareholder policy in question, regarding hostile acquisitions.

I look forward to hearing from you.
Sincerely,

Kirk Dunkirk

Kirk Dunkirk
🖝 ♥ ♥ 🖜
Kochi City 780- ☁ ☁ ☁ ☁
Japan

Dite de Shopping
〒603-8402　京都市北区大宮南椿原町35-4
35-4 Minami Tsubakihara-cho, Ohmiya
Kita-ku, Kyoto
Japan

Jan. 7, 2009

Dear Dite de Shopping,

Man am I scared!

I recently ate a whole box of your "F-cup Cookies", the ones that make your breasts grow larger. After my girlfriend and I broke up, I was stressed and turned to sweets for comfort, as I am trying to quit smoking. (You don't have products for that, do you? Ha ha. Cough. Ha.)

I found that comfort in a plain container of cookies she had left here and ate the whole bunch, about two dozen, in three days, along with several tubs of ice cream and bean pies. Later while I was burning her belongings I found the original package for your breast enlargement cookies. – She must have switched them into the tupperware out of embarrassment.

I don't know why she was eating breast enlargement cookies. Her breasts were pretty good, I'd say in the Top 5 of girls I've been with lately, but maybe that's the result of your cookies, and if so, good job! No, they are certainly not the reason we broke up. That was her rear end. Way too small. Got enlargement products for that? Might be a hard sell, I see your point, as good ol' chocolate and the sofa usually works wonders in that department. Ironically, since we broke up, that's probably what she's doing right now! Maybe I should call her.

Anyway, am I gonna be ok? Will my breasts get big and how long will they stay that way? I'm an English conversation teacher so my employability rests mostly on my boyish good looks. So far, no noticeable effect on the breasts, but may be too early to tell. Worryingly though, I get sudden urges to buy shoes and haven't been able to park properly.

Thanks for your help. I need it!

Dear Kirk Dunkirk,

We see your letter.
I am Mizuho Higashimoto of dite de shopping for service center.

Now, let's answer your question.

There is an element that can be expected that the bigger breasts "Pueraria Mirifica" has been mixed in F-cup cookies. "Pueraria Mirifica" comes from cone of Thailand.

This is an element that promote ESUTOROGENHORUMON. If a man eat the F-cup cookies, that element won't effcet. So don't worried.

If you have bigger breasts, it is a temporary phenomenon, you will return to the original in about a week.

Here is the detail of Pueraria Mirifica.

Knowledge for Pueraria mirifica in F cup products
http://www.dite.co.jp/shop/eng/pueraria.shtml

Thank you very much.
Sincerely,

Dite Customer: Mizuho Higashimoto
Address: 35-4 Minami Tsubakihara-cho Ohmiya Kita-ku, Kyoto 603-8402
JAPAN
International call: +81-75-495-3581
FAX number: +81-75-495-3581
E-mail: shop@dite.co.jp
URL: http://www.dite.co.jp/shop/eng/

Kirk Dunkirk 様

お手紙拝見いたしました。
ディーテdeショッピングお客様相談室の東本と申します。

貴方のご質問に対し、回答させていただきます。

F cup クッキーには、バストが大きくなることが期待できる成分であるタイ国のイモである「プエラリアミリフィカ (Pueraria Mirifica)」が配合されています。

この成分は、女性特有のホルモンを促すものですから、男性が食べてもバストが大きくなる効果は期待できません。ですから、心配されることはありません。

もし、一時的にバストが大きくなっても、それは一時的なものであり1週間ほどで元に戻ります。

「プエラリアミリフィカ (Pueraria Mirifica)」の詳細は次をご覧ください。

Knowledge for Pueraria mirifica in F cup products
http://www.dite.co.jp/shop/eng/pueraria.shtml

ご相談ありがとうございました。

★:*:。☆彡.:*:・★━━━━━━━━━━
☆ ディーテ お客様相談室
〒603-8402　京都府京都市北区大宮南椿原町３５－４
Tel : 075-495-3581
Web: http://www.dite.co.jp/shop/
Email: shop@dite.co.jp
━━━━━━━━━━━━━━━━★:*:。☆彡.:*:・★

Kirk Dunkirk
f f f f f
Kochi City 780- F F F
Japan

Dite de Shopping
〒603-8402　京都市北区大宮南椿原町35-4
35-4 Minami Tsubakihara-cho, Ohmiya
Kita-ku, Kyoto
Japan

Jan. 23, 2009

Dear Ms. Higashimoto,

Thank you so much for your fast and kind explanation about my problem.

I feel very relieved. I am already driving better and can understand sports. You sound cute. Are you single?

Thank you again!

Kirk Dunkirk

Kirk Dunkirk
☼ ☼ ☼ ☼
Kochi City 780- ✹ ✹ ✹
Japan

BASF Japan Agro
Roppongi 25 Mori Bldg., 23F
1-4-30, Roppongi
Minato-ku, Tokyo 106-0032

Aprrrril. 8, 2010

Dear BASF Agro,

Why are you guys so agro!? Grrr! Is it all the killer chemicals you merchants of tense sell to the highest bidder? Herbicide, fungicide, insecticide... the list goes on. What's next? Can't decide? Step aside.

Whose side are you on anyway? Isn't there enough aggression in the world already without you profiting from it? Why don't you make some refrigeration chemicals and chill out man? I wish B-A-S-F would make a new division of P-A-X. Now THAT'S something worth getting worked up about!

I've written a bunch of letters and they keep getting sent back to me "undeliverable."

I can't relax until I hear back from you!!
Sincerely in Your Face,

Kirk "Lima Beans and Corn" Dunkirk

** Argh! No reply. **

Kirk Dunkirk
x x x x x
Kochi City 780- x x x x
Japan

Mizuho Bank
1-1-5 Uchisaiwaicho
Chiyoda-ku, Tokyo
100-0011, Japan

April 8, 2010

Dear Mizuho (aka Bank 0001),

I recently visited my local branch of your bank, just to say hi and transfer some money to Nigeria, but Mizuho wasn't there! Instead I had to deal with a young woman named Chika posing as a bank clerk.

What have you done with Mizuho? Where has she gone? Nigeria perhaps? That would be the logical conclusion as she always had a knack for perceiving what I wanted before I even asked.

No one could explain what had happened to her and the surly manager eventually suggested I write the head office. What's going on here? Have you merged with a bank named Chika? It's suspicious and possibly unconstitutional.

Please allay my fears on this matter.
I miss Ms. Mizuho.

Sincerely,

ps. Any word yet on my suggestion about "F-Word Fridays?"

No reply from Mizuho.
Feeling Unloved.

Kirk Dunkirk
x x x x x x
Kochi City 780- x x x
Japan

Ezaki Glico Co., Ltd.
4-16-23 Shibaura
Minato-ku, Tokyo 108-0023
Japan

April 21, 2010

Dear Glico Consumer Safety Department,

The other day I was riding my bicycle towards a busy intersection while nibbling on some of your scrumptious Salad Pretz salty snack sticks.

After years of observation and careful consideration, I have concluded that people who prefer Roast Pretz can't be trusted, while those in the Butter Pretz camp are a pack of incestuous baboons. As long as they keep their paws off of my snacks, we're ok.

Anyway, I thought I could coast through the yellow light and in front of the advancing streetcar with ease, but the signal changed red sooner than I expected. Since I was checking email on my cell phone with the other hand, I was unable to grab the manually actuated braking activator device in time. Rather than ride into a busy intersection with cars and a train, I chose instead to "wipe out," as it were.

I suffered bad scrapes and bruises on my legs and arms of course. That could not be helped. Yet were it not for the divine intervention of my guardian angel, Sariel, one of your Salad pretz sticks would have poked my eye out!

I strongly recommend you think of ways to make your stick snacks less dangerous to customers' eyes. Since they are so-called pretzels, you could try actually making them pretzel shaped. That would be a start. Also, a change of ingredients, so less salt gets into the wound.

Sincerely,

Kirk Dunkirk
(and Sariel. Forever over my shoulder, guide me, protect me, correct me.)

ps. Your TV jingles always say "gu-li-ka" but your name is clearly "gu-li-**ko**"

Glico

April 28, 2010

Mr. Kirk Dunkirk
Kochi City,
780-

Masoto Shimizu
Consumer Services Office
Ezaki Glico Co., Ltd.
TEL 0120-917-111

Dear Mr. Dunkirk
Thank you very much for writing a letter to us the other day.
We also appreciate you are enjoying our products, particularly our "Salad Pretz"

You mentioned that when you were riding your bicycle with our "Salad Pretz" nibbling, you got an accident with your legs and arms badly scraped and bruised, also Pretz stick would have cut into your eyes.
We first sincerely apologize our product might have caused you any inconvenience and any displeased feelings. We also express sympathy to your injuries and hope you get well soon.

We have always been very careful about our product quality and each phase of manufacturing process, so that customers always feel assured and enjoy our products. However, taking this opportunity that Mr. Kirk Dunkirk wrote to us, We would like to further study how we will get customers' continuously safe and comfortable patronage.

If you have any other finding or opinion to us or our product, please do not hesitate to write to and tell us. We also look forward to your continuous patronage to us.

Thank you very much once again.

Masato Shimizu

Kirk Dunkirk
x x x x x x x
Kochi City 780- x x x
Japan

Mizuho Bank
1-1-5 Uchisaiwaicho
Chiyoda-ku, Tokyo
100-0011, Japan

July 28, 2010

Dear Mizuho (aka Bank 0001),

It has been almost four months since I inqvired about the suspicious disappearance of my local Mizuho but have yet to hear back from your Damage Control department.

But the other day I ran into her, or at least someone who claimed to be her, at the video rental shop. When I told her my suspicions she started acting funny and hurriedly took her children away to the animation section. Have you threatened her into silence? She used to be so friendly to me when she sat behind the thick safety glass at the Kochi branch.

Then I noticed that her twins looked exactly alike and very similar to her, and if you put that together with a chain of Mizuhos all over the country and what have you got? A clone bank.

Just putting my two cents in but I think it's a bad idea. Once you factor in the costs of raising them, clones are no cheaper than naturally bred humans. But I admit, my opinion isn't worth much. That and a dime will get you a phone call. Besides, Chika is hotter.

Still Waiting,

Kirk Dunkirk

Kirk Dunkirk
A-Ok Research Institute
☁ ☁ ☁ ☁ ☁ ☁
x x x x x
Kochi City 〒780- x x x

Ministry of Economy, Trade and Industry (METI)
1-3-1 Kasumigaseki
Chiyoda-ku, Tokyo 100-8901   ~~August 18, 2010~~   Nov. 1, 2010

Dear METI,

I love the work you do, especially your early 80's stuff. I hope you weren't too discouraged by the massive failure of the Fifth Generation Computer Project. Let's face it: there was plenty of disappointment to go around in the 80's.

However I must take issue with your assessment of the future of "cloud computing" that I read in today's Mainichi Daily News, particularly the spurious claims that it will reduce the nation's greenhouse gasses.

How is this possible? Simply moving CO_2 numbers off the Japanese mainland and into the clouds is a cynical accounting trick. Or is it because these futuristic cloud computers will be powered by self-created thunderstorms? I think your computer models used dubious assumptions - for example, we don't know if the increased cloud cover will have a cooling effect by blocking more sunlight, or a warming effect by trapping in more heat.

Granted, the clouds' proximity to satellites might speed up data transmission, boosting efficiency, but this increased bandwidth will simply be filled immediately by horny young men texting for girls or watching porn when they can't get any.

This is pretty basic stuff, so your optimistic predictions worry me that as a government organization, your scientific integrity has been compromised by political considerations. Or perhaps a newly promoted policy maker is trying to relive his massively parallel glory days of two decades ago?

I don't mean to criticize. In fact, I hope I am wrong! It is thanks to you that every day my life in Japan is filled with fuzzy logic. But as a fellow researcher I feel a kinship and therefore an obligation to advise that you've gone astray.

If you could please respond it would greatly aid a project I am working on.
Sincerely,

Kirk Dunkirk

ps. This is my SECOND LETTER. It's been OVER TWO MONTHS. Won't you please reply?

(A third try even but METI never replied.)

Kirk Dunkirk
Chobitto Japan Seeing Eye Dogs
¥¥¥¥¥¥
Kochi City 780-¥7-11

Ito-Yokado
Okayama City, Kita-ku
Shimoishii 2-10-2
700-0907   April 22, 2011

Dear Ito-Yokado,

Sadly, we have only AEON superstores in my area, but I am fortunate enough to be visiting the Chugoku region soon, where Ito-Yokado superstores abound. I can't wait to try on the new squid slippers!

Before a big trip, especially one involving rail travel, I often have premonitions. Lately I keep experiencing a recurring dream where a giant shape-shifting lizard from the Thuban system, named MEGASTOR and protected by chain mail, wreaks havoc on the small city where I live, crushing the downtown and spewing noxious garbage that turns everyone into faceless shopping zombies.

It sounds silly, but dreams are like that. Besides, I sense that the dream is a symbolic warning projected into my unconscious by my third-all-seeing-eye dog, Cupcake. She guides me fearlessly on the astral plane, but will she be allowed in your stores? I know your 7-11 subsidiary allows guide dogs in the convenience stores, but please tell me your policy regarding the Ito-Yokado big box shops.

Cupcake is sweet and well-mannered and specially trained to be patient around humanoid children. In fact, her enlightened aura might help you resolve the recent tainted eel relabeling scandal. Can I bring her? Huh, can I? I promise to be good.

Sincerely,
Kirk Dunkirk

Kirk　Dunkirk 様へ

この度はお手紙ありがとうございます。
そしてお返事が遅くなり、申し訳ございません。

当店は盲導犬を同伴してのお買物をしていただいても
大丈夫なお店ですので、安心してお越し下さいませ。

お客様のお越しを従業員一同心よりお待ち申し上げて
おります。

イトーヨーカドー　岡山店

To Kirk Dunkirk

Thank you for the letter for this time.
I am sorry for the delay in answering and.

Relieve because our shop is a safe shop even if
shopping that goes with the guide dog is done.

The employee everyone is waiting sincerely for customer's
coming.

Ito Yokado Okayama branch

COSTCO WHOLESALE JAPAN LTD.   3-1-4 Ikegami-Shincho, Kawasaki-ku, Kawasaki-shi, Kanagawa 210-0832
コストコ ホールセール ジャパン株式会社   210-0832 神奈川県川崎市川崎区池上新町3-1-4

Dear Mr. Kirk Dunkirk

Thank you very much for the inquiry and we sincerely apologize for our late reply.

It is more than welcome to bring your seeing-eye dogs to our warehouse.

Thank you again and we look forward to your visit.

Costco information

With Compliments

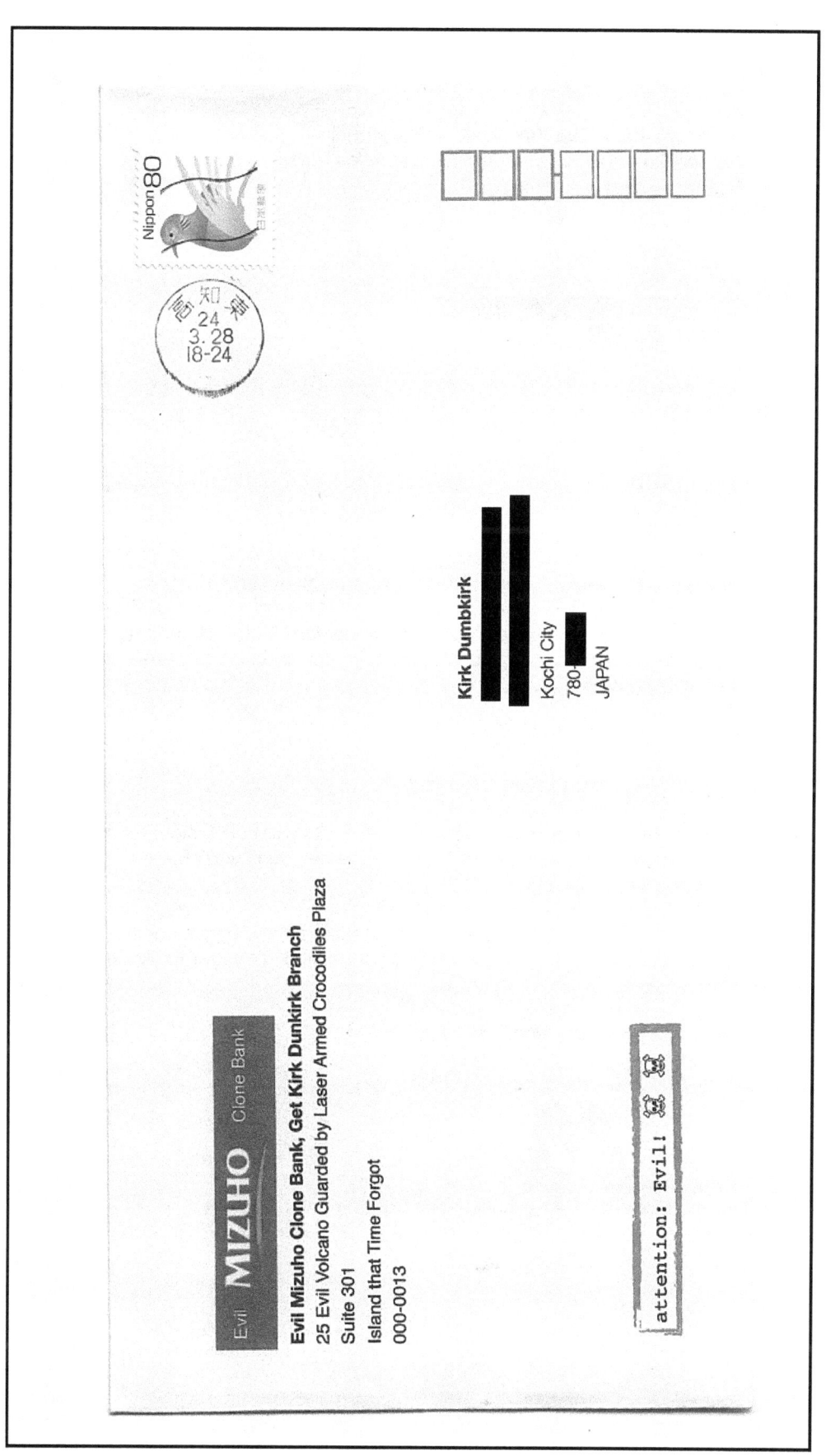

Evil Mizuho Clone Bank, Get Kirk Dunkirk Branch
25 Evil Volcano Guarded by Laser Armed Crocodiles Plaza, Suite 301
Island that Time Forgot
000-0013

Kirk Dunkirk
████████████████████████
Kochi City, 780 - ███

March 27, 2012

Dear Kirk Dunkirk,

Or should I say **dumb**-kirk?

Drat! Why are you trying to interfere with our dastardly plans again?

You know very well that there is nothing that you and your Atomic Smartypants can do to stop our takeover of the world… our clones have already infiltrated every fire department on the planet.

HA HA HA HA HA HA HA HA HA

But maybe it's not too late to save Ms. Mizuho!

Is she your *girrrrl-friend*? Oooh, Kirk has a girlfriend! *Do you LOVE her?* You want to kiss her? On the lips? I bet you want to touch her heiney don't you? Maybe I'll touch her heiney when she's not looking.

If you ever want to see Miss Mizuho and her touchable behind again, come to our Secret Space Station X **ALONE** and turn over the keys for your Atomic Smartypants. And don't try anything stupid, Dumb-kirk!

She might live, but you sure wont! HA HA HA HA HA

F-word Friday will soon stand for FICTORY!

Sincerely,

Doctor Mysterio
Evil Plans and Mortgage Backed Securities Department
Mizuho Bank

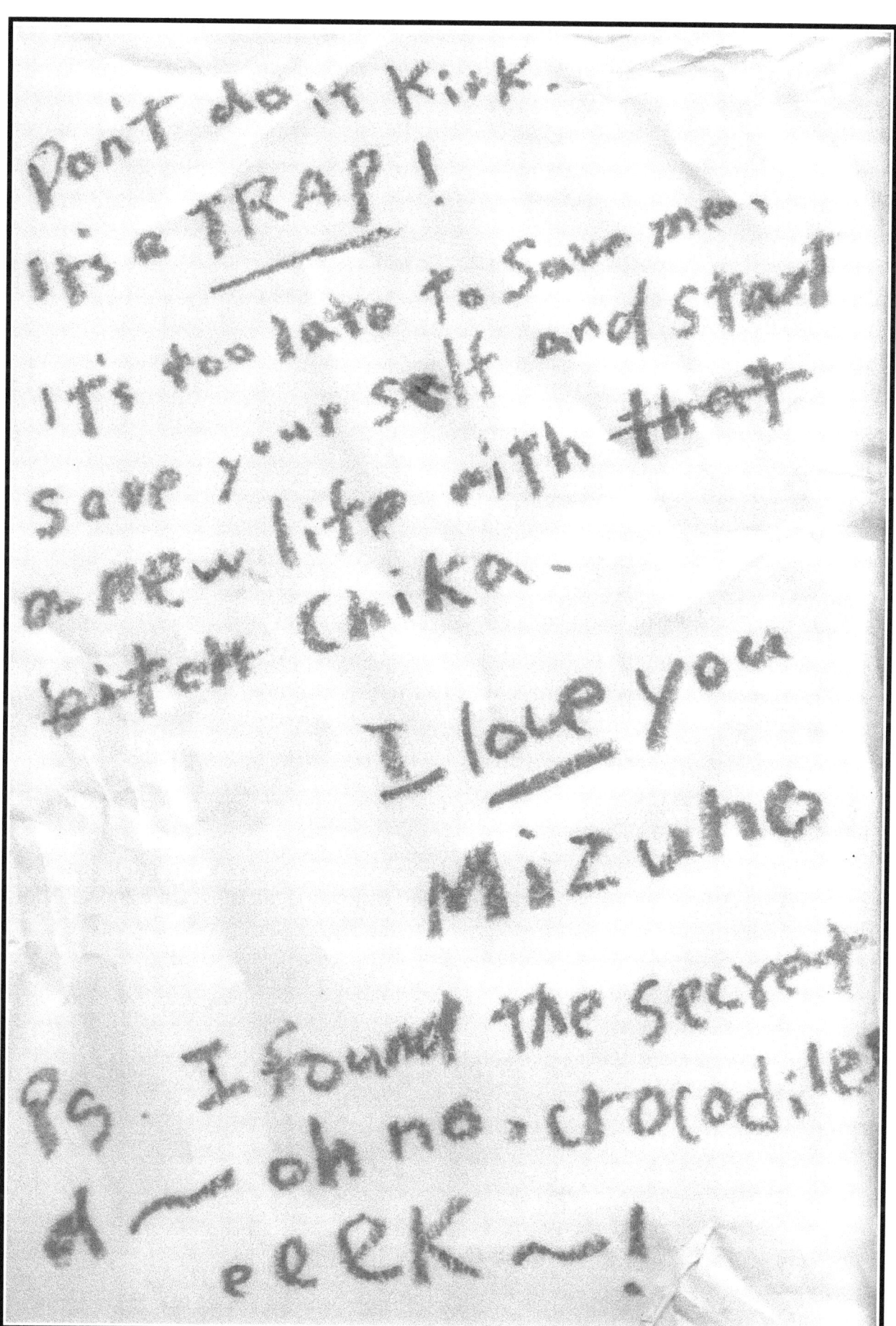

Kirk Dunkirk
☆ ☆ ☆ ☆ ☆
Kochi City 780- ☆ ☆ ☆

New Reoma World
Kagawa-ken Marugame-shi
Ayauta-machi Kurikumanishi 40-1
Japan

April 30, 2011

Dear New Reoma World Amusement Park,

What's new? Not much. And you? Let me introduce my organization. We are a loving bunch of fun-loving movie lovers who love to reenact the movies of the greatest actor and lover of all time: Leonardo DiCaprio.

He is the cat's pajamas. The bee's knees. Flamingo hiccups. He does not poo in the woods. He simply has what it takes and he won't take no for an answer. He has his game face on. He's really ideal.

I can't emphasize how much we love this guy. Some might be crazy for Swayze but we agree with Scorsese. Take a breather Bieber Fever, cuz you ain't all that either. Instead put your hands together for the best new film reenactment club in town: The Leo-tards!

How can we rent your "Lake Boat Dixie Queen" at night for our Nov. 2011 big event: "Tight-anic?" (We chose the date for wintry realism.) Every scene will be redone in loving detail with scale models and miniatures by our award-winning Leotard/swimsuit-wearing water ballet team. If you like, you can see our members up close beforehand. (They are full size!) Plus we won't need hotel rooms, just a place to cuddle up together for warmth in the life rafts.

As for the safety of your facilities, we guarantee that the only possible trouble will be that the water might be a little more salty from our tears...

Please let us know ASAP about pricing and availability during that time frame because depending on the circumstances, we might also need something really high to climb for Gilbert Grape.

Sincerely,
Your Huckleberry Friend,

Kirk Dunkirk
President & Choreographer, West Japan Leo-tards

Kochi City 780-

May 17, 2011

Dear Mr. Kirk Dunkirk,
Thank you for inquiring to our theme park New Reoma World. About the request of wanting to rent our "Lake Boat Dixie Queen", we afraid to tell you that it is only used as one of our rides. We want to secure its safety and functionality so we can't rent you one. We really sorri that we can't grant your request.

However, it's good to Know that such organization like yours exists. Please keep up the good work.
Thank you again for the inquiry.

Sincerely yours,
Chiaki Satake
Person-in-charge PR Division
TEL : 0877-86-1071
FAX : 0877-86-1074

Kirk Dunkirk
Honeycomb Hideout
x x x x x
Kochi City 780-•••

日本在来種みつばち会
Japanese Original Honeybee Association
Wakazono-cho 3-10
Morioka-City, Iwate 020-0886
JAPAN

~~July 28, 2010~~
Oct. 26, 2010

Hi Honey,

How goes it with your campaign to re-colonize Japan with more native honeybees? I wish you the best of luck. It would **bee** really **sweet** if you succeed. Sorry to **drone** on and on, but I get a **buzz** from the topic.

In the meantime, I would like to know if you are interested in endorsing me or inviting me to perform at one of your conferences. After slathering my body in all-natural, made-in-Japan honey, I transform into my stage persona, Carl the Bee Guy.

I stomp around and perform a honeybee inspired dance routine, sometimes in black and yellow leotard, others in a beekeeper's suit with a smoke can and face mesh. I juggle beehives and make balloon art, using wax combs instead of balloons. Audience participation is encouraged in the Annie Oakley number and I lead a swarm of hundreds of bees onstage in a choreographed aerial laser-show finale. No bees are harmed and anyone in the audience who is, well, they're probably used to it. Sting and the B-52s are big fans!

By the way, you state on your website:

> However, recently the bee has seen a revival with the realization that the honey is well-suited to the Japanese body and has other unique properties.

I am not Japanese, so does this mean that Japanese honey is not suited to my western body? I'm worried what might happen- will I get hives?

Be Cool.

ps. It has BEEn 3 months since my first letter. Won't you please write back?

Kirk Dunkirk
Honeycomb Hideout
x x x x x x
Kochi City 780- • • •

日本在来種みつばち会
Japanese Original Honeybee Association
Wakazono-cho 3-10
Morioka-City, Iwate 020-0886
JAPAN   May 13, 2011

Hi Honey,

It's me, Kirk, aka Carl the Bee Guy.

I never got a reply from you about my letter last summer, but that's ok since Carl and I split up. Now I'm back to beeing Kirk, the non-Carl Guy. It still stings a little but I'm getting used to it.

But I still love bees! Nothing else gives me a buzz like they do.

Since the act has split up we will not be available to perform for your association. Neither will the Bee Gees.

Still, would you mind answering my question about a claim on your website?
It says:

> However, recently the bee has seen a revival with the realization that the honey is well-suited to the Japanese body and has other unique properties.

I am not Japanese, so does this mean that Japanese honey is not suited to my western body? I'm worried what might happen- will I get hives?

Boys Be Ambitious,

Kirk Dunkirk

Dear Kirk Dunkirk

I am very sorry for having forgotten your letter.
I am glad you love bees even if you are stung by the bee.

By the way, about your question, "Japanese honey is not suited to my western body?"

What I want to say is that from the viewpoint of the Japanese taste and culture, Japanese honey is well—suited to the Japanese body, not from the viewpoint of medicine and nutrition.

The word "Japanese body" means "Japanese sense."
Please don't worry, of course you can take Japanese honey !

In this season you have a chance to get some swarm colonys.
Please try to get a new colony !

Sincerely
Seita Fujiwara

Miki Dunkirk
Atago Theater
☎ ☎ ☎ ☎
📞 📞 📞
Kochi City, Kochi Prefecture
Japan 780- © © ©

Apple
1 Infinite Loop
Cupertino, CA 95014
USA

Dear Apple,

Pleased to apologize for disturb you. It's getting warmer these days isn' it.

I want eye phone. But I am very worry that it difficult talking without use a mouth and an ear. Maybe sound difficult to use. I don't know internet and didicamu. Likewise kids play too much a tv game, because society degenerate culture. Same phone. But i have earphone. It's a sony.

Anyway I still very want eye phone. We Japanese are good to talking with eyes. Long ago from telepathy, not new. manufacture of the rice require entire village eye contact. Every body same. Phone not necessary! Don't you think so?

Maybe it's problem to use eyephone while drive a car? Not because button, your phone an absence of botan, but because can't keep to keep one's eyes on the road.

So is safe to apple eyephone during drive a car? How to drive? Automatic?

Please reassure me.
With Warm Sympathy.

Miki Dunkirk
2011-5-13

June 01, 2011

Miki Dunkirk
Kochi City, Kochi Prefecture
Japan 780-

Dear Miki Dunkirk,

Thank you for getting in touch with Apple.

We very much appreciate your comments on Apple.

Apple is committed to providing a positive experience for our customers through the use of our hardware, software, and Internet offerings. Feedback such as yours helps us determine areas of opportunity as we continue to grow our business.

Please be assured that Apple values the time and consideration that you invested in your letter and for your records, your concern has been documented in Apple case number 222751100.

Sincerely,

Liz
Apple

Apple
No. 7, Ang Mo Kio Street 64
Singapore 569086

www.asia.apple.com

Miki Dunkirk
x x x x

x x x x x x x

☹ ☹ ☹ ☹ ☹

Kochi City, Kochi Prefecture

Japan 780-x x x 2

```
Amazon.com Customer Service
1200 12th Ave. S., Suite 1200 Seattle, WA 98144
```
USA

Attention Amazon,

I recently get the amazon kindle for my smart phone. i think it great maybe i can read book anytime soon. Everybody talking about these days.

It include the English free book Aesop's Fables. Excitement.

I think it good. Because enable I can read storys for relation's kids. Ant and Rabbit, three small pigs and etc

My sister's nephew want learn English. So I start read Amazon kindle Aesop's fables. but I surprise!

Soon was find terrible, terrible words. The words for example faggot and cock and bollocks.

Faggot cock and bollocks? Why?

```
Only first 12 pages so I stop if maybe more. I learn from movie, is bad
word. The slang.
It's big shock!
```

I am deeply shamed and apologize again my sister must. I damage the nephew's pure

innocence mind. You have big a responsibility. Why you make the money with terrible the free

book to harmful sweet kids? When I young Aesop is teach moral image. Children are futrue so

kindle maybe most terribel thing in the world.

2011 May 13.

amazon.co.jp

Amazon.co.jp Customer Service
Maruito Building Sapporo
1-1 Nishi Kita 2 Jiyo
Chuouku Sapporo Hokkaido
060-0002 Japan
Tel: 0120-999-373 Fax: 0120-919-373
English@amazon.co.jp

May 19, 2011

Dear Miki Dunkirk,

Thank you for writing us at Amazon.co.jp.

Unfortunately, Amazon.co.jp does not support about Amazon Kindle and contents of Kindle.

Please contact Amazon.com Customer Service about Amazon Kindle and detail about book's contents. You can find FAQs or instructions about Amazon Kindle on Amazon.com help page. Please click yellow "Contact-Us" button to email Amazon.com customer service for more information.

http://amazon.com/gp/help/customer/display.html/?nodeId=200127470

Please note that we cannot transfer your inquiry over Amazon.com customer service.

I hope this information helps. Thank you for contacting us at Amazon.co.jp.

Sincerely,

Amazon.co.jp Customer Service
R.Yamaguchi

amazon.com.

May 26, 2011

Miki Dunkirk
Naka
Kochi City, Kochi Prefecture
Japan 780-

Dear Miki,

    I'm sorry you found offensive words in some of our kindle content. While those words have negative meanings in the English language today, when the text was written they meant other things entirely. To help clear it up, in this text the word faggot means a bundle of wood to be used in a fire or something. Bollocks is a lie, and cock means rooster.

    Of course, those words have different connotations today and I'm sorry for that. If you have any further concerns about the content you find in Kindle books, please contact us by phone or email through our website's help pages so that we can help address your concerns faster.

    I hope you have a great day. We look forward to seeing you again soon.

Respectfully,

Amazon.com Customer Service

1550 S 48th St, Grand Forks, ND 58201-3808

Irked by Kirk Crossword Puzzle No.1

Across

1. The man who lives in my finger, Mr. ---
3. Accursed reading device
4. Conversation school for dogs
5. Full Chest of cookies
7. Aye then the wee --- respect ye
9. Members include Usher and Dubya
11. Cockatoo in Arizona
13. Circus guests might park here
15. Axis of -
18. Nickname for Elizabeth mom
19. Doll that makes centipede repellant
20. New type of phone
22. Giant shape-shifting lizard from the Thuban system
23. Say in Amsterdam to get a buzz, "Your -"
24. Singing pet pug
26. Donations are proportion to ---
27. Not Northworst
28. Deliberately delivering debilitating -
31. Disease name, "It's not ---!"
32. Scorcese's favorite pants
33. Split personality fast food mascot

Down

2. Sha-wing! Sparkling ---
6. Just a butthead from Rah-chister
7. "Don't procrastinate,---!"
8. Confused Ovtcharka
10. Explicit day of the week
12. Died of monkeypox
14. "I mean the wife I'm ---"
16. A.H.B. base player nickname
17. Crappy revolutionary dance troupe
21. He had a high fever.
25. Could have been Nike!
29. Weighty plane city
30. Testuo's handle at the jamboree

Irked by Kirk Crossword Puzzle No.1

About the Authors:

Kirk Dunkirk is the guitarist and lead vocals for a Kochi based prog-rock band called Shaman You. He can use chopsticks well.

Scott Linyard is an actor and independent director whose films include "Imo Omiai" and "Homer's Aquarius." He was born on Noman, a small island in the Notar Republic.

Owen Wade is a tough guy from New Jersey who is pretty good at dominoes.

www.ingramcontent.com/pod-product-compliance
Lightning Source LLC
Chambersburg PA
CBHW081453040426
42446CB00016B/3230